'Then it was Destroyed by the Volcano'

'Then it was Destroyed by the Volcano'

The ancient world in film and on television

Arthur J. Pomeroy

Duckworth

First published in 2008 by
Gerald Duckworth & Co. Ltd
90-93 Cowcross Street, London EC1M 6BF
Tel: 020 7490 7300
Fax: 020 7490 0080
inquiries@duckworth-publishers.co.uk
www.ducknet.co.uk

A catalogue record for this book is available
from the British Library

ISBN 978 07156 3026 6

Typeset by Ray Davies
Printed and bound in Great Britain by
MPG Books Ltd, Bodmin, Cornwall

Contents

Acknowledgements   vi
List of Illustrations   vii

Introduction   1

1. The Actress and the Playwright   7
2. Hymns to the Ancient World in (the) Buffyverse   13
3. The Peplum and Other Animals   29
4. The *Odyssey*, High and Low   61
5. Alexander the Hero   95
6. 'It's a Man's, Man's, Man's World' – except for Xena and Buffy 113

Notes   115
Filmography   138
Bibliography   141
Index   145

Acknowledgements

I would like to express my thanks to Susanna Braund, who originally suggested that I submit the proposal for this book to Duckworth, and especially to Deborah Blake who not only accepted the idea with enthusiasm, but has continually encouraged me along the way. I would also like to express my appreciation to the other staff at Duckworth for suggestions for publicity and technical assistance.

I would like to thank Claire Thomson for an invitation to the 'Blood, Text, and Fears' Conference held at the University of East Anglia at Norwich in 2002 and Paula James and David Scourfield for an invitation to the one-day seminar held at the Open University (Milton Keynes) in January 2004 on 'Classical Themes in Fantasy and Science Fiction in Contemporary Television'. Thanks too to Martin Winkler, Hanna Roisman, and the other organisers of the Kinema panels at the American Philological Association in San Francisco 2002 and San Diego 2007. I am particularly grateful to Ward Briggs for sending me a copy of his APA paper of 2007 on Walter Hill's *The Warriors*. Martin Winkler, David Scourfield, Tim Lucas and Theo Angelopoulos have replied to my queries with great generosity.

At Victoria University of Wellington, New Zealand, I would like to thank the Faculty of Humanities Research Committee for assistance with travel to conferences and the Central Library for Interloan assistance. My colleagues in the Classics Programme, Diana Burton, Peter Gainsford, David Rosenbloom, and Matthew Trundle, have not only endured my obsessions, but also assisted with references to texts both Classical and cinematic. David Tulloch read the manuscript and offered excellent advice on what to cut and what to keep; Angela McCarthy made numerous perceptive comments on the Alexander chapter. In particular, I would like to express my unreserved gratitude to Dr Harriet Margolis of the Film Studies Programme for reading all sections of this book and offering numerous critical comments that have improved it immensely.

Finally, I would like to dedicate this to the memory of my teacher and mentor, Dr Alex Scobie, who introduced the study of folklore and popular culture to Victoria University and whose continuing influence on students and colleagues through his humanism and scholarship is inestimable.

List of Illustrations

1. Willow paints Greek on Tara's back in the episode 'Restless',   15
   first aired May 2000, from *Buffy the Vampire Slayer*.
2. Nagiko uses the back of Jerome for calligraphy practice in   15
   Peter Greenaway's *Pillow Book* (1996).
3. A female dress: Andromeda and companions in peplums from   47
   The Giant of Marathon (1959).
4. Hercules (Reg Park) is confronted by a group of identical,   53
   genetically manipulated Atlantidean super-warriors in
   Hercules Conquers Atlantis (1961).
5. Smoke and mirrors: Hercules regards an ethereal Deianeira   55
   in *Hercules at the Centre of the Earth* (1961).
6. Telemachus arrives at the shore of Pylos, where Nestor is   69
   sacrificing, in *L'Odissea* (1968).
7. 'I have returned.' In *The Return of Ringo* (1965), the ragged   75
   peasant metamorphoses into Captain Montgomery Brown in
   full military uniform standing at the door of the church where
   Paco Fuentes is about to marry his wife.
8. *Ulysses' Gaze* (1995): the colossal statue of Lenin sails up the   91
   Danube on its barge.
9. Alexander and his companions, from the opening credits of   108
   Reign: the Conqueror (1999).
10. An art deco fantasy of Babylon from *Reign: the Conqueror*   109
    (1999).

Joan: There's a moral laxity around. Herpes and AIDS have come as the great plagues to teach us all a lesson. It was fine to have sexual freedom, but it was abused. Apparently the original AIDs sufferers were having 500 or 600 contacts a year, and they are now inflicting it on heterosexuals. That's bloody scary. A good reason for celibacy. It's like the Roman Empire. Wasn't everybody running around just covered in syphilis? And then it was destroyed by the volcano.

Playboy: That's bending public health and ancient history a little out of shape.

Joan Collins interviewed for *Playboy* (31 [1981] no. 4)

Introduction

In mid-1997, I was on research leave in Berkeley, California. My apartment possessed a small television, but there was little worth viewing – except for one programme, a sleeper hit of the previous season then in repeat on the Fox Network. This was *Buffy the Vampire Slayer*, a series combining nods to old-style Universal horror movies, the angst of high school dramas, and faux kung fu action, all wrapped in a quirky humour that was decidedly non-standard for American television. As the show progressed, I began to note references to my own field (I am a Classicist, dealing with ancient Greece and Rome) and discovered that other academics were also finding much of interest in the series. An invitation to present a paper at a general conference on *Buffy* (and, by then, the spin-off *Angel*) at the University of East Anglia at Norwich in 2002 was followed by another request to participate in a one-day seminar on Classical themes in televisions series held at the Open University (Milton Keynes) in January 2004. On a rather different topic, I had noted 'quotations' from Leni Riefenstahl's *Triumph of the Will* (1935) incorporated into Ridley Scott's *Gladiator* (2000). A paper delivered in a special Kinema panel at the American Philological Association in San Francisco 2002 became one of the chapters in Winkler 2005.[1] Other investigations, particularly in the world of Japanese animation, led to the presentation of 'Alexander as Hero' at the American Philological Association meeting in San Diego, 2007.

This book is intended to tie together my research and show *why* the ancient world has been and continues to be important to the modern by studying different themes in its film and television presentations. In part it results from my background as a Roman social historian – I want to place these depictions of the past in a social and cultural context. My training also allows me to comment on the accuracy of reproduction, but I hope that I generally only do this when exactitude is required. Detailed analysis of technical aspects of the past for its own sake can be as fascinating as a film expert talking on the finer points of lighting and camera technique – a little goes a long way. Purpose is paramount.

In recent years, the burgeoning field of reception studies has focussed on the way individuals and societies interpret the past by reproducing it in their age. In the main, such studies have concentrated on literary forms and the plastic arts, at least in part because cinema is such a modern

1

invention (the Lumière brothers made their first films just over a century ago). As a Classicist in New Zealand I might be tempted to concentrate on 'high' art responses to my subject, for instance in the writings of a number of significant authors that reflect their study of Classical literature at school and university, whether through the original languages or in translation. Such an approach, however, runs the risk of ending in pure introspection. In contrast with poets such as James K. Baxter and Ian Wedde, the film directors Jane Campion, Vincent Ward, and Peter Jackson have greater international recognition. From the viewpoint of reception studies, the films made by these directors are sadly lacking in allusions to the Greek and Roman worlds.[2] After all the cinema of Aotearoa/New Zealand has other points of *national* reference at present. Yet the *international* appeal of the ancient world has global effects: two television programmes filmed in New Zealand (*Hercules: the Legendary Journeys* (1995-9) and *Xena: Warrior Princess* (1995-2001)) were crucial for the development of the local film industry. Popular culture cannot easily be escaped.

International or 'Hollywood' cinema continues to be interested in the ancient world as shown by the number of films in ancient settings produced since *Gladiator* (2000) through to *300* (2006) and to this year (2007)'s *The Last Legion*. More are on their way: we await news on the Vin Diesel project *Hannibal the Conqueror* ('with a script in Greek, Latin, and Punic'). Individual national cinemas also clearly show a desire to connect with the ancient past. Such interest may appear understandable for Greek film-makers, yet the lack of films on the ancient world from Italy in recent decades appears puzzling. The intention of this book is to attempt to answer such questions by examining the features of the past that have resonated in moving images at different times and places, taking exploratory samples from the mass of material in film and television.

My first chapter considers the significance of the past through the somewhat wobbly memory of a British actor working in North America in the mid 1980s and her late-night recollection of cinematic depictions of the Roman world. It is instructive to compare Joan Collins' view of Nero's Rome, one presumably shared by many in Middle America, with that of the considerable French audience who enjoyed the novels of Alexandre Dumas in the nineteenth century. Although *The Count of Monte Cristo* is pre-cinema, its dramatic features give some indication of popular theatrical depictions of the ancient world that were the basis of the earliest silent films.

In the Western world, Greece and Rome have long functioned as marks of origin guaranteeing the quality of any product to which they are attached. In the nineteenth and twentieth centuries, for example, the study of Greek and Latin helped define an educational elite whose influence has declined only in the last half century. Television's *Buffy the Vampire Slayer,* the subject of my second chapter, by its populist use of these languages subverts their exclusionary message. It is therefore not surprising that the media regularly publicised academic conferences on a series whose heroine's image was likely to be found in women's magazines – presumably these gatherings were seen as signs of the impending apocalypse predicted by Joan Collins. Yet a good deal of the series' postmodern attraction lies in its deceptive image. *Buffy* was always a niche product, catering to audiences ignored by the big three television corporations in the United States and mainstream channels elsewhere. Its allusions to the past not only include vernacular images (e.g. the skeletons from the 1963 *Jason and the Argonauts*) but also, for instance, quite recondite references to Greek literature filtered through high culture.

The confusion of 'high' and 'low' art in *Buffy* is not, however, simply a twenty-first-century phenomenon, as can be seen in examination of one national cinema. Italy dominated the production of feature films before the First World War. Even after Hollywood eclipsed Italian output, the lavish early Italian productions, often featuring Greek or Roman settings, remained part of the national imagination. As will be seen in Chapter 3, from being occasional recreations, films set in the ancient world became a staple part of the local film industry in the late 1950s and early 1960s. The appeal of these 'peplums' locally and internationally (particularly in the lucrative North American market) reveals complex changes socially and economically in this period. Intended above all to entertain, Italian sword and sandal movies have often been dismissed as 'low' art. Such a verdict would not lessen their cultural importance, yet, as I hope to have shown, at least some contributions to the genre show a directorial vision that would qualify them as auteurist productions. Furthermore, a sub-set of the peplum, the muscleman film, shows the remarkable continuity of one theme from the earliest silent creations to modern films that exploit the star appeal of Arnold Schwarzenegger, as well as the television series *Hercules: the Legendary Journeys* and *Xena*.

In contrast with Hercules, who, with his oversized strength and appetites, has lent himself to comic and camp treatments, the other great travelling hero, Odysseus, receives more respectful treatment. Chapter 4 considers six different versions of *The Odyssey*. *Ulysses,* the Kirk Douglas star-vehicle of 1954, is a proto-peplum, mixing fantasy elements with the traditional Hollywood adventure movie. Tessari's *Return of Ringo* (1965), recreates the suspense of Odysseus' return to Ithaca in an Italian western, illustrating how one stream (*filone*) of film-making may flow into another, without altering the essential core of action: the climax to which the story builds. By contrast, Rossi's 1968 Italian television series *L'Odissea* situates itself securely within the European humanist tradition. The hero is located in a wider social setting, and depictions of consumption – including a remarkable Polyphemus episode – serve to highlight the conflict between the desire to satisfy one's individual appetites and a necessary concern for the welfare of the group.

3

Godard's *Contempt* (1963) sets up an opposition between pre-war European cinema and commercial modern styles, allowing the director to use the *Odyssey* as the background to a complex (or perhaps deliberately incoherent) treatment of sexual politics. The inability of modern cinema to recreate Odysseus' journeys also reflects the way films set in the ancient world fell out of style internationally by the mid-60s. When *The Odyssey* returned, it would be in another country and clothed in comedy. In *Oh Brother Where Art Thou?* (2000), the Coen brothers recreated the archetypal road movie as a story of the depression-era South, thus allowing them to exploit the darker subject matter of American film (chain gangs, the Ku Klux Klan and racism, political corruption, and stories of doomed bank-robbers). Yet, by mocking such material à la Preston Sturges, the Coens can also suggest the possibility of a better future.

For Theo Angelopoulos the story of Odysseus is a national myth that reflects the travails of the Greek psyche. His borrowings from American film (for instance, the musical cues of 1950s Vincente Minnelli films) only underscore Greece's social and political dilemmas since independence as a nation dependent on emigration and subject to intervention by foreign powers. In *Ulysses' Gaze* (1995), Angelopoulos extends the theme of the journey to explore the wider history of the Balkans in the twentieth century. The voyage ends in a besieged Sarajevo with the slaughter of the innocents: the violence of history cannot be escaped, but the art of the past, be it drama, poetry, or music (all regular aspects of Angelopoulos' films), still offers hope.

My last chapter emphasises the variations in national cinemas through the prism of a specific historical story. Because of the speed and extent of his conquests, Alexander the Great has provided a model for European imperialism for two millennia. Yet the various portrayals of his deeds are much more ambiguous. Robert Rossen, who had first-hand experience of the abuse of political power in the 1950s, sought in his *Alexander the Great* (1956) to show that military victory can lead the way to social change – if the opportunity is taken. By contrast, in the new millennium, Oliver Stone's *Alexander* (now without the title, 'the Great') is subject to intense external forces as well as inner demons. The Macedonian king's aims and his desires are too complex to be more than glimpsed by others, although many, including the film-maker, have sought to portray them visually. Yet both of these film depictions strike a chord for an America grappling with its global power, desirous to undertake 'the White Man's burden' but unsure of destiny's road. By contrast, the 1941 Indian depiction of *Sikandar* saw him as an adventurer and interloper who should return to enjoy his own native land – a clear anti-British sentiment at a time when the independence movement was close to achieving its goals. Finally, the recent Japanese animated retelling of the Alexander story, *Reign: the Conqueror* (1999) suggests an alternate international cinema. Created using talents from northeast Asia and the United States, a European myth is drawn in a western style, but told using Japanese tropes that have become familiar worldwide. With the destruction of distinct cinematic styles may come the apocalypse – or renewed creativity. In sum, the Pompeian volcano may preserve the past as well as hide it.

A note on films and television series discussed: I have normally used an English title, rather than the original name of foreign features. In some cases, a film may exist in an English language version that is markedly different from the one I adopt: so *Hercules Conquers Atlantis* is the title I use for *Ercole alla conquista di Atlantide* (1961),[3] but the available (cut, with new material added) American version is called *Hercules and the Captive Women*. Even more confusing is *Goliath and the Dragon*, a hacked treatment of *The Vengeance of Hercules* (*La vendetta di Ercole*, 1960). I prefer *Hercules at the Centre of the Earth* (*Ercole al centro della terra*) for *Hercules in the Haunted World*, although there is a very good recent reissue of the film under the latter name (with a choice of subtitles or the English dub provided by the Italian producers rather than the camp Woolner brothers version). For the *Odyssey* films, I have used the title *Ulysses* for the Kirk Douglas version, but *L'Odissea* for the television series in order to distinguish it from Homer's epic. All films and television series treated in detail in this book, with the exception of *Sikandar*, are available on DVD. Some of the foreign language films are readily available in English language dubbed versions and/or with English subtitles (*Contempt* is available in a splendid Criterion edition), but a number need to be sourced from various DVD regions and will require players that can handle multiple zone encoding and NTSC and PAL formats. The Japanese interest in 'macaroni westerns' means that the cowboy films of Giuliano Gemma, including *The Return of Ringo*, are once more available.[4] Japanese animation has become an international phenomenon: as a result, almost all significant titles are available, usually with a choice between English subtitles or dub. French and German companies have reissued full versions of many Italian films set in the ancient world, from the peplum period and earlier. These are often to be preferred for picture quality over sometimes abysmal US-sourced reissues. We await the availability of the magnificently restored *Cabiria* screened at Cannes in 2006. Most of Angelopoulos' films are available on DVD with English subtitles from various sources, but in the meantime Japanese DVDs (Greek language, Japanese subtitles) must be used for *Reconstruction, The Hunters, Megalexandros, Voyage to Cythera*, and *The Beekeeper*. A reissue of *L'Odissea* with English subtitles would be a venture worth investigating by the Classical associations of English-speaking countries. In the meantime, a two-DVD set is available in Italian, with Italian subtitles for those whose written language skills are better than their oral ones. I certainly cannot claim to have mastered the various languages of the films discussed in this book, but can at least assert that my infinitesimal knowledge has often been improved to the level of merely inadequate by my researches.

Written 26 September 2007, a day marked by the eruption of Mt Ruapehu.

1

The Actress and the Playwright

In 1984, *Playboy* published an interview with the English actress, Joan Collins, then at the height of her fame as Alexis Carrington in the television soap *Dynasty*.[1] Fuelled by several bottles of champagne, Collins talks about her life, her loves, and her times. When questioned about her use of drugs, she recalls once smoking marijuana. Yet if passing joints was a communal rite of the 1970s, it is a practice that is no longer safe. She would never do that again – or even smoke a cigarette or drink from a glass that had touched another's lips. This was the height of the AIDS panic, and Joan Collins is quick to blame the promiscuity of the homosexual community for the spread of the virus. Punishment for the sins of a minority is now being inflicted on the heterosexuals within the community:

> It's like the Roman Empire. Wasn't everybody running around just covered in syphilis? And then it was destroyed by the volcano.[2]

Celebrities are hardly good sources of information on health matters or history, but the very mention of ancient Rome in this regard is significant. The cause of the downfall of the Roman Empire has been a favourite topic through the ages. In the fifth century AD, non-Christians attributed the disasters of the times to failure to observe time-honoured pagan practices. The Christians, still hopeful of the arrival of the final apocalypse, retorted that this was God's due punishment on a sinful world. Alongside scientific solutions, such as lead poisoning or climate change, proposed in modern times, moralising explanations have continued to thrive. While Edward Gibbon's *Decline and Fall of the Roman Empire* was an Enlightenment response that saw Christianity as sapping the moral fibre of Roman society, screen presentations of the godless immorality of the imperial power have upheld the Christian tradition. Uniting the eschatological portrayal of the punishment of the Great Whore of Babylon in the Book of Revelation and the public spectacle of Roman games and feasts, cinematic depictions of the Roman world reinforced the message of the triumph of Christian virtue over pagan vice.

Henryk Sienkiewicz's 1895 novel *Quo Vadis* had pointed the way by depicting the persecution of Christians under Nero and also showing the elegant debauchery of the imperial court under its *magister elegantiae*, Petronius.[3] The mixture of aristocratic decadence and humble faith was irresistible. The novel was quickly adapted to the stage as a play, turned into a film and returned to live performance as an opera.[4] In the same period, Edward Bulwer Lytton's 1832 blockbuster, *The Last Days of Pompeii,* had also been revived by the new medium of film, particularly in the 1913 silent Italian melodrama, *Gli ultimi giorni di Pompeii* (dir. Mario Caserini) that featured both evil Egyptian priests and a climactic eruption of Vesuvius. Wilson Barrett's 1895 play, *The Sign of the Cross,* can be added to the mix, with a similar theme to *Quo Vadis* in its description of the Great Fire of Rome in AD 64 and the subsequent Neronian persecution of Christians. It too was adapted to film (dir. Frederick A. Thomson, 1914). The new world of sound cinema saw Cecil B. deMille's extravanganza version of this story (1932, starring Charles Laughton as Nero and Claudette Colbert as Poppaea), and later Mervyn LeRoy's *Quo Vadis* (1952) featured a ripe performance by Peter Ustinov as the Roman emperor. In the meantime, the *Last Days of Pompeii* (dir. Ernest B. Schoedsack, 1935) had been remade as the story of a humble blacksmith turned gladiator. The hero's path crosses with that of Christ before the final reckoning of the eruption of Vesuvius by the simple expedient of telescoping the fifty years that passed between the crucifixion and the destruction of Pompeii. Despite the lurid poster that is reproduced on the cover of this book, the film is sadly lacking in the sexual promiscuity that had previously been a feature of films set in Roman imperial times. Rome often promises more than it presents: 'SEE! The Shameless Orgy As Drunken Pompeii Abandons Itself To The Goddess Isis' is the slightly hysterical message of the United Artists poster for the 1959 Steve Reeves vehicle, *The Last Days of Pompeii.* Yet, as will be seen in Chapter 3, what passed for an orgy in middle America now was little more than a rowdy Friday night on the town in Pompeii.

It is likely that some mix of all these films, recalling the corruption of Rome, in combination with televangelistic warnings of God's punishment in the form of AIDS visited on the sinful 1980s, just as he had passed judgement on Pompeii, lies behind Joan Collins' unforgettable summary of ancient history. She herself had enjoyed a rare sympathetic role as Esther in the extravaganza *Esther and the King* (1960), a retelling of the biblical romance between the Persian king and a Jewish princess that was as faithful to the original text as most Hercules movies have been to Greek mythology.[5] Her knowledge of the Roman world derives indirectly from popular sources that happily meld events and cultural practices. The Great Fire of Rome of AD 64 and the eruption of Vesuvius in AD 79 are readily interchangeable. Extravagant banquets and orgies or in the cruelty of the gladiatorial games and the spectacle of condemned prisoners being publicly mauled by wild beasts are equivalent signs of excess. Linking behaviour and disaster scenarios thus offers a warning to hedonists of later ages. Films about Rome allowed the audience to enjoy the vicarious pleasures of such behaviour criticised from a safe distance.[6] In brief, daily life in ancient Rome was simply a forerunner to the tales of the rich and decadent in modern America, the harbinger for *Dynasty* and *Dallas*. It would hardly be stretching the point to suggest that *Playboy's* depiction of the hedonism of Hollywood was but further confirmation of the social conformity of its readers who desired such escapism.

The Joan Collins summary of Roman history could be taken as indicative of common impressions of the ancient world in the late twentieth century, generally derived at third hand via film or television. One response would be to deplore such ignorance and to seek to improve public education, for instance, by hiring experts in the field as advisors. Yet this would also put at risk the very prestige of the academic field of Classics. Harvard professor Kathleen Coleman, as consultant for *Gladiator*, was unable to persuade the film's producers to make the battles in the arena conform with historial evidence rather than with earlier cinematic trreatments. Oxford don Robin Lane Fox might be judged more effective in his screen role as part of the cavalry charge at Gaugamela than through his advice to Oliver Stone on how to film the battle.[7] Documentaries on public interest television channels are likely to preach to the converted, an educated élite.

In fact an educational Eden, where experts could impart their knowledge to the empty vessels of the public, has probably never existed. There is something quaint in this model, similar as it is to the one adopted by museums of the nineteenth century. Public exhibitions were designed to increase the knowledge of the less educated public during their leisure time. Yet it is debatable whether these efforts were any more effective in encouraging the adoption of the values of the governing classes by the proletariat than the didacticism of twentieth-century film was in promoting conservative Christian values.

An alternative approach is for the academic to admit defeat in the culture wars – Richard Burt's critic as 'loser'. The recognition of the loss of any real power over popular culture is at the same time a celebration of freedom from the cult of academic superstars.[8] This, in turn, has drawn criticism for appearing to patronise youth culture and for reverting to the stereotype of the (academic as) lone hero riding off into the sunset.[9] Others have suggested the role of the researcher as detective, perhaps Sherlock Holmes, possibly Philip Marlowe or Sam Spade, or, more worryingly, as Mike Hammer: self-parody coming full circle.[10] Gideon Nisbet's *Ancient Greece in Film and Popular Culture* (2006) is an excellent recent introduction to 'trash culture' and the ancient world. Yet there is the danger that such studies will once more reinforce the dominance of a particular subculture (academic Classicists) over other groups. I am also concerned about the limitations of such an approach, which avoids the foreign and difficult (no subtitled remakes of Greek tragedy, for instance). The academic thus becomes a cultural tourist, slumming it with media and cultural studies, whereas the role of a good taste gatecrasher, enjoying the canapés of the high culture vultures as well as plebeian sausage rolls, is to my mind every bit as congenial.

In brief, popular culture need not be restricted to slackers, losers and Bogans.[11] This can be seen in the shared knowledge of Greek and Roman antiquity that is expected of (or at least appreciated by) both creator and consumer in the case of Alexandre Dumas' novel, *The Count of Monte Cristo*. Numerous abridgements, pictorial versions (most notably in *Classic Comics/Classics Illustrated*), and film and television adaptations have led to the popular belief that the story is simply adolescent literature.[12] But the novel clearly appealed to a wide spectrum of the French public, who eagerly consumed it in serial form (in eighteen parts) and then as a book of over a thousand pages. Most notably, it features at least a hundred Classical references, that is, approximately one Classical reference per chapter.[13] Examination of these suggests reference points quite different from the simple 'Nero as persecutor of good Christians' that appears in American film.[14]

It is questionable how many readers would remember the story of the African Caesellius Bassus, who persuaded the emperor that there was a cave in North Africa filled with wealth left by Dido. But the narrator recalls this treasure-hunt episode from Tacitus' *Annals* (16.1-3) when the Abbé Faria attempts to buy his way out of the Chateau d'If (ch. 14) and on several other occasions recalls Nero as *cupitor impossibilium* (e.g. ch. 63, in effect comparing the Count's cave with Nero's Golden House).[15] The fabulous treasure of Monte Cristo is thus not only related to the cave of Ali Baba (ch. 23) and the orientalist world of Sinbad the Sailor, underlined by Dantès' use of the pseudonym Sinbad when engaged in acts of philanthropy: it has even earlier historical antecedents in the Western imagination. Nero's unrestrained imagination and inventions are thus more important than his moral failings amid the spectacular innovations of nineteenth-century industrialism.

A similar mix of Classical and Eastern can be seen in Dumas' depiction of the Greek princess Haidee who has fallen into slavery and is now in attendance on the Count.[16] The daughter of the late Ali Pasha, once ruler of Yanina and much of northern Greece, she presents a striking picture of femininity with her traditional dress and her skill in playing the guzla. But she is also well educated and can converse with the Count either in modern Greek (Romaic) or the language of Homer and Plato (ch. 77). Her very name recalls the heroine of Byron's *Don Juan*, Haydee the pirate's daughter, and so brings into play European romantic ideas about ancient Greece and the new Greek nation created after liberation.

The past also offers models of leadership in an age of revolution in Europe. The Roman brigand chieftain, Luigi Vampa, not only shows himself to be a man with an interest in bettering himself through education, but is a precursor of the bandit turned popular leader that we will see later in Angelopoulos' *Megalexandros*. First, as he holds Albert de Moncerf prisoner (ch. 37), he is reading Caesar's *Commentarii* (i.e. his *Gallic Wars*). By the conclusion of the novel, when detaining Baron Danglars (ch. 114), he has moved on in his reading material to Plutarch's *Alexander*. Such men will provide the impetus for Italy's *Risorgimento*.

Other references situate *Monte Cristo* within a romantic tradition that is derived from Classical mythology. Particularly significant is the title of ch. 51, 'Pyramus and Thisbe'. In the Ovidian version of this story (*Metamorphoses* 4.55-166), Pyramus and Thisbe are lovers separated by family hatreds who can only communicate through a gap in the wall between their houses. They finally agree to meet at night outside the city, but their hopes of freedom are disappointed. Thisbe appears first, but is frightened off by a wandering lioness. Pyramus, arriving later, finds only Thisbe's shawl, torn and stained with blood – although this is actually the blood of an animal that the lioness had recently consumed. Assuming the worst, he stabs himself and as he lies dying, Thisbe arrives and joins him in death. In Dumas, the chapter title with its mythological reference thus introduces the romance of Maximilian Morrel, the son of the Count's early benefactor, and Valentine de Villefort, the daughter of his enemy who had sentenced him to lifelong imprisonment in the Chateau d'If, star-crossed lovers whose assignations take place across the wall of the de Villefort estate. Thisbe's apparent unhappy end in Ovid foreshadows Valentine's later feigned death and burial to escape the poison of her stepmother. In Dumas' version, however, at the last moment the Count dissuades Maximilian from imitating Pyramus by committing suicide (ch. 105) and the story has a happy ending as the novel concludes with the lovers' reunion in Marseilles (ch. 117).

It is unimportant whether the reader detects these allusions as coming from Ovid's version of the myth or its re-enactment in Shakespeare's *Midsummer Night's Dream* (Act V scene 1), particularly when Dumas incorporates a considerable amount of the tragic love story from *Romeo and Juliet* as well. After all Dumas began his career as a noted playwright and his novels have strong dramatic (and comic) underpinnings that have encouraged their adaptation to film and television.[17] It is significant, however, that the writer and his audience can draw on their knowledge of romantic tales, ancient and modern. Greek and Roman themes had been the staple of theatre and opera since the Renaissance; the fabricated exoticism of the East was a nineteenth-century addition to add variation to standard tales.[18]

The contrasting accounts of the ancient world from Joan Collins and Alexandre Dumas should act as a reminder that ancient Greece and Rome are not stable points of reference, but continually shifting in the public imagination throughout the world. The French public of the late nineteenth century had at least a general education in the Classics, if not from schooling, then certainly from popular entertainment on the stage. In the United States, religious education, particularly stressing the tribulations of God's children, the Old Testament Jews and the New Testament Christians, became the basis of numerous Hollywood films. Each treatment shows the traces of its historical setting. In particular, French colonial expansion into Africa at the time when Dumas was writing *Monte Cristo* recalled the glories of Roman imperialism. The theme of Manifest Destiny in American political thought can be seen in the triumph of the Chosen People, now identified with the citizens of the United States. But the nation's success would always be open to the withdrawal of God's favour and manifestations of divine wrath. Each of our examples is also marked as the culmination of a series of past interpretations: if Dumas frequently recalls the romanticism of Byron and even earlier authors, Joan Collins' view of Rome harks back to the cinema of the first half of the twentieth century, to a style of film-making that, at the time of her interview, had been extinct for several decades. As such it reveals its origin in the conservative reaction in America to marked social developments of the 1960s and 70s, particularly the rise of feminism and the public display of gay culture. Novel and interview, then, should be seen to serve as time capsules. In order to try to perceive the ancient world's position in contemporary popular imagination, more recent material needs to be studied. For this purpose, I have chosen the television series *Buffy the Vampire Slayer* (1997-2003), the subject of the following chapter.

2

Hymns to the Ancient World in (the) Buffyverse

Body language

It is possible to describe *Buffy the Vampire Slayer* briefly as a long-running television series of the horror genre, initially given a High School setting, with touches derived particularly from Hong Kong action movies. Buffy Summers is a schoolgirl who finds that her role in life is to dispose of the vampires and other monsters that abound in her Southern California town, often after kung fu fighting sequences (stylised in the same way fencing is in stage drama). In this she is assisted by school mates Willow Rosenberg, (Ale)Xander Harris, and school librarian and Buffy's mentor ('Watcher') (Rupert) Giles, who together form the so-called Scoobie Gang.[1] The mixture of youth culture and traditional narrative (could there be a more conventional horror figure than the vampire?) creates an ironic undertone. This allows for both the playful ('I'm Buffy and you're … history') and the serious (for instance, the unexpected death of Buffy's mother Joyce from natural causes is all the more shocking and poignant for occurring in a series where violent deaths are commonplace). In many ways the series represents late twentieth-century post-modernism where traditional American teen coming-of-age stories happily coexist with Bollywood romance and storylines may be derived from the adventures in Crusader movies or may be Eisenstein-style tales of saving workers from satanic exploitation. Any references to the worlds of ancient Greece and Rome are thus all the more significant as evidence of the place of the Classical world in modern popular culture.

An opening point is the episode 'Restless' (Season 4, Episode 22). The opening credits have finished. The scene changes from the Scoobie Gang (Buffy, Willow, Giles, and Xander) fast asleep in front of the television screen in the Summers household to a view of a student dorm room. There Willow's new lover, Tara Maclay, is lying face down on the bed, watching their kitten play.

> Tara: It's strange … I mean I think I should worry, that we haven't found her name.
> Willow: Who? Miss Kitty?
> Tara: You'd think she would have told us her name by now.
> Willow: She will. She's not all grown yet.

13

Tara: You're not worried?
Willow: I never worry here. I'm safe here.
Tara: You don't know everything about me ...
Willow: Have you told me your real name?
Tara: Oh, you know *that* ...
    They *will* find out, you know. About you.
Willow: I don't have time to think about that. You know. I have all this
    homework to finish.

So far, the sequence of images – which musical clues indicate is Willow's dream – appears to focus on essential entities that are indissolubly linked to the true names of humans and even kittens. It is insufficient simply to impose a name. Instead, the real name will reveal itself in good time. In the first flush of love, Willow is confident that she knows the true Tara.[2] But what will 'they' find out about Willow? The dream setting tends to confirm for the viewers that Willow's anxiety stems from her unwilling-ness to make her lesbian relationship with Tara public. Or is Willow's basic fear of public exposure the source of all her insecurities? This is a theme that dates back from the very first season of *Buffy*[3] and is reinforced by Willow's recurrent terror of stage fright. In this episode this will manifest itself when she finds that she is appearing in *The Death of a Salesman*, but a totally unfamiliar version that somehow now features a milkmaid and a cowboy.

Willow's immediate response to these anxieties is simply to concentrate on her homework. She has been writing something with a brush and ink. Now, as the camera pulls back, it is revealed that it is Tara's back that is being used for her calligraphy practice:

ΠΟΙΚΙΛΟΘΡΟΝΑΘΑΝΑ
ΤΑΦΡΟΔΙΤΑΠΑΙΔΙ
ΟΣΔΟΛΟΠΛΟΚΕ
ΛΙΣΣΟΜΑΙΣΕΜΗΜ
ΥΣΑΙΣΙΜΗΔΟΝΙΑΙ
ΣΙΔΑΜΝΑΠΟΤΝΙ
ΑΘΥΜΟΝ
ΑΛΛΑΤΥΙΔΕΛΘΑΙ
ΠΟΤΑΚΑΤΕΡΩΤΑ
ΤΑΣΕΜΑΣΑΥΔΑΣ
ΑΙΟΙΣΑΠΗΛΟΙ
ΕΚΛΥΕΣΠΑΤΡΟΣ[4]

For most of the audience, the writing is indecipherable, another little mystery amid many in this episode. The Greek capital letters without accents or word separation add to the difficulties. But the word 'Aphrodita' on the second line is easily recognised and the few viewers who have studied Classical Greek may then recognise what is being written.

14

1. Willow (Alyson Hannigan) paints Greek on Tara (Amber Benson)'s back in the episode 'Restless', first aired May 2000, from *Buffy the Vampire Slayer.*

2. Nagiko (Vivian Wu) uses the back of Jerome (Ewan McGregor) for calligraphy practice in Peter Greenaway's *Pillow Book* (1996).

Buffy's creators appear to have chosen Sappho *Ode* 1 as the first poem, at least in modern editions of Sappho, by the first named lesbian and indeed the original Lesbian, since the Greek poetess lived on the island of Lesbos around 600 BC. In this way, Willow's writing both reveals the love that dares not speak its name and hides it beneath a foreign script. The very act of writing on the naked body of the beloved is in itself a visible sign of consensual desire.

It is also probable that in 'Restless' (first aired 23 May 2000) Joss Whedon or Todd MacIntosh, the head makeup artist for the series,[5] is paying homage to Peter Greenaway's *The Pillow Book* (1996). In that film, the heroine takes pleasure in having her body written on first by her father and then by her lovers, until such time as she finds a partner who himself enjoys being inscribed. Greenaway's themes are complex, but perhaps most significant for understanding what is happening to Tara and Willow is the blessing with which *The Pillow Book* begins:

> When God made the first clay model of a human being He painted in the eyes ... the lips ... and the sex.

> And then He painted in each person's name lest the person should ever forget it.

> If God approved of His creation, He breathed the painted clay model into life by signing His own name.

The theme of naming is thus referenced, but whereas in Greenaway's film this is a mark of endorsement, a signature or even a warranty from the approving gaze, in *Buffy*, while the dream Tara may readily accept the rite of naming and approval, Willow remains hesitant.

It is not simply that in this version there is a substitution of Greek for Japanese, of one unfamiliar script for another. The words inscribed markedly differ in content too. Consider the first nine lines of the Hymn to Aphrodite:

> Gleaming-throned Immortal Aphrodite.
> Snare-weaving child of Zeus, I pray to you:
> Do not with pains and sorrow repress
> My spirit, Mistress,
> But come here, if ever at another time
> hearing my words from far away, you listened
> And leaving the golden home of your father
> You came
> Having yoked your chariot.

In contrast with the poems derived from Sei Shonagon's *Pillow Book*, which play on the metaphors of book and body,[6] Sappho's verse is a prayer and an incantation, a spell that fits in perfectly with Willow's depiction as a Wicca.[7] It may even foreshadow Willow's desire to be the dominant partner in her relationship with Tara, a theme that figures so prominently (and finally, tragically) in Season 6. What Tara regards as a sign of approval may turn out to be a charm created by Willow, removing her rights of choice as an individual (cf. Season 6, Episode 6 'All the Way', where Willow uses Lethe's Bramble to make Tara forget their quarrels).

'Restless' is a favourite episode among devotees of *Buffy* because of its complex depiction of the main characters through their dreams and through the numerous allusions to episodes previously screened. To use the parlance of the series, there is a geekiness in this self-referentiality that explains why the show was so popular with critics and appreciative viewers at a time when the general public preferred the untaxing fantasy of magical females provided by *Charmed*.[8] The value of recognising internal references and cultural quotations created a coterie of insiders, a fan club that could pride itself on possessing an esoteric knowledge denied to the rest.

The multiple intertextual references in the series also probably account for the remarkable interest in *Buffy* among academics, including among Classicists.[9] The possibility of an annotated Buffy recalls the complexities of Hellenistic poetry or the efforts of the Neoteric poets of Republican Rome. For instance, the *Smyrna* of Cinna (the poet who comes to an unfortunate end at the hands of an enraged mob in Shakespeare's *Julius Caesar*, killed as conspirator or for his bad verses) needed extensive commentaries even at first publication. By contrast the epic poems of Homer had required explication only hundreds of years after their composition, when the language became too archaic for general understanding. Similarly, *Buffy* will certainly require elucidation for the viewer a century from now who will be unfamiliar with West Coast American language and culture from the turn of the millennium. But after broadcast each episode had immediately acquired annotation on the emerging internet, which allowed both academics and the wider community to contribute to the preservation and explanation of the show. Television programmes, once notoriously ephemeral, were now readily available in the high quality medium of DVDs. Officially sanctioned texts of the scripts were often provided, along with commentaries from the directors and writers. Joss Whedon was no longer an employee providing product for Twentieth Century Fox to screen, but had become an *auteur*, whose work could be studied and critiqued (and who might readily respond in electronic space to queries from his viewers). Media interest in academic conferences on *Buffy* added to the confusion between commentator and object. What if media studies in turn focussed on this phenomenon? In the computer age, infinite looping might now become the Siren Song for academics lured onto the rocks of popular culture ...

First things first

Perhaps the cure for the self-importance of academics is to remember that for all the art-house effects and allusive internal references in *Buffy*, the series' basis is Joss Whedon's script for the originating film, *Buffy the Vampire Slayer* (dir. Fran Rubel Kazui, 1992), a reassemblage of teenage horror and high school, valley girl comedy tropes. In particular the television episode, 'Restless', acknowledges its debt to the horror genre through references to Wes Craven's *Nightmare on Elm Street* series.

Willow's magic has summoned up a *name*-less terror, not Freddy Krueger but the First (Slayer), the Primeval One. But as the first female to have the essence of the demonic implanted in her, she also appears here as the Prime Evil One.[10] The First Slayer, labelled 'Primitive' in the original script, uses the individual anxieties of Willow, Xander, and Giles to suck the life out of them. Only the practical Buffy rejects the game and refuses to allow herself to be treated as a horror victim. Having originally tried to fight the Primitive, she finally decides simply to refuse to believe in her opponent. 'That's it. I'm waking up.' And when the Primitive attempts to trap her in her dreams by changing the scene to the Summers' living room, Buffy is rather bored with the entire performance:

> Are you quite finished? ... You just have to get over the whole primal power thing. You are not the source of me. ... Also in terms of hair care, you really want to say 'What kind of impression am I making in the workplace?' 'Cause that particular look –

Victory is actually assured when the heroine refuses to allow herself to be isolated from her network of friends and assume the stock role of lone and isolated protector of the community[11] – in effect, a rejection of the climactic battle between the good (in the form of the heroine) and evil (Freddy Krueger) that typically completes a *Nightmare* film. There is no need for a fight to the death between the two females and Buffy's friends will now be restored to life, even if apparently killed in their dreams. But the didactic message is not allowed to overwhelm its vehicle. What might appear all too serious is undercut by fashion advice: Southern California taste rejects the wild look and the world is saved once more.

Buffy's grounding in the mundane thus creates an anti-heroism. The star's superhuman feats are undercut not, as often occurs in super-hero movies, by displaying the gap between human and superhuman and a resulting inability to cope with daily life (Hercules' discus once hurled is likely to disappear over the horizon), but by displays of almost excessively typical behaviour for her social group (shopping, going to the local nightclub).

SHE SAVED THE WORLD
A LOT

2. Hymns to the Ancient World in (the) Buffyverse

This lapidary inscription from the close of Season 5 encapsulates the destiny and temporarily tragic fate of the series' heroine. But the colloquial grammar of the second line undercuts the pomposity of the epitaph and permits the insertion of personal grief by her sister and the friends whom she died protecting. This is typical of the series: various apparently contradictory themes underpin the world of Buffy Anne Summers and permit numerous permutations of what would otherwise be stock plots. *Buffy* is set in an almost timeless present (the late twentieth century is the closest dating permitted),[12] but predicated on a history that dates back to the origins of the human race. After Season 3, the spin-off *Angel* allows for the possibility of 'cross-overs', convergent plotlines between the two shows. This occurs even in Season 5 of *Angel*, one year after the conclusion of *Buffy*, creating the interesting paradox of the virtual crossover. Buffy herself seems to be the stereotypical cinematic blonde, except that instead of becoming the screaming victim of various assailants in the tradition of horror or slasher movies and Italian *giallo* films, she is more than capable of resisting and dealing with the worst that may challenge her. Her name perhaps suggests a counter-cultural statement on the part of her parents, but her high-stepping kung fu kicks when fighting recall the physical undertones of the colloquial use of the adjective 'buff'.[13] And while Buffy may initially appear to possess the vapidity traditionally associated with attractive young females, this impression is likely to be part of her desire not to draw excessive attention to herself.[14] She is, after all, the Slayer, the one living female who can challenge the demonic world. She inhabits the stereotypically Californian city of Sunnydale. Unfortunately, this is situated on a Hellmouth, which attracts the worst elements, such as vampire masters, mayors who have sold their souls to the devil, intergalactic felons, and even original malevolence ('the First Evil'). All of these have as their aim an apocalypse that will destroy the human world and replace it with an alternative, demonic dimension. Buffy has to save the world, a lot.

Beneath all this lies a creation myth, popularised by H.P. Lovecraft in the period after the First World War, according to which mankind replaced earlier creatures, forcing them into the depths or outside the human dimension. But these displaced peoples always wish to return and thus pose a continual threat that must be warded off. That is the cosmogony that is relayed to Buffy by her Watcher, Giles, in the second episode of *Buffy* ('The Harvest'):

> This world is older than any you know. Contrary to popular mythology, it did not begin as a paradise. For untold eons demons walked the Earth. They made it their home, their ... their Hell. But in time they lost their purchase on this reality. The way was made for mortal animals, for ... for man. All that remains of the old ones are vestiges, certain magicks, certain creatures.[15]

This mythology underpins many modern examples of the horror genre. The strongest protection for the human race is likely to be someone whose strength is increased by demonic blood, for instance the half-human, half-vampire *dhampir* of Slavic folklore.[16] Such a figure appears quite frequently in Japanese animation horror, such as D. in *Vampire Hunter D.* (dir. Toyoo Ashida, 1985). In Narumi Kakinouchi's *Vampire Princess Miyu* OVA[17] (dir. Toshiki Hirano, 1988), Miyu, the vampire Guardian, is doubly liminal. Half-human and half-demon, burdened with the duty to return the 'Old Ones', the *Shinma*, to the darkness, she is also tragically frozen in adolescence as a perpetual schoolgirl.[18]

But while the first Slayer may have been created from human female and demon, Buffy, although trapped in her role as Slayer and not infrequently resentful of the limitations this imposes, is fully human and matures from teenager to young adult. The dubious nationalist and racial implications of the Lovecraft model are also clearly reduced as the show progresses and the audience comes to sympathise not only with the human side of the heroine's love interest, Angel, a vampire cursed to feel remorse for his earlier deeds, but also with the punk stylings of Angel's rival, Spike. In *Angel*, humans and demons are shown as being able to co-exist peacefully. Good and evil are a matter of ethics, not genetics. Indeed, a demon with a Bassett hound appearance, Clem, features as a benevolent ally in the final two series of *Buffy*. Although Watchers, vampires (among them, the notorious Dracula attracted by the equal fame of his slayer adversary) and demons (including vengeful Chumash Indians) all have their own stories, the burden of history need not weigh heavy on the present. The very last episode of *Buffy* ('Chosen') provides a remarkably optimistic conclusion in what might appear as the end of History. Democracy, or at least female collectivism, triumphs universally as all women are now potential slayers and Buffy may now retire from her duties. Freedom does come at a cost: both Sunnydale's Hellmouth and its mall are now permanently closed.[19] Still, there will always be a Hellmouth in Cleveland – there are *some* problems that are clearly insoluble.

What's academia got to do with it?

In the 144 42-minute episodes of *Buffy* (leaving aside the further 110 episodes of the *Angel* spin-off) there is enough material to create a mini-world, and scholars have set out to explicate the various cultural and social issues raised.[20] Some tension naturally arises between creators and interpreters. The producers of the show have both encouraged and sought to keep at arm's length dedicated fans and academic audiences, as the commentary by David Fury and Marti Noxon to Season 6, Episodes 1-2 ('Bargaining') amply illustrates. Yet Joss Whedon himself is happy with the attention:

2. Hymns to the Ancient World in (the) Buffyverse

It's always important for academics to study popular culture, even if the thing they are studying is idiotic. If it's successful or made a dent in culture, then it is worthy of study to find out why. Buffy, on the other hand is, I hope, not idiotic. We think very carefully about what we're trying to say emotionally, politically, and even philosophically while we're writing it. The process of breaking a story involves the writers and myself, so a lot of different influences, prejudices, and ideas get rolled up into it. So it really is ... something that is deeply layered textually episode by episode. I do believe that there is plenty to study and there are plenty of things going on in it, as there are in me that I am completely unaware of.[21]

As a spiritual guide, Buffy has gained almost divine significance. 'What would Buffy do?' mocks the fundamentalist Christian problem solving of 'What would Jesus do?', but is also a query that is approached with considerable seriousness by devotees.[22] After all, if Buffy did not die for our sins, she certainly died to save the world – twice. One volume of essays has been dedicated to the philosophical implication of the show.[23] Accordingly, there would appear to be room for those with interests in the ancient world to make their contribution, particularly since the study of Greece and Rome has long had a strong interdisciplinary base. At the same time, it must be remembered that the show's dominant value is irony, which allows it to escape the trap of extolling *specific* cultural values. While (Rupert) Giles, the Oxford-educated librarian played by Anthony Stewart Head, may be as attractive a role model to academics as the legendary Latin master, Mr Chips,[24] Willow's fantasy of academia and scones in a foreign place is simply an educational utopia, not reality.[25]

As it happens, neither Willow nor Buffy can break away from their natural environment and enrol in U(niversity of) C(alifornia), Sunnydale, modelled on the University of California, Los Angeles (UCLA), whose campus was used, along with that of California State University, Northridge, for establishing shots. The college drama within the programme lasts less than two seasons (4 and 5) before the heroine is forced to suspend her education in order to take care of her new sister, Dawn. Buffy is thus prevented from a 'normal' middle-class educational progression, graduating from High School, taking a liberal arts degree, and then moving on to graduate work or employment in the white-collar world. Yet she had already shown herself to be disenchanted with academic matters after boyfriend Riley Finn moved on in Season 5: 'New semester, new classes. Whole new vistas of knowledge to be confused and intimidated by.' While Tara shows real enthusiasm for the educational experience ('This one's going to be fun. Greek Art's gonna touch on so many things – mythology, history, philosophy.'), Buffy has her stake ready: 'The professor spit too much when he talked. It was like being at Sea World. "The first five rows will get wet." '

In fact, by contrast with normal experience, education is not a prime factor in social hierarchy in *Buffy*. Xander is regularly depicted as an underachiever, most suitable for army service or blue-collar employment. Yet Giles, despite his trove of (mainly useless) information, is fit for little regular employment once the school in which he was the librarian was destroyed at the end of Season 3 and in later seasons ends up as the proprietor of a dilapidated magic shop whose recent owners have met unfortunate ends at the hands of the customers. Even Willow, who appears well adapted to an academic environment and has excellent employment prospects afterward, derives much of her learning from unorthodox, magical sources that threaten to take over her life. Throughout the series the 'Scoobie Gang' are misfits who contribute to society in the main by acting outside social norms. A course in Greek Art will not, therefore, make Buffy a better person, especially as it is merely a choice between this class and one on Central American Geopolitics. Given the present location of her ex-boyfriend Riley Finn on military service – and perhaps also alluding to Buffy's geographical dyslexia from the 1992 movie[26] – our heroine is faced with one of the banalities of student life: classes are often taken mainly because of timetabling constraints, not for reasons of interest.

Don't talk Latin in front of the books

Western society frequently regards those with knowledge of the ancient world with considerable esteem, if for no other reason than that few possess such esoteric learning. Still such people are rarely classified along with expert trainspotters, tiddlywinks champions, and other possessors of rare skills. The very term 'Classics' has considerable intellectual cachet, especially since it confuses Greek and Roman authors who have gained a place in the literary canon with the much longer list of approved writers throughout history. Appropriate education in elite schools or near-cabbalistic initiation through academically challenging, and hence exclusive, classes in colleges and universities is regarded as the essential path to knowledge of these authors. Social and intellectual snobbery go hand in hand.

This point is made clearly by Sol Yurick in his newly composed introduction to his novel, *The Warriors* (originally published 1965; reprinted 2003). The novelist sarcastically describes how film critics abased themselves before the product of higher culture after learning that Walter Hill's 1979 film version of the story of a New York street gang fighting its way home through hostile territory was based on an ancient Greek classic. Pauline Kael, the *New Yorker* columnist, as Yurick acerbically relates, even inquired whether the tale was based on the *Odyssey*.[27] In fact, Kael was not far off the mark with respect to the novel. Hinton's *katabasis* while walking through the subway tunnel between 96th and 110th streets has Homeric echoes and Hector's distinctive appearance in a mixed race gang ('blond, wavy hair', p. 140) recalls the Homeric epithet *xanthos* (although in the *Iliad* that descriptor is reserved for the Argive, Menelaos). Even the giant nurse whom three of the gang members attempt to rape in her drunken state resembles the Laestrygonian mother of *Odyssey* 10.112-13 or an ogre's wife. Classical parallels can easily be found. But Yurick is contemptuously dismissive of film critics and regards Hill's work as escapist violence saved only by considerable visual flair.[28]

While attacking the intellectual snobbery of upper-class New York society, Yurick is also making a political statement. The movie lacks the (dominantly Marxist) theme of the book: that even street gangs form naturally into political groups. Yurick had observed this behaviour as a social worker in New York during the 1950s. Xenophon's *Anabasis* (*The March Up Country*) provides a Classical antecedent when the army as a collective assumes many of the features of a Greek city (*polis*).[29] Yet there could hardly be a greater contrast than that between the Classical Greek and contemporary American worlds. Xenophon's mercenaries succeeded in fighting their way through the Middle East to the comparative safety of the Greek world and the author himself, while exiled from Athens for his participation in the campaign, was given an estate on their territory by appreciative Spartan authorities. In Yurick's book, however, the Coney Island gang, the Warriors, after all their battles find themselves back in their home territory, but still imprisoned by poverty and social injustice.

The recent DVD version of the film (2005; labelled 'ultimate director's cut') takes the illustrated version of the *Anabasis*, mentioned briefly in the novel, as the framing of the story, emphasising the comic-strip violence and episodic nature of the tale, while also foregrounding the heroism of its protagonists. By contrast, in Yurick's novel the *Anabasis* has a different function. For gang member Junior, the comic-book version is his favourite read. 'The Junior didn't follow the words too well unless they were printed big, or dark. But he could follow the whole action from the pictures. It was about ancient soldiers, Greeks, heroes who had to fight their way home through many obstacles, but in the end they made it.'[30] Yet, rather than offering a comforting mythology for modern life, the passage underlines the fact that Yurick's gang members are painfully uneducated and the stories of a past age offer a heroic view of struggle that is far removed from the random violence of their environment.

If Yurick explicitly rejects any argument for the equal legitimacy of high (Greek literature) and low culture (graphic novels and film), *Buffy* both parodies high-culture references and exploits them for their resonances. For instance, Buffy's knowledge of Victor Hugo's *Notre Dame de Paris* is shown to be derived from at least a third remove. When asked whether she had completed reading this lengthy tome for the class assignment, she replies: 'I rented the movie.' 'Oh, with, um, with Charles Laughton?' 'I don't know. Was he one of the singing gargoyles?' (Season 5, Episode 14 'Crush'). Tara here identifies the highly esteemed 1939 RKO *Hunchback of Notre Dame* with Laughton playing Quasimodo,[31] but Buffy has headed straight for the Disney animation of 1996. At the same time, for the viewer, Quasimodo's doomed love for Esmeralda is an evocative parallel to Spike's infatuation with Buffy that drives the narrative in this episode.

Allusions to Greek mythology in the series are similarly indirect. There is an homage to the master of stop-motion animation, Ray Harryhausen, when we briefly glimpse Giles fencing against a skeleton created by Anya's inept spell-casting (Season 6, Episode 8 'Tabula Rasa'). The reference is to a famous scene from *Jason and the Argonauts* (1963) where the hero and companions are confronted with the 'Sown Men', skeletons who spring up from the dragon's teeth. In this case, there is a small visual joke that many viewers acquainted with fantasy films would note. A more poignant reference to the same film is likely to have already occurred in Season 5, Episode 17 'Forever', where Spike is shown fighting the ghora demon, while Dawn steals its eggs as a necessary ingredient in the resurrection of her mother. This echoes Jason and Medea's battle with the Hydra for the Golden Fleece in the 1963 film and thus hints at aspects of the characters in the television series. Spike is already seeing himself in the role of a romantic warrior on a quest, while Dawn wishes to be Medea to his Jason, suggesting both infatuation and a developing but dangerous interest in witchcraft. Other parallels to Greek mythology suggest themselves – for instance, Spike's fiery death at the end of the series parallels that of the Greek hero, Heracles, on Mount Oeta. Yet this too is likely to be at several removes from Greek literature, perhaps filtered through the writings on mythology of Joseph Campbell that influenced *Star Wars* and seem directly or indirectly to influence *Buffy*.[32]

In other cases, knowledge of mythology provides a comic element. In Season 1, Episode 4 'Teacher's Pet', Xander babbles on about Greek food and Greek salad, while Giles as interpreter expounds at length on archetypes, such as Greek Sirens. In the meantime, Natalie, the seductress teacher, who also happens to be a She-mantis or kleptes-virgo, prepares for her snack. Xander's research into cloaks of invisibility as a feature of Greek divinities (Season 1, Episode 11 'Out of Mind, Out of Sight') is amusing both because of the character's normal lack of research skills and because it is provides an erroneous solution. Buffy's response ('This girl's pretty petty for a god') deflates the mythical aspects and makes a significant observation for episode's plot. The high school student Marcy has been treated as invisible by her classmates and in time has literally acquired this attribute, which turns out to be very helpful in gaining revenge on those who have ignored her. In both of these cases, male speech is shown to be considerably less valuable than female action, as Buffy is required to come to the rescue once again.

Demonstrating one's knowledge of arcane material (including Greek mythology) thus acts to impress an audience, even if the practical value of the material is much less clear. Even more impressive, as we have seen, is the use of the languages of the ancient world. In many cases, oral use of unknown languages signifies a remarkable skill restricted to the practitioner. The formula 'Abracadraba', which merely displays knowledge of the first four letters of the alphabet, is perceived as magical by the illiterate and uninitiated. Willow's prayer to bring Buffy back to life (Season 6, Episode 1 'Bargaining') is unintelligible to most. But 'Adonai, Helomi, Pine' and 'O Mappa Lamma, Adonai, Helomi' is authentic kabbalistic Hebraic from the *Almadel*,[33] designed to invoke the presence of a helping angel. Actual understanding of the text is not required: the strange nature of unknown language – or languages – is sufficient. For instance, the formula 'Eko eko azarak', popular with modern Wiccan,[34] seems to have been popularised by the early twentieth-century witchcraft practitioner Gerald Gardner, even if the words may have existed earlier.[35] The most likely linguistic explanation is a mixture of Greek (*echo* = 'I have') and Hebraic (Azarak as a proper name) that may be happily interpreted to mean whatever the devotee wishes. But just as Sappho's poem indicates the lesbian relationship between Tara and Willow, the wiccan formulae in the series suffice to mark the pair's interest in white magic. Academics may wish to explain such material, but there are other groups who have their own claims to appropriate representation.[36] Their interests may not coincide with those of academia, or even of the series' scriptwriters, as the furore that broke out over the killing of Tara and the consequent ending of one of the few positive portrayals of a lesbian couple on primetime television indicates.

Greek possesses a particular social cachet, as shown by the use of Greek letters to signify college fraternities, a social system whose origin in Classical revivalism in the United States is now generally forgotten. But in *Buffy* such signs are simply marks of the unknown. Jonathan's demon (Season 4, Episode 17 'Superstar') has a sign described by Tara as 'like a Greek letter, only not'. And while Giles recognises the terrifying killer of Faith's watcher as *kakistos*, 'the worst of the worst' (Season 3, Epsode 3 'Faith, Hope, and Trick'), to Buffy he is merely an exotic item for consumption, 'taquitos'.

Latin, however, is another story. The language of power, of legal maxims and the Catholic Church, it has a solemnity and dread that makes it a regular feature of the horror genre.[37] Giles, the disgraced ex-Watcher, catches the point exactly. Faced by his impotence when the gang needs to solve an encoded computer programme, he bitterly remarks 'Whatever happened to Latin? At least when that made no sense the church approved' (Season 4, Episode 20 'The Yoko Factor').[38] Latin also denotes time-honoured tradition, as the inscription on the demon-slaying scythe of Season 7, denying its use to anyone except the Slayer, shows ('non tibi est, ei solae tractare licet'/ 'It is not for you; she alone is permitted to wield it': Episode 19 'Empty Places'). It is not just a dead language (such as ancient Sumerian): it is an undead language, no longer a living tongue but still maintaining its power. Scary.

The taxonomic use of the language since Linnaeus also accounts for

Latin's regular appearance, its ability to rise from its coffin, in the horror corpus.[39] *Buffy* makes infrequent use of this feature, although it is likely that Spike's girlfriend, the wonderfully insane Drusilla, gains her name from the bizarre (Livia) Drusilla, sister of Caligula, whose incestuous relations with her brother featured in the television adaptation of Robert Graves' *I, Claudius*.[40] But while Latin may be the language of Gregorian chants, it is also mainly the preserve of pedants and bores. So Giles makes a public display of his learning when checking the books on revivication rituals: 'Ah ah ah uh uh uh uh, the book is translated from the Sumerian and rather badly.' (Season 2, Episode 1 'When She Was Bad'). But by the time he has actually decoded the text, the Scoobies are already being kidnapped. The theme recurs in *Angel* (Season 4, Episode 15 'Orpheus') when Fred waxes lyrical about the Pergamum Codex: 'I think some of the really obscure passages are actually Latin translated from a demonic tongue, and they're kind of a hoot. All this stuff about Bacchanals and spells and – actually I think it's probably funnier in Latin. You know how that is sometimes ....' As with glasses, girls with excess knowledge of Latin are unlikely to attract amorous attention – and Willow responds by quickly mumbling 'I'm with someone' and leaving. Nor is Latin simply the preserve of gentlemen. Giles' ex-chum from Oxford, Ethan Rayne, uses his knowledge of the language for petty mischief, conjuring up Janus to confuse Sunnydale (Season 2, Episode 6 'Halloween'). Dalton, a rare example of an educated vampire, makes an unwise display of his knowledge in attempting to translate DuLac's book. In return he earns himself a slapstick beating from Spike (Season 2, Episode 9 'What's My Line, Part 1'). He may well be, as Spike puts it in his charming south London idiom, 'a wanker, but the only one with half a brain'. But intelligence, as with residual emotion, is regarded with suspicion by the mainly zombie-like and irrational creatures of the demon world. Hence it is hardly a coincidence that Dalton is the first victim of the Judge, a Golem-like figure of mindless and emotionless destruction (Season 2, Episode 14 'Surprise').

How authentic is the use of Latin in *Buffy* and *Angel*? Take, for instance, the following example from *Angel*, regularly transmitted on web pages as 'alli permutat anima kimota'. The name of the episode (Season 3, Episode 4) 'Carpe Noctem' is perfectly good Latin, 'Seize the night', a play on the Epicurean maxim 'Carpe Diem' ('Seize the day', i.e. enjoy yourself while you may). But the transmutation spell by which the geriatric Marcus exchanges bodies with Angel is not. Latinists, who often face the task of recovering an original text from scribal miscopying, would seek to emend. 'Alli' quickly changes to 'alii' ('to another', dative case). 'Kimota' is recognised as a mishearing of 'commoda' (an adjective defining 'anima': 'a suitable soul') or perhaps 'commode' ('right away'). But shouldn't 'permutat' ('it changes') be a command? So then, 'alii permutet anima commode' ('let the soul change into another immediately'). But a glance at a Latin

26

dictionary indicates that the verb *permuto* is used not with a dative, but with an ablative. 'Alia permutet anima commode!'

Such emendation of Latin texts is a splendid intellectual pastime, one that has on occasion been compared to solving crossword puzzles, much to the annoyance of senior professors at learned institutions. It is certainly possible to follow the same process of exposition and correction with all the foreign languages quoted in Joss Whedon's universe. There is, however, a slight problem. Whereas editors of texts seek to restore a text according to the original intention of writers who are expressing themselves in their native tongue, it is not at all certain that the Latin texts in the television series were originally syntactically correct. Oral report has it that graduate students in Latin at the University of California, Los Angeles, were telephoned and required to provide translations in rapid time. Errors in transmission and garbled enunciation by actors who have not been trained in Latin (or Greek, or Sumerian, etc. etc.) can easily add to the confusion. Foreign, but vaguely familiar sounding phrases and maxims offer an aural wallpaper, the exact nature of whose design is really of little importance.[41] Indeed, in the line discussed above 'kimota' may be right – as the palindrome of 'atomic', it is the action word that causes Marvelman/Miracleman to transform into superhero, the equivalent of mixing Latin and abracadrabra.[42]

Throughout *Buffy* Latin is likely to be parodied or used as simply part of the rigmarole of spell-casting, 'that stuff with the Latins and the herbs', in Buffy's description (Season 2, Episode 17 'Passion'). As might be expected, Xander, the class clown, figures prominently, mangling even pig Latin: 'Ood-gay, idea-yay, Anyay' (Season 6, Episode 3 'Afterlife'). When Willow defends the power of spells by noting that they require concentration and being attuned to the forces of the universe, his supporting remarks ('Right, one can't go *librum incendere* and expect ...') immediately cause the tome he is reading to ignite. He hurriedly extinguishes the flames by shutting the book, but not before Giles chides him in a manner which links Latinity with profanity: 'Xander, don't speak Latin in front of the books.' (Season 4, Episode 17 'Superstar').[43] Latin may be the prime language for spells, but it's the sound that matters. So when Oz expresses ironic perplexity ('Did I mention I didn't take Latin?'), Willow responds 'You don't have to understand it. You just have to say it – I hope' (Season 2, Episode 22 'Becoming Part 2'). Latin may be fun: 'Fiat lux' ['Let there be light'] is 'better than using a flashlight like some doofus' (Season 5, Episode 4 'Out of Mind'). Yet use by the ignorant can be dangerous (Ethan Rayne's Halloween tricks), ridiculous (so Jonathan's creation of a Ground Hog's Day scenario for Buffy at the Magic Shop: Season 6, Episode 4 'Life Serial'), or even soul-destroying (as in Willow's addiction to *Potestas* ['Power'] that Amy can exploit: Season 6, Episode 12 'Doublemeat Palace'). When a wiser Willow uses Latin, it is only as the necessary means to an end: 'Via, concursus, tempus, spatium, audi me ut imperio.[44] Screw it!

27

Mighty forces, I suck at Latin, ok? But that's not the issue. I'm the one in charge and I'm telling you to open up, portal, now!' (Season 7, Episode 15 'Get It Done').

Joseph Farrell has described the traditional method of teaching Latin as operating

> under the watchful eye of a teacher who will respond by pointing out and discussing at length and in meticulous detail each and every one of the student's mistakes. This is a type of education that teaches humility as well as Latin and that equates humility with ignorance of Latin, pride with knowing it well.[45]

While Vergil famously has Aeneas' father Anchises declare that it was the duty of the Roman rulers to beat down the proud and spare the downtrodden,[46] applying imperial methods in the classroom is no longer common or even likely to be tolerated. In the secular world of the late twentieth century, knowledge of Latin is no longer essential for success,[47] but merely one option among many.

If the language of the Romans, so familiar from inscriptions that reflect the glory of their empire, still asserts power, the actual process of Rome's conquests is less often considered. It is typical of *Buffy* that Spike, who as a vampire has been around much longer than the Scoobies and has international experience, should cut through the liberal guilt felt about the ill-treatment of the Chumash Indians of Southern California, after avenging native American demons gatecrash Buffy's Thanksgiving dinner. 'You won. All right? You came in and you killed them and you took their land. That's what conquering nations do. It's what Caesar did. And he's not going around saying, "I came, I conquered, I felt really bad about it." The history of the world isn't people making friends. You had better weapons and you massacred them. End of story.'[48]

This sobering view of history raises the question of whether the ancient world is a privileged source of cultural capital,[49] or, more democratically, is but one choice in a multicultural world. The Classicist who ventures into this field with displays of hard-earned expertise runs the risk of beginning as trendy and ending as bore of the week. Sleazy college student, Parker Abrams, like Joan Collins, looks for guidance to cinematic depictions of the ancient world; 'Some party, huh. Last day in Rome' (Season 4, Episode 3 'Harsh Light of Day'). Buffy's reply is worth pondering: 'Better. No old Romans.'

3

The Peplum and Other Animals

'Joey, do you like movies about gladiators?'

Consideration of *Buffy* suggests that the world of Greece and Rome has a place in modern popular media, but ancient material is employed under restricted conditions (e.g. the use of ancient languages in standard horror scenarios) and is in competition with other cultural forms that have now become internationalised, such as Chinese martial arts. The past is generally taken to support conservative trends in American life, although in the one memorable appearance of Sappho's poetry it may also serve as a model for the present. An expert who offers excessive commentary on this risks seeming a pompous prat or simply superfluous. A more sensible alternative to trying to co-opt popular culture for academic purposes, to 'correcting' misunderstandings of the ancient world, would be to examine popular culture itself in its historical and national settings.

For this purpose, I have chosen in this chapter to concentrate on the Italian action films featuring hyper-masculine heroes that achieved international success as 'sword-and-sandal epics' (Italian: 'sandaloni') or 'peplums' (the term preferred by French film critics) in the late 1950s and the first half of the 1960s. Their modern reputation is as a *mauvais genre*, a type of film that breaks all the standard rules of decorum – not epic enough for the gravity of the ancient world, too ironic or kitsch to provide a suitable didactic message. In brief, if high art is taken out of the ancient world, the result may be seen as not merely vulgar, but downright tasteless, not 'Classical', but simply dated.

In the Zucker/ Abrams/ Zucker disaster movie spoof *Airplane* (1980) Captain Oveur (Peter Graves) utters the infamous words given at the start of this chapter to a boy visitor to his cockpit. Its obvious incongruity (not to mention moral incorrectness) highlights the difficulties faced in taking sword-and-sandal films seriously. Buff men without shirts, indeed dressed in what look like miniskirts or tutus, cannot help but seem camp to modern audiences. That many of these heroes began their careers as muscleman performers in Mae West's Las Vegas Sahara revue (1954-7) makes sniffy comparison with Chippendales performers that much more pointed.[1] Even *300* (2006), glorying in its display of mighty Spartan abdominal muscles, has not been able to escape the weight of cinematic history. Both homoerotic and homophobic, the film exhibits remarkable levels of testosterone and, in places, a comic-strip grandeur. But the depiction of the *agoge*, the brutalising education of Spartan youths, un-comfortably recalls Alan Parker's depiction of the sexual degradation his protagonist suffers when imprisoned in Turkey (*Midnight Express* 1978) – an image that also clearly fires the imagination of Captain Oveur in his interrogation of little Joey ('Joey, have you ever been to a Turkish prison?').

A first requirement for understanding is to set the sword-and-sandal films within the history of the Italian movie industry. This can be achieved by considering the depiction of the gladiator Spartacus up to the 1950s. Then, avoiding the restriction of considering only the sub-species of gladiator movie, I will examine cinematic adaptations of Bulwer-Lytton's Roman melodrama *The Last Days of Pompeii*, including the 1935 American version, to trace the effects of national and Hollywood productions on Sergio Leone's 1959 film. At this point it will be possible to examine the nature of the peplum, a phenomenon that enjoyed a quite limited geographical and temporal existence.[2] To conclude, an examination of two Hercules films made in Italy in 1961 will show the opportunities presented by the mythological form and the cross-currents of influence with other cinematic genres.

'I'm Spartacus'

Long before Stanley Kubrick's classic 1960 version of the tale of the gladiator who defied Rome, based on Howard Fast's politically committed novel from 1951, Spartacus was a well-known figure of Italian film. Giovanni Vidali's *Spartaco* (1913) depicts a valiant – and clearly hetero-sexual – gladiator who has rebelled against Rome only because he has been refused the right to marry his beloved Narona, the daughter of the Roman general Crassus. Love conquers all, since the maiden reconciles the rebellious gladiators who have taken refuge on Vesuvius with her father's forces, throwing herself between the two battle-lines to prevent bloodshed, like one of Livy's Sabine women. Troubles still lie ahead, when a rival tries to make it appear that Spartacus has killed Crassus' brother. Only at the last minute is the hero saved from being torn apart by lions in the arena by the discovery of the real murderer. Instead of Spartacus dying, the villain suffers a well-deserved fate of being torn to pieces by wild beasts, while everyone else, including the happy Roman spectators, appears to live happily ever after.

Spartaco is in many ways the prototype for the genre. First, it uses small amounts of historical detail – for instance, the clash between the Roman general, Crassus, and Spartacus, the Thracian leader of a band of escaped gladiators (and runaway slaves) that took place in southern Italy 71 BC – to lend credence to the story. Next, archaeological material is added, such as the accurate depiction of gladiatorial armour and the amphitheatre in which Spartacus fights so successfully and where he undergoes condemnation *ad bestias*. However, the siege of the rebel forces on Vesuvius (by the praetor Glaber, not Crassus) had taken place two years previously and ended in a famous slave victory.[3] Furthermore, while the amphitheatre at Pompeii dates from about 70 BC, the Colosseum at Rome, the site of the games in the film, was not inaugurated until 80 AD by the emperor Titus.[4]

The love story is another modern addition, although from a literary source. Raffaelo Giovagnoli's 1874 novel *Spartaco* featured a romance between the hero and a Roman matron, a theme still visible in the 1960 film version (in which Jean Simmons plays the British slave-girl Varinia, a latter-day version of Narona).[5] The sudden dangers from which the hero and heroine are rescued in Vidali's film and the happy ending are, however, pure cinematic melodrama. One obvious parallel is the rescue of the hero from the arena at the conclusion of *The Last Days of Pompeii*, a novel that was also popular with Italian silent film-makers. But the melodrama is also strangely 'authentic', since it might have been borrowed from the world of the ancient Greek love romances. Indeed, if a pedigree were needed for the 'sword-and-sandal' genre, these Greek novels would readily provide one. Composed in the Roman era, but set in an ill-defined classical Greek past, they are full of unlikely plot twists to wring the maximum pathos out of the perils of their Pauls and Paulines. These romances may have been the pulp fiction of the ancient world, but they undoubtedly enjoyed considerable popularity.[6]

Riccardo Freda's *Spartaco* (1952) recalls Vidal's parallels with Bulwer-Lytton's novel through its use of sets at Cinecittà constructed for the 1948 remake of *Last Days of Pompeii* (*Les derniers jours de Pompeii*, dir. Paolo Moffa), but in other respects is closer to Giovagnoli's novel than to Vidali's version. Its hero is a Thracian who has risen to become a Roman officer and then been condemned to slavery for protecting his people against atrocities ordered by his commander. Freda reportedly said that he had initially wanted to expose the basis of Roman imperialism in slavery, but had been prevented by the strongly pro-Roman attitude of the film censorship of the time.[7] Yet the storyline of the film clearly rejects any idea of an eternal struggle by the slaves against Rome: Spartacus is willing to come to a peace agreement with Crassus, since he knows that he cannot withstand Rome's military might forever, but his lieutenant Oenomaus deliberately provokes a conclusive battle while his leader is absent. Spartacus out of loyalty has no choice but to rejoin his men and die in a losing struggle. Yet the final scene of the film shows Amytis, the Thracian slave who has become his lover (played by the ballet dancer Ludmilla Tcherina), taking up the hero's sword as a sign of the eternal struggle for freedom.[8] It is difficult not to think that the contradictions of production were too great. Giovagnoli's romance is reproduced with awareness of Vidali's version. Tcherina's balletic expertise is used for an exotic dance on board a ship in a flooded Colosseum after which Spartacus must rescue her from the lions that have been let loose to devour her by the decadent Sabina, daughter of Crassus. As Sabina, Gianna Maria Canale appears in one of her classic vamp roles, seducing the ingenuous Spartacus but unable, in the end, to bind this man of the people to a life of luxury.[9] After the success of Kirk Douglas in the 1959 film, Freda's effort (released in the US in abbreviated form as *Sins of the Romans*) was almost forgotten. Yet in its very incoherence in trying to balance the power of Rome and the slaves' desire for a better life, popular politics and aristocratic power, spectacle, romance, and the aspiration for a better future set in a distant past, it well reflects post-war Italy.[10]

In short, it may be argued that there is as much of a tradition for the distortion of history in its literary or dramatic representations as for its respectful recreation.[11] The story of Spartacus has been as radically altered in modern times as that of Alexander was after his death. The same process can be seen in the constant rewriting of versions of Hercules (or Ursus, Maciste, Samson, Goliath, and Colossus – all representing an archetypal strong man).[12] It is impossible to avoid the effect of American distributors' alterations to Italian sword-and-sandal movies, which is in part responsible for the mockery expressed in *Airplane* or *Mystery Science Theater 3000* or even Disney's *Hercules* (itself mediated via Las Vegas).[13] The modern audience's reception of the past will then be filtered through its knowledge of such later judgements. Yet it is also possible to read *back* through Western (and even Eastern – see Chapter 5) responses to the past, not to discover an original narrative but rather to recover an 'authentic' multiplicity of stories in the Classical tradition. Indeed, the exploration of 'bad taste' or 'tasteless' genres, such as the peplum, offers an opportunity to free the study of the past from constant association with high culture and good taste.

The volcano explodes

In 1834 recent discoveries in the Kingdom of Naples inspired Edward Bulwer-Lytton to write a novel, *The Last Days of Pompeii*, whose climax would be the city's destruction. The expansion of rail transport throughout Europe would soon create a need for entertainment on long journeys, and Bulwer-Lytton's nineteenth-century equivalent of airport novels more than adequately catered to the passengers' desires.[14] With its turgid mix of melodrama opposing Greek culture to Roman brutality in AD 79 Pompeii, *The Last Days of Pompeii* became remarkably popular. It was soon adapted in the film era and became a staple of Italian silent cinema, beginning with *Gli ultimi giorni di Pompeii*, directed by Luigi Maggi (1908).[15] Two more versions followed in 1913: Giovanni Enrico Vidali's *Jone o Gli ultimi giorni di Pompeii* and Eleuterio Rodolfi's *Gli ultimi giorni di Pompeii*.[16] A 1926 silent version directed by Carmine Gallone and Amleto Palermi provided superior orgy scenes and footage of an actual volcanic eruption. All have a similar narrative derived from Bulwer-Lytton's novel: Glaucus, a Greek inhabitant of Pompeii who has returned from abroad, is in love with the beautiful Ione; the blind flower-girl, Nydia, is in turn besotted with Glaucus; and Arbaces, the debauched priest of Isis, lusts after Ione. Arbaces lays the blame for a murder he has committed on Glaucus, who is condemned to death in the arena. Then, in a sudden dramatic reversal, Nydia reveals the true culprit. At this very moment, Vesuvius explodes. Glaucus and Ione escape through the self-sacrifice of Nydia to sail off to Athens and live happily ever after as Christians, while Arbaces perishes spectacularly in the eruption.

These films have been discussed at length by Maria Wyke, who has shown their links with the continuing discoveries by Italian archaeologists and also with pyrodramas of the late nineteenth century that were based on Bulwer-Lytton's novel.[17] Entertainment could thus pose as edification of the masses. The punishment of the guilty and the saving of the innocent also fitted well with Christian moralising of the time as Pompeii had often been identified with Sodom and Gomorrah. The last-minute reprieve of the hero and condemnation of his accuser is a crowd-pleasing turn that Vidali also used in his *Spartaco*: the audience identifies with the masses watching in the amphitheatre and their desire for vengeance. That the villain in Bulwer-Lytton's story is an oriental who threatens the chastity of white women also caters for the racial stereotyping and colonialising fantasies of the period. Viewers could leave the theatre satisfied that virtue is rewarded and that the guilty suffer in the end.

The 1935 Hollywood 'remake' produced by Merian C. Cooper and directed by Ernest B. Schoedsack is a marked contrast. It is introduced by an extraordinary disclaimer: 'Although this story is an original one, and the characters and the plot have no relation to those in the novel by Sir Edward Bulwer-Lytton, acknowledgment is made of his description of Pompeii which has inspired the physical setting of this picture.' Maria Wyke regards this as a sign of fading American interest in the Pompeian excavations. It may also indicate depression era budgetary exigencies, as painted backdrops are used together with inexpensive sets to depict a rather generic Roman town with working-class quarters as well as seaside villas that illustrate its protagonist's social progress.

The narrative differs completely from that of earlier films of the same name. Marcus the blacksmith, a decent, hard-working blue-collar everyman, becomes embittered when his wife and son are run over and killed by an out-of-control chariot. Disillusioned with life, having had to sell everything in an attempt to provide medicine for his injured son, he becomes a gladiator, working his brutal way to top billing until an injury prevents him from pursuing his career.

Next, he provides 'muscle' for slavers in Africa and then decides to seek his fortune as a horse-trader in Judaea. This brings him into contact with the corrupt Roman governor, Pontius Pilate, who surreptitiously arranges for Marcus to raid the local tribesmen and split the profits with him. At the same time, Marcus' adopted son (the child of one of his victims in the gladiatorial arena) is critically injured but healed by Christ, who is shortly afterwards condemned by a visibly distraught Pilate.[18]

Having gained his fortune, Marcus retires to Pompeii where he becomes the producer of entertainment in the amphitheatre. However, his now youthful son has rejected his father's lifestyle and is secretly assisting slaves to escape certain death in the arena. When the boy is captured along with the runaways, his father, the impresario of the games, is ironically unable to save him from meeting his fate before the eyes of Pompeii's citizens. Only the sudden eruption of Vesuvius saves the day. Marcus now realises that the greatest good in life is not money. Happiness lies instead in maintaining his family and following the teachings of the holy man of Judaea. Marcus lays down his life to save his son and the boy's beloved. He awakens amid the destruction to a heavenly chorus as he is summoned by the Lord into the next life.

The film is in many ways an answer to Cecil B. DeMille's epics, such as *The Sign of the Cross* (1932), since it offers unsubtle religious moralising but without DeMille's spectacle of Roman orgies and sin. Partly gangster movie (the hero abandons any concern for other members of society in his desire for wealth, only to discover that his success is hollow), partly boxing film (Marcus, whose very name suggests a generic common Joe, rises up the bill, surrounded by sycophantic supporters while displaying indifference for the lives of the fighters he defeats), it also borrows from Christian depictions of miracles in films such as *Ben Hur* (dir. Fred Niblo, 1925). The themes of the protagonist's rejection of society's values, his downfall when he believes he has achieved success, and the possibility of final redemption were particularly popular in the Depression era, since they criticised the heartlessness of the rich while reaffirming the human dignity of the poor and emphasising their eventual reward (although not necessarily in this life). There is a limited amount of social criticism in the story, such as in the depiction of the lack of medical treatment available for the poor (aside from religious faith) and their vulnerability in the face of contemptuous treatment by the wealthy and corrupt politicians. Still, Marcus' methods of redressing these wrongs are depicted as socially harmful. Family is presented as the great bond that must be preserved, a common theme in Hollywood films. But in the Depression, when numerous white males were suddenly forced to travel in search of work, the emphasis on familial values would have struck a particular nerve. Most notably, the film does not advocate change by overthrow of the established order under any circumstances. Unlike Spartacus and his gladiators, the escaped slaves sentenced to the arena do not attempt to rebel to gain their aims, but rather wish merely to flee to a land that is free from Roman influence. As America has not yet been discovered, this utopia remarkably turns out to be Ireland. Since the climactic battle in the arena in this film occurs between these pacifistic potential Celts and British barbarians on horse-back (which suggests a possible model for the battle of Carthage scene in *Gladiator* (dir. Ridley Scott, 2000)) it is likely that producer Merian C. Cooper was here seeking to exploit ethnic prejudices already present in his audience. Pompeii itself is reduced to the setting of a spectacular volcanic eruption, a warning of the uncertainties of life in this world in comparison with the guarantee of salvation for those who believe in the next.

Paolo Moffa's post-Second World War French-Italian production *Les derniers jours de Pompeii* (completed in 1948, released in 1950) returns to Bulwer-Lytton and builds on its understated Christian themes. In the novel a Christian priest converts Ione's brother, Apaecides, who is murdered by Arbaces, the priest of Isis, when he threatens to reveal his tricks. The blame for the killing is then placed on Ione's lover, Glaucus. Moffa, drawing on themes familiar from cinematic adaptations of Sienkiewicz's *Quo Vadis*, stresses the persecution of all poor Christians by the Roman government. In this manner, placing faith in Christianity could be portrayed as an authentically Italian response to the violence of those in power, be they the forces of Fascism or of the German occupation. As Wyke notes, this was but one of a number of Italian post-war depictions of persecution in ancient times, including Biasetti's *Fabiola* (1948), a tale of the mistreatment of Christians before Constantine's adoption of Christianity as Rome's official religion. All were funded by the Christian Democrats as part of a programme of establishing their claim to be the real voice of Italy between the (Communist) left and (Fascist) right.[19] As with Cooper's film, a subplot now dominates, but the change in emphasis restricted the story's appeal. *Les derniers jours de Pompeii* did well at the box office in Italy but appears not to have had any great success elsewhere.[20]

Gli ultimi giorni di Pompeii (1959), directed by Mario Bonnard and Sergio Leone,[21] takes the lack of interest in Pompeii for its own sake a step further. The scriptwriters included Ennio De Concini, who had worked on Pietro Francisci's *Labours of Hercules* (1958) and *Hercules and the Queen of Lydia* (1959) as well as Vittorio Cottafavi's *Revolt of the Gladiators* (*La rivolta di gladiatori,* 1958) and who would go on to script numerous biblical and peplum[22] efforts through the 1960s. More notable from hindsight are the names of Duccio Tessari, Sergio Corbucci, and Sergio Leone himself, who all graduated from the sword-and-sandal genre to produce the finest Italian westerns of the 1960s. Wyke regards the film they produced as pure entertainment created out of now empty signifiers,[23] since there are no explicit ethical and political messages. However, closer examination suggests that the changes in the diegesis and the visual portrayal of Pompeii reveal a number of interesting developments in historical film.

Most obvious is the star factor in the casting of Steve Reeves as Glaucus after his two very successful Hercules outings for Francisci.[24] That an ex-Mr Universe (1950) should be chosen for the leading role is also less surprising in an Italian context, since the Punic Era epic *Cabiria* had in 1914 launched the strongman career of the Genoan longshoreman Bartolemeo Pagano, who starred as the male protagonist's servant, Maciste.[25] In fact, Maciste was not the first gentle giant of the silver screen: that honour goes to the character of Ursus 'the Bear', the heroine's bodyguard, played by Bruto Castellani who enjoyed a major role in the 1912 version of *Quo Vadis*. Furthermore in Vidali's 1913 *Spartaco,* Mario Guaita, a well-known body-builder, had depicted on screen a populist strong man and unifying leader – thus strikingly foreshadowing the development of modern Italian politics. Yet Maciste's performance in *Cabiria*, where he bent prison bars and fought off puny enemies, surpassed those of all his predecessors and paved the way for approximately thirty more films of which he was the star. Helping the weak while avoiding trouble, Maciste appeared as the embodiment of Italian manhood (despite appearing in blackface!) and was clearly a model for propaganda photographs of a bare-chested Mussolini posing as a man of the people in the 1920s and 1930s.

Unlike the bald Pagano (and *il Duce*), however, Reeves had an impressive full head of hair, slicked back in 1950s style, and may even have set a trend for such coiffure among the body-building fraternity in the period. He also was notable for his fine, almost feminine features that together with his physique gave him a Classical image. Thus his appearance appealed to both male and female audiences. That a leading man born in Glasgow, Montana might become a major star in Italian movies would initially seem unlikely. Part of the answer lies in the Americanophile atmosphere left over from the liberation of Italy in the Second World War. Particularly in the south of Italy and Sicily, the United States was seen by many as the best hope for the future, a place to which large numbers of the population migrated. There was even, as some Sicilian separatists fantasised, a dream of political union with the United States. In Italian political thought a clear distinction was made between Fordism (a capitalist form of industrialisation by piecework valuation of labour, originating in America) and Americanism (philosophy put into action, i.e. deeds, not words, but without the Fascist emphasis on action for its own sake) that could overcome the stultifying social structures of Europe.[26] Who best to represent this than an American country boy whose superb physique marked him out as a man of action?

Italian films of the period were regularly dubbed because of technical difficulties in sound recording in the presence of noisy film cameras. So it was irrelevant whether the lead actors could speak Italian or not. Indeed *Gli ultimi giorni* stars not only Reeves as Glaucus, but also the respected Spanish actor Fernando Rey as Arbaces. Christine Kaufman (German) is cast as Ione, Barbara Carroll (American) as Nydia, and Anne-Marie Baumann (French) as Julia, no longer Bulwer-Lytton's daughter of a rich

Pompeian senator and rival for Glaucus' affections but now the concubine of the governor of Pompeii. Commercial Italian cinema thus became internationalised in its use of acting talent, which in turn encouraged investment from foreign distributors and the export of such films. In the case of *Gli ultimi giorni*, Spanish and German as well as Italian production companies provided financial backing. In short, for the first time since *Cabiria*, whose success in America was at least partly thanks to the strong Italian immigrant community, Italian-made films depicting the world of Greece and Rome could compete with their Anglophone counterparts such as *Helen of Troy* (dir. Robert Wise, 1956) or *Ben Hur* (dir. William Wyler, 1959) in an international market.

In Italy, sword-and-sandal films came to be aimed at second- or third-tier cinemas in inner city or provincial locations as cheap entertainment for the lower classes (workers or farm labourers, often illiterate or semi-literate) in pre-television days. The dubbed soundtracks, rather than subtitles, appealed to this audience. Muscleman movies also provided a reassuring sense of the worth of masculine labour in an era of rapid industrialisation, particularly in Italy's north, both for southern migrants who provided the human capital for these developments and for those left behind. The emphasis in such films on the protection of the weak from overpowering forces also struck a nerve with the underprivileged and exploited.[27] It is not merely the muscular power of the hero that allows him to succeed against often apparently overwhelming odds, but an inner moral strength that permits his body, nearly naked and unassisted, to withstand torture and pain on behalf of others.[28] The semi-religious over-tones hardly need explication.

Non-Italian audiences would find other reference points. Particularly in the United States, the Hercules films were subject to major advertising campaigns by the promoter Joseph E. Levine. Buying the rights to *The Labours of Hercules* in 1959 for $120,000, Levine launched a saturation campaign of promotion. The film, now relabelled simply *Hercules*, cost around a million dollars in advertising but was rewarded with an $18 million dollar return at the box office. The entrepreneurial Levine revived Barnum and Bailey showmanship in lavish – and garish – Hollywood parties and distributed 700 4-lb chocolate Hercules figures to members of the media.[29] The attraction was the implied sexuality of bare-chested or scantily dressed body-builders and similarly clad starlets in what Levine termed 'God, sex, and spectacle' films. Much more was promised in the advertising than was actually produced on screen (another good principle of showmanship) but the films catered for an increasing demand at the time. The titillation of muscle-building had already been part of Mae West's mid-50s Las Vegas revue. Now the *Hercules* movies and *Sodom and Gomorrah* (1961), a rare venture into the biblical adventure genre by an American director (Robert Aldrich) with a mainly Italian cast, filmed in Morocco and at Cinecittà, provided Levine with all his requirements. The use of wide-screen CinemaScope and Technicolor[30] in such films made them much more attractive than black-and-white small-screen television. A substantial increase in disposable income for postwar American youth also allowed frequent attendance at the cinema (either regular theatres or the drive-ins), which became part of the dating process. This in turn created a demand for films that were visually entertaining in terms of the mise-en-scène, action sequences, and the stars' physical attributes. Peplum movies with mythological heroes (e.g. Hercules) and Classical settings (e.g. Rome or Pompeii) not only suited these needs very well, but were also more 'respectable' than the low budget science fiction and horror fare provided up to this point by, for instance, American International Pictures.

Leone's *Gli ultimi giorni di Pompeii* is in some ways exceptional. It has connections with 'Hollywood' blockbusters such as *The Robe* (dir. Henry Koster, 1953) and *Ben Hur* (1959) – both actually produced at Cinecittà – in its mix of Christian and Roman themes, its international cast, and its relatively high production values for an Italian sword-and-sandal film. In the United States it was distributed by United Artists, a much more respectable label at the time than Levine's Embassy Pictures. Yet the links with the more plebeian entries in the peplum canon are also considerable. For instance, the screening time is less than two hours, a concession to the audience's attention span and comfort at a time when American mega-movies were often exceeding three hours' running time.[31] Commentators have also mentioned *contaminatio* from the western genre in scenes where masked bandits on horseback rob the villas, the Roman equivalent of ranch houses, around Pompeii. The murder of the hero's father in one of these raids introduces the stock theme of vengeance, also commonly associated with cowboy films. Still, these are commonplaces of action movies and care must be taken not to read into this feature Leone's future success with Italian westerns. The elasticity of cinematic genres can easily be illustrated by the fact that *A Fistful of Dollars* (1964) was itself a remake of Kurosawa's samurai film *Yojimbo* (1961). And Kurosawa had in turn most likely been inspired by Dashiell Hammett's hard-boiled detective novel *Red Harvest* (1929). As will be seen in Chapter 4, it would be equally easy to convert a classical story (the return of Odysseus), already frequently treated in the sword-and-sandal style, into a western (*The Return of Ringo*, 1965) as to incorporate western elements into films set in the ancient world. In brief, Italian 'genres' such as the peplum are extremely permeable, as the plotline of *Gli ultimi giorni* reveals.

The story begins with the centurion Glaucus (Reeves) returning to Pompeii after the wars, a change from Bulwer-Lytton's Greek protagonist of the same name coming back from a sojourn in Athens. The new version retains the stranger-in-town scenario, while Glaucus' military background establishes the protagonist as a leader of men and a Roman (despite his Greek name) who will be able to fight for his ideals. His initial contact with the heroine Ione now occurs when the latter loses control of her chariot and Glaucus manages to stop the runaway horses. The reason for inserting this non-canonic episode is clear: saving the damsel in distress fosters an immediate relationship between the two leads. It may also be a reminder of Reeves' deeds as Hercules, since a mere year previously he had saved Iole when her horses had bolted at the beginning of *The Labours of Hercules*. But this time he does not uproot a tree to throw in the horses' path to halt their flight. Glaucus is no superman. He simply races along-side Ione's chariot, grasps the reins, and brings the horses to a halt, a daring feat but one that is not uncommon in westerns.[32] When a banquet is held at the villa of Ione's father, the consul of Pompeii, the hero's status as protector of the weak is further developed. He saves Nydia, in this version Ione's blind servant, from abuse at the hands of the local praetorian soldiers.

As already noted, a major addition to the standard plotline is the raiding of the homes of the wealthy around Pompeii by black-masked horsemen, who leave as their mark the sign of the cross. Thus they implicate the adherents of the new Christian religion in these atrocities, which include the murder of Glaucus' father. When Nydia, who is revealed to be a Christian, accidentally makes the leader of the praetorians aware that she and her fellow-believers are meeting on the slopes of Pompeii (compare the slave escapees in the 1935 version), this information leads to the capture of the entire group. Believed to be the bandits responsible for the carnage in the area, they are sentenced to death in the arena. In the meantime, Glaucus and his friends (in particular, the resourceful Pompeian thief, Antonius) have discovered that the hooded raiders are in fact the local praetorians acting on behalf of Arbaces. The priest of Isis is no longer a rival for Ione's affections, but in this version of the story implicated as one of the leaders of a sinister organisation that threatens the city. When Glaucus seeks to warn the consul, it is revealed that Ione's father's concubine Julia is also part of this plot, the purpose of which is to pay for an army to expel the Romans from Egypt. In what is perhaps another borrowing from *The Labours of Hercules*, where Hercules drops through a hidden trapdoor before recovering to dispatch the tyrant's soldiers, Glaucus, warding off the conspirators, falls into a hidden pit beneath the Temple of Isis. He fights his way out, battling a crocodile on the way. But in the meantime Julia has murdered the consul to prevent his intervention and placed the blame on Glaucus. Instead of saving the city, our hero is consigned to being eaten alive by wild beasts, along with Ione who, like Nydia, has refused to deny her Christian faith. Love triumphs: Glaucus breaks free from his cell in time to battle the lion that is about to devour his beloved and the other Christians. His companions arrive armed at the amphitheatre, disguised as gladiators, where they stage a surprise attack on the praetorians. At this moment, the volcano erupts and panic ensues. Julia and Arbaces perish in the Temple of Isis.

Glaucus and Ione, together with Nydia and the slavegirl's sweetheart, Antonius, after evading numerous dangers, escape by boat from the destruction while molten lava and ash descend on Pompeii.

Leone has made changes to the story great and small. The assignment of a consul to govern Pompeii is a relatively minor adjustment of the historical post of *duumvir* (more or less one of two mayors for the city). The presence of praetorian guards (the stock villains of many films set in Roman times, including *Gladiator*), however, is a major invention in the Pompeian context, since they are the elite troops assigned to the emperor, not a consul. The exploits undertaken by Steve Reeves add to the entertainment. Although not up to the standard of twenty-first-century choreography, his fight with the lion is at least the equal of Victor Mature's battle with the tiger in *Demetrius and the Gladiators* (1954), itself borrowed for Russell Crowe's arena exploits fifty years later. Even Glaucus' struggle with an apparently rubber crocodile in the pit beneath the Temple of Isis has some point, since it reinforces the Egyptian themes associated with Arbaces and Julia in the film.

While the singing of Negro spirituals by condemned Christians in prison preceding their execution is a noticeable anachronism, it certainly contributes emotionally. The most obvious reference is to the Christian martyrdoms depicted in *Fabiola* (1948). At the same time, the style of singing introduces a cinematic comment on the post-civil-war history of the United States. In a reversal of D.W. Griffith's *Birth of a Nation* (1915), riders in black masks who leave the mark of the cross behind after their outrages are persecuting true Christians, while the good citizens of Pompeii refuse to admit what is going on around them. The similarities to the developing civil rights movement in the US need hardly be stressed.

Most striking, even bizarre, is the introduction of the Egyptian liberation sub-plot. Arbaces in Bulwer-Lytton's novel was described as 'the descendant of the dread Egyptian kings', secretly mocking the ritual practices of the ignorant Pompeian adherents to the cult of Isis.[33] But he never intends to reclaim regal power. The suggestion in Leone's film that Julia will become the new Cleopatra indicates a megalomania that befits the revenge themes of a Fu Manchu story or the megalomaniacal scheming of the villain in a James Bond movie. Yet this plot also resonates with the theme of a life-or-death struggle between Italy and the East that underpins the death of Dido in Vergil's *Aeneid* and Livy's account of the Punic Wars. The innate conflict between Italy and Africa, between Roman virtues and Semitic perfidy, had figured prominently in Italian cinema at least since *Cabiria*. Leone might even be alluding to the film that served as a Fascist justification for the Abyssinian campaign, *Scipio l'africano* (1937), in which Hannibal explicitly refers to his childhood vow to hate Rome eternally. But there are surely contemporary overtones in addition to generic references from the historical film tradition. For all Leone's reluctance to incorporate explicitly political messages into his work,[34] it can hardly be coincidental that the military police and the politicians of Pompeii are co-operating in criminal activities and their subsequent cover-ups. In post-war Italy, corruption amongst the ruling political party and the carabinieri allowed the re-establishment of the power of the Mafia and other criminal organisations.[35] *Gli ultimi giorni di Pompeii* is thus no advertisement for the dubious politics of the Christian Democrats, but with its revanchist plot offers a warning that there are still hidden forces in Italian society, thought to be defeated, that may wish to return to power.

The question remains of the relationship of the Leone film to the historical reality of the ancient world. Is it only the volcano erupting (a rather weak special effect in the movie, created as it appears to be by a fireworks display on a rather plain hill) that connects this tale of crime and punishment with actual events of AD 79? Bulwer-Lytton had based his story around the discovery of human remains that in a typical archaeological reconstruction had been identified with the owner of the House of Diomedes:

> In the garden was found a skeleton with a key by its bony hand, and near it a bag of coins. This is believed to have been the master of the house – the unfortunate Diomed, who had probably sought to escape by the garden, and been destroyed either by the vapours or some fragment of stone.[36]

The impression of a woman, one of twenty bodies excavated in the basement of the house, was taken to be the owner's daughter and given the name Julia in the novel. In the 1959 version, Diomedes has disappeared and Julia is no longer the spoilt rival for Glaucus' affections, but instead the secret villain. Yet something of the immediacy of 'the City of Pompeii … disinterred from its silent tomb, all vivid with undimmed hues'[37] remains in the film. Early scenes depict the townspeople rushing past a triangular building at a cross-road, This is surely based on a well-known structure (regio VII, insula 12, house f) close to the Stabian baths – which is regularly identified in archaeological texts as a *lupanar* (brothel). Excavated in 1862, it was unknown to Bulwer-Lytton. Yet Leone uses the building not for its notoriety, but for its architectural shape, as it permits a view down two roads simultaneously. At the close of the film, after the eruption, there is a poignant tableau: instead of bustling traffic, there are only destruction, fires and bodies to be seen. This is a trademark Leone shot, relying on widescreen photography for its emotional impact, which predates his depictions of the futility of war in the battle of the bridge in *The Good, the Bad, and the Ugly* (1966) or the Goya-esque scene of slaughtered civilians of *Duck You Sucker* (*Giù la testa*, 1971).

Viewers with a keen eye for scenery will also spot, at the beginning of the film as Glaucus and friends arrive in Pompeii, the Latin notice

VALENTIS
FLAMINISNERONIS
PERPETUIGLAD PAR•XX

painted on the wall above a shop just inside the city gates, as well as

OFFICINA
UBANI
OFFECTORIS

inscribed on a wall on the way to the Temple of Isis. The first is an abbreviated version of a well-known inscription[38] that announces that Decimus Lucretius Satrius Valens the priest (*flamen*) for life (*perpetuus*) of Nero, the son of the emperor (i.e. Claudius), will put on twenty gladiatorial fights (*paria*), together with ten fights sponsored by his son, on five days, 8-12 April.[39] The second is a sign for the workshop (*officina*) of Ubanius the painter (*offector*), the identification given to the building listed as region 9, block 3, house 2 at Pompeii. The viewer may also briefly observe high on a wall a copy of the *Mosaic with Street Musicians* (signed as the work of Dioscurides of Samos) that was recovered from the 'Villa of Cicero' close to Pompeii and is now in the Museo Archeologico Nazionale at Naples. In the main these visual touches are probably designed merely to provide a touch of authenticity by reproducing what in its original setting is sometimes described as 'urban wallpaper'. Yet the inscriptions and pictures may also have been selected from a wealth of similar material for the relevance of their themes to the story (gladiatorial games and the carnival of Isis).

The production and set design for *Gli ultimi giorni* was in the hands of Ramiro Gómez, who performed the same function two years later on Leone's *Colossus of Rhodes* (1961). While history is always subject to the narrative demands of film, the variances are now more striking. *Colossus* depicts a fabulous colossal statue astride the harbour being used as a mechanical defence for the city against Phoenician pirates. At the conclusion of the story a catastrophic earthquake destroys it. Leone has apparently combined the giant siege-tower (the *helepolis,* 'city-taker') that the Antigonid king of Macedonia, Demetrius Poliorcetes, constructed and lost to the Rhodians in his 304 BC attack on the city with the statue of Helios that the islanders erected from the spoils taken from the besiegers to commemorate their victory. Completed in 280, an earthquake did destroy the legendary figure in 224 BC, but it did not topple into the sea as depicted in Leone's film. The set design for Rhodes also is a mish-mash of styles (including Minoan art of the second millennium BC at the entrance to a hidden labyrinth within the royal palace) rather than being limited to those current at the time of the film's setting in 280 BC. [40]

It would be easy to pass judgement on these two Leone efforts as simply displaying third-hand knowledge of the ancient world, viewing Pompeii through a lens that had been fashioned by Bulwer-Lytton and Rhodes after the engraving by Marten Heemskerk (1572) that depicted its extraordinary colossus. The storyline of both films is similar: the protagonists (Steve Reeves, Rory Calhoun) face two women (Julia and Ione, Diala and Myrte), one of whom turns out to be plotting in secret with the evident villain against the city and whose schemes are foiled in the end only by a catastrophic natural disaster. But while the Rhodes of *Colossus* is a melange of archaeological elements, *Gli ultimi giorni*, despite its disappointing volcano, shows considerable attention to the daily life of Pompeii. With his portrayal of a bustling centre that abruptly ceased to exist in AD 79, Leone achieves a pathos that had been absent in earlier screen versions. The historically accurate depiction of the wayside shops of vendors of hot food (*popinae*) and of public water fountains projecting into the streets and hampering foot traffic lends an air of 'authenticity' to the Pompeian street scenes and intensifies the loss after the ensuing catastrophe.

The Latin inscriptions in *Gli ultimi giorni*, if not readily decipherable by the audience, at least have the look of the genuine article. By contrast, Ridley Scott's *Gladiator* presents abominable cod-Latin such as LUDUS MAGNUS GLADIATORES for *ludus magnus gladiatorum,* 'the main gladiatorial school', perhaps on the grounds that the audience would not recognise the genitive plural form of *gladiator*.[41] As already noted in examining the television version of *Buffy the Vampire Slayer*, viewers can usually recognise Latin in inscriptional form, although not necessarily understand it. By contrast, *The Colossus of Rhodes* manifests a singular lack of Greek. The reason is simple: apart from some relatively familiar Latinised forms (*kyrie eleison*, for example), the language is simply not comprehensible to modern audiences, one small linguistic group excepted. Where it is used in historical film, such as in *The 300 Spartans* (dir. Rudolf Maté, 1962) when the Spartan queen Gorgo passes over a shield with the instructions *ê tan ê epi tas* ('either with it or on it')[42] or Leonidas refuses the Persian call for surrender with *molôn labe* ('come and get it'),[43] it is incomprehensible. There is either a bizarre request for translation, as when one of the Spartan women asks what the queen said, or immediate explanation by the speaker (Leonidas' procedure). While the modern Greek accent of Queen Gorgo (Anna Synodinou) might have confused a Doric-speaking Spartan, the self-translation of Leonidas all too clearly reveals a well-known dramatic trick: all speech in such films is magically 'dubbed' into a single language. In *The 300 Spartans* both Persians and Greeks speak English (if with different accents, depending on the origins of the actors), although in Italy they would naturally speak Italian and German in Germany. Since the version of the apophthegms in the film is in Classical Greek, even modern Greek audiences would also await a translation. Clearly, despite the efforts of a sympathetic scriptwriter and producer

(Russian-born George St. George) and the patronage of the Greek royal family and government hoping to create an origin myth of Greek unity in defence of freedom when faced by foreign threats,[44] spoken Greek is too unfamiliar for non-native viewers to have any resonance in itself. Greek letters, by contrast, particularly capital letters, may have their use as cinematic decoration, as the credits to English language Alexander films (1956, 2004) illustrate. The difference in treatment is easily explained: the Roman alphabet is derived from Greek and Greek forms are regularly used for mathematical symbols. Hence there is a limited use of Greek inscription to provide a gratifying touch of the foreign without being too exotic.[45] But nothing matches the power of Roman capitals to give an immediate sense of the grandeur of the past, a trick that has not been lost on the creators of *Rome* (2005-7) in their use of an inscriptional background for the opening credits.[46]

In sum, while *Gli ultimi giorni* was made during the heyday of spectaculars set in ancient times and has an Italian director and a leading man who had acted as a muscleman in Hercules movies during this period, there are clear objections to placing this film and the later *Colossus* within the peplum genre. The production values are too high, which perhaps robs the films of the charm of the hotchpotch designs created out of discarded props from earlier films that characterises most of the Italian sword-and-sandal efforts between 1958 and 1965. For that, Christians, and a volcano, try the distinctly derivative *79 A.D.* (*Anno 79: la distruzione di Ercolano*, 1962, dir. Gianfranco Parolini), aka *Les dernières jours d'Hercolanum* (France) or, not bothering to disguise its origins, *Die lasten Stunden des Pompeii* (Germany). *79 A.D.*, a Three Musketeers-style adventure in which Brad Harris saves the emperor Titus from a planned coup organised around Herculaneum, was filmed back to back with *The Old Testament* (dir. Parolini, 1962) using the same actors and many of the same props as in the earlier film. To show the end of Herculaneum, a town that is never otherwise seen in the movie, a simple solution was found: the footage of urban destruction is simply taken from the 1959 film. Leone's connections, however, are less with the mass production of Italian peplums and closer to the Hollywood-produced efforts set in the ancient world that in the 1950s and early 1960s had funnelled considerable amounts of money into Cinecittà and Rome.[47] The set-design for Pompeii aims at presenting both elements of authenticity for cityscapes and the grandeur of Italian opera scenery for the interior of the Temple of Isis.

These striking visual effects were to be multiplied in *Colossus*, particularly in a duel between the hero and enemy soldiers on the very shoulders of the monumental statue of the sun god, Helios, at Rhodes. This is, perhaps, itself an homage to the remarkably exciting escape over the shoulders of the idol of Baal by the heroes in *Cabiria*. By the time he directed this, his second historical film, Leone could also incorporate a wry sense of humour that would be developed in his westerns. For instance, having Dario (Rory Calhoun) lost in a necropolis for mummified Rhodian kings is a splendid touch. But the opening of the film is particularly significant. A band of rebels make a daring raid from the sea on an underground prison involving much knife-throwing and arrow-shooting, a clear borrowing from the cowboys-and-Indians tradition. As they escape, one of the guards picks up a large club and strikes a gong, ushering in the opening credits.

The allusion to the loin-cloth clad strongman who introduced J. Arthur Rank productions is an amusing nod both to the Atlas/ Hercules mythology within which the figure of the Colossus exists[48] and to the classic English war dramas distributed by the Rank Organisation which the commando raid in Colossus recalls. In 1962, when Jacques Siclier penned his article 'L'âge du péplum' for the prestigious French cinematic journal *Cahiers de cinéma*, Leone was listed as but one of eighteen specialist 'artisans' working on such films in a virtual Italian cinema assembly line.[49] By contrast, Vittorio Cottafavi and (to a lesser degree) Riccardo Freda had already qualified as *auteurs*, though even they were seen as being restricted by the genre to the role of new versions of Alexandre Dumas.[50] Freda's reputation has suffered by comparison with that of his frequent collaborator Mario Bava: for instance, *Maciste in Hell* (*Maciste all'inferno,* US: *The Witch's Curse*, 1962), despite one scene in Hell that would do Hieronymus Bosch proud, cannot match its model, Bava's *Hercules at the Centre of the Earth* (1961).[51] It is also unfortunate that his best effort in the genre, *The Giants of Thessaly* (*I giganti della Thessaglia*, 1960), a version of the Golden Fleece legend, was quickly overshadowed by *Jason and the Argonauts* (dir. Don Chaffey, 1963) whose stop-motion monsters supplied by Ray Harryhausen inspired many future filmmakers, including the young Peter Jackson.[52] Cottafavi's inventive fantasies *The Revenge of Hercules* (*Goliath and the Dragon*, 1960) and *Hercules Conquers Atlantis* (*Hercules and the Captive Women*, 1961) certainly deserve wider release in their original form, rather than in their truncated American versions.[53] But Leone's *Colossus of Rhodes* still remains a landmark in depictions of the ancient world.

Gli ultimi giorni and *Colossus* should thus be viewed as part of a long Italian film tradition dating back to the silent era, but also, in particular aspects, incorporating American (and even English) film mythology as well. Rather than remaining a genre specialist, Leone was to master a number of styles. He is famed for his westerns, with versions set in Spain (from the ground-breaking *Fistful of Dollars*, 1964, through to *Duck You Sucker*, 1971) and the United States (particularly his operatic masterpiece, *Once Upon a Time in the West*, 1968, but also the substantially Leonean *My Name is Nobody*, 1973). Yet his elegiac vision of past eras is perhaps best expressed not in a western, but in an American gangster film (*Once Upon a Time in America*, 1984). And at the end of his career, he was readying a war movie based on the siege of Leningrad in 1941-44. A unifying thread runs through all this: these films are all set in past eras that have become associated with cinematic genres (sword-and-sandal, western, gangster, war). Within each genre, one of the most important requirements for the creative director is consistency with prior depictions of the subject in film. A war movie, for instance, that does not look like one will confuse the audience, while emotional depth may be gained by allusions to well-known earlier productions. Little is to be gained by demanding 'authenticity' in Leone's westerns, given that his American models were already composed of invented elements. So too his sword-and-sandal efforts should be seen as part of the process of classical reception. Drawing on a nineteenth-century novel that had already been transformed by operatic and cinematic depictions, in *Gli ultimi giorni di Pompeii* Leone continues the process of change by making use of new opportunities in set design while incorporating more recent adventure elements from Italian and foreign sources. It will not do to complain that this is 'too improvised',[54] since this is the very process through which *Once Upon a Time in the West* was created.[55] *Gli ultimi giorni* was certainly a commercial success in Italy, with audience receipts that placed it among the top four peplums of the period.[56] If it is not regarded as a great artistic achievement, the reason is not that, for a film with a specific historical setting, it borrows too heavily from peplum movies and other styles, but, paradoxically, because Leone had yet to mythologise his subject matter completely. One cannot make a tasteful film *de mauvais genre*.

Le péplum – qu'est-ce que c'est?

So far I have generally used the English term 'sword-and-sandal' film to describe historical and mythological films set in the ancient world, rather than the other common term, *peplum*. The invention of the term is often attributed to Jacques Siclier, writing in *Cahiers du cinéma* in 1962. In fact, the term 'film à péplum' was, as Siclier indicates, already in use in France as a neologism for spectacle films. Peplum, the Latin form of the Greek *peplos*, originally described a type of female dress (a woman's sleeveless long robe, such as seen on statues of Athena), such as worn by Mylène Demongeot in the still from *The Giant of Marathon* (*La Battaglia di Maratone*, 1959) that introduces Siclier's article.[57] It is likely that its use as a metonymy for the type of film in which peplums might be worn was originally a coinage of Yves Martin, a member of Bertrand Tavernier's film club Nickel Odéon at Lyons. On his way to one of the muscleman films that were regularly screened at a local commercial theatre around 1960, he announced that he was 'going to see a peplum', a jocular remark equivalent to 'I'm off to see women in diaphanous robes'.[58] Subsequently misunderstanding of Siclier's title, 'L'âge du péplum', as referring, not to women in classical garb, but to men in short tunics or even loincloths resulted in the modern use of *peplum* (or the Latin plural *pepla*) for Italian sword-and-

46

3. A female dress: Andromeda (Mylène Demonguet) and companions in peplums from *The Giant of Marathon* (1959).

sandal films of the 1950s and 1960s. There is even now a dedicated *Festival of Peplum Film* (in 2007 in its nineteenth year) that takes place annually at Arles in the last week of August, with outdoor showings in the Roman theatre.[59]

Actual definition of the subject matter of what is also called the 'sword-and-sandal' genre is much more difficult. Under normal circumstances, it excludes actual biblical stories, although film versions of Lew Wallis' 1880 novel, *Ben Hur*, despite the biblical setting, are included. Indeed there is considerable cross-pollination, as the 1935 *Last Days of Pompeii* or Leone's contribution to *Sodom and Gomorrah* (1961) show. It is clear that the description *peplum* is most often used for strongman movies involving certain recognisable characters (Hercules, Maciste, Ursus, Samson, and Goliath) even if the rest of the subject matter is non-Classical. Thus, *Maciste alla corte del gran khan* (aka *Samson and the Seven Miracles of the World* (1961; dir. Riccardo Freda), *Ursus il terrore dil kirghisi* (aka *Hercules Prisoner of Evil*, 1964, starring Reg Park), or *Sansone contro i pirati* (*Samson vs. the Pirates,* 1963), or even non-Herculean Steve Reeves vehicles such as *Morgan il pirata* (*Morgan the Pirate*, 1960; dir. André De Toth) and *Sandokan, la tigre di Mompracem* (*Sandokan the Great*, aka *The Pirates of Malaysia*, 1964) are sometimes described as belonging to the genre, despite their non-canonical subject matter. Claude Aziza would use the term for any film depicting the period from the beginning of the world to the fall of Constantinople (1456).[60]

A logical alternative, to which I subscribe, is to restrict the use of *peplum* to the group of films depicting the ancient world made in Italy by Italian directors in the period 1958-65, a brief period that generated large numbers of entries in this category. This treats these films not as a particular genre, but rather as a *filone*, a trend in filmmaking that has a currency at a certain time and place and then is replaced by another style (as, for instance, Italian westerns and later *gialli* replaced historical fantasy).[61] Such a definition both reinforces the connections between the output of Italian film-makers, while permitting sub-genres (gladiator or strongman or historical action hero) to be studied separately or as their forms interrelate. Because of their budgets, such films do not fit in the category of Hollywood 'block-busters' (contrast Cottafavi's *Legions of Cleopatra*, 1960, with Mankiewicz's *Cleopatra*, 1963, or Corbucci's *Son of Spartacus*, 1963, with Kubrick's *Spartacus*, 1960) and must rely on popular appeal to earn enough revenue for the next feature. Some may be striking in construction and visual appeal, but most use stock plots and themes familiar to their audiences to provide reliable entertainment. Similar efforts made by non-Italians or outside the specified time period (precursors or revivals) will instead best be described as 'mythological or 'fantasy' (e.g. Columbia Pictures' *Jason and the Argonauts*, dir. Don Chaffey, 1963) or 'muscleman' (cf. Arnold Schwarzenegger's first role in *Hercules in New York* (dir. Arthur Seidelman, 1970) which because of its contemporary setting is excluded from the company of historical films). 'Spectacular'[62] or 'historical' films, such *Cabiria* or *Gladiator*, as a result of the production companies' substantial investment require a wider audience and have greater pretensions.[63]

It is significant that Siclier himself appears to have wanted to restrict his definition of *péplum* to non-historical mythological fantasies involving strongman heroes, Italian creations who might challenge Hollywood archetypes such as Tarzan or Superman for the affections of their national audience.[64] For a brief period, Italy was able to compete successfully with America in particular through the figure of Hercules. America has since then embraced the hero, most notably in Kevin Sorbo's television series *Hercules: the Legendary Journeys* which in turn spawned a female equivalent in Xena, herself a descendant of the archetypal Amazon, Wonder Woman. Disney's *Hercules* (1997) may be seen as indicating the now complete domestication of the strongman. While Hercules may battle numerous monsters, it is his stalwart heart displayed in his willingness to sacrifice himself for true love, not his physical strength, that earns him immortality. The intentions may be good, but the pure escapist delight of large-chested heroes and heroines in improbable scenarios has been lost.[65] Rather than competing with American superheroes, Hercules, like Schwarzenegger, has been co-opted into the Hollywood pantheon.

48

3. The Peplum and Other Animals

Reg Park, an alternative Hercules for the 1960s

At the beginning of feature film-making, the ancient world offered a veneer of respectability to the new art of 'photo play' and costumed displays of masculine strength had not yet come to be associated with the Thunderdome of *Mad Max 3* (1985) or World Wrestling Entertainment. *Cabiria* (1914) can in many ways be seen as a development from orientalising Italian grand operas such as *Aida*, adding new spectacular displays, such as the eruption of Etna, Hannibal crossing the Alps with his elephants, and Archimedes setting fire to the Roman fleet at Syracuse by the concentrated light of mirrors. The thrill of the circus was also included. Fulvius Axilla climbs into Carthage using Roman legionaries in gymnastic formation to provide a human ladder up the walls. There are no safety nets visible, so the audience may admire both the skill and the physical bravery of the actors in this scene. Furthermore, in the figure of Maciste a popular hero was being created. Axilla's faithful servant, he helps rescue Cabiria from being sacrificed to Baal and saves his master's life as well as his own when they are captured and imprisoned at Cirta by not only organising their escape but also finding a refuge in the royal storehouse where he may indulge his gargantuan appetite. While Axilla may be the ostensible hero, it is the faithful Maciste who brings the poison from Masinissa as his last gift to Sophonisba and restores Cabiria to freedom and the promise of a new life in an Italian home.

By contrast, a film that is in many ways a remake of *Cabiria*, *Scipione l'africano* (1937), needs no one to bend prison bars and break chains. There is a strongman, but it is Scipio Africanus himself, the conquering general and hero of the Italian people, a man who speaks on their behalf before the aristocrats of the Senate and is ready to lead his country in a war of revenge. The disaster of Cannae, where 60,000 Roman soldiers were killed by Hannibal and his Carthaginians, is to be repaid by a conclusive Roman victory at Zama. The figure of Scipio rather obviously prefigures Benito Mussolini whose attack on Ethiopia in 1935-6 was intended to avenge the shame of the Italian defeat at Adowa in 1896.[66] As a result, propaganda overpowers spectacle. A new character, Velia, representing the best of Roman womanhood, replaces the Greek heroine Cabiria. Velia suffers from brutal Carthaginian enslavement and the lusts of an ogre-like Hannibal, but never forgets her true love, Italy (her boyfriend comes off decidedly second best in this context). Such a virtuous heroine needs to be matched by a scheming villainess, who is provided in spades by Francesca Bragiotti (wife of the American actor and (later) politician, John Lodge) as Sophonisba. Gone is the feline grace of Italia Almirante-Mazini, the story of her youthful romance with Masinissa, and her noble, if histrionic, death in the 1914 film. Bragiotti's queen is pure vamp, using her wiles to trap two African kings (Syphax and Masinissa) in order to advance the cause of Carthage. But through this adoption of noir style, Sophonisba's death is robbed of most of the pathos that had inspired its depiction by writers, painters and composers since the Renaissance and becomes merely the just outcome of her earlier actions.

As already discussed, partly in reaction to the Fascist depiction of the strong leader, films in the post-Second World War period downplayed the physical strength of the Classical hero and focussed on the self-sacrificing aspects of his character. Paris, the hero of *Helen of Troy* (dir. Robert Wise, 1956), has to be provoked into showing his ability as a boxer, while the Greek villain, Achilles, displays egotistical arrogance toward Greeks and Trojans indiscriminately. Although in 2000 the tagline for *Gladiator* was 'A hero will rise', Maximus turned out to be remarkably traditional in his concern for family values and sense of social responsibility. An exception is Robert Rossen's 1956 portrait of Alexander the Great, whose traditional power is also his tragedy.[67] The success of Francisci's *Labours of Hercules* (1958) lay in its reversion to the original mould of Maciste for his hero, once again celebrating physical strength. Now, however, whenever Hercules does serve a master, the king is no threat to others. So, borrowing from the Argonaut legend, Pelias, the ruler of Iolcos is portrayed as a petty tyrant, fearful of Jason's return and suspicious of Hercules' strength. At the end of the film, it is Hercules who has gained the love of the beautiful princess Iole, but Jason who is the new ruler. In the sequel, *Hercules and the Queen of Lydia* (1959), Hercules has first to escape from the clutches of Queen Omphale and then attempt to intervene between Eteocles and Polynices as they battle for the throne of Thebes. Royalty does not feature well in these stories, generally performing the approximate function of a videogame Superboss – a final opponent for Hercules to defeat after he has bested various wild animals and fantastic monsters on the way.

Rather than discuss the canonic Steve Reeves Hercules films that opened the way for the brief bloom of peplum cinema, I wish to focus on two productions that appeared in August and November 1961 respectively: Cottafavi's *Hercules Conquers Atlantis* and Bava's *Hercules at the Centre of the Earth*. Both appeared under the aegis of the Italian production company SpA Cinematografica and starred the English-born, South African domiciled body-builder, Reg Park. Park had sufficient acting ability that some aficionados argue that he was the best Hercules of the period, surpassing even Steve Reeves. That he could star in both films is indicative of the rapid production of peplum movies, almost equivalent to the shooting schedules of modern television series that, like the peplums, also often rely on stock footage and reuse of sets. Both directors for these films had lengthy experience in the genre. Bava had lent his technical expertise (uncredited) in set design, lighting, and photography to *Ulysses* (1954, dir. Mario Camerini) and then to Francisci's two *Hercules* films before completing *The Giant of Marathon* (1959) in place of Jacques Tourneur.[68] Today much less well known than Bava, Cottafavi's ironic versions of the ancient world include *The Revolt of the Gladiators* (*La rivolta dei gladiatori*, aka *The Warrior and the Slave Girl*, 1958), *Messalina* (*Messaline Venere imperatrice*, 1960), and *The Legions of Cleopatra* (1960). The Italian director Gianni Amelio held the last in sufficient esteem to make it his choice when the European Union asked thirty directors to pick films for restoration in the late 1990s. Luc Moullet, a confirmed Cottafavi fan, wrote that he preferred *The Revenge of Hercules* (1960, aka *Goliath and the Dragon*, a version unfortunately butchered by American International Pictures who intercut scenes from a film of that name on which they had begun production) to any of the films in the Venice Festival of 1960,[69] while Bertrand Tavernier has listed Cottafavi's *Amazons of Rome* (*Le vergini di Roma*, 1961) as one of his favourite films.

Hercules Conquers Atlantis[70] begins with Hercules (Reg Park) in service to the king of Thebes, Androcles (Ettore Mani, a peplum regular). This arrangement is common in the cinematic treatment of the hero – for instance Hercules assists Aeson in his first outing in *The Labours of Hercules* (1958) – but is also a part of the mythological tradition. In the best-known Hercules tale, the demigod was condemned to serve king Eurystheus who set the now canonical twelve labours in an attempt to eliminate this dangerous servant. Where Hercules gains absolute rule for himself, as in Euripides' and Seneca's *Hercules Furens* or in Cottafavi's *The Revenge of Hercules* (1960), the danger looms that strength and power may combine into an unhealthy potion. For instance, in the latter film Hercules as ruler of Thebes calmly prevents his younger brother Hyllus (Sandro Moretti) from visiting the daughter of his enemy, king Eurystheus of Oechalia, by tying him to a tree. The scene (as often with Cottafavi) is comic, but also somewhat disturbing. In *Hercules Conquers Atlantis*, Hyllus[71] (now played by Luciano Marin) appears once more, but this time as Hercules' son, smooching with the barmaid and brawling ineffectually in the local tavern. Only after completing his meal does Hercules bother to rescue Androcles ('I'm the king of Thebes'), Hyllus, and Timotheus the midget (Salvatore Furnari, another Cottafavi regular, often used to undermine Hercules' heroic pomposity) with the minimum of fuss from this unseemly affray. Contrary to other depictions of his character, Hercules is the level-headed one in this group of ne'er-do-wells, trying to keep his son on the straight and narrow. But trouble is never far away: in this case it appears in the form of a strange red eclipse and an indistinct figure predicting a rain of fire and blood over Greece. A consultation with the prophet Teiresias, seen conducting a torchlit ceremony, possibly the Mysteries, but looking remarkably like a Christian bishop presiding over his flock, helps only a little. The threat is from the West, from outside the straits of Gibraltar. Unlike his audience, Hercules is unaware of the legend of Atlantis and the confusion is continued at the stock council of the leading kings of Greece, usually seen in such films as either preparing to attack Troy or defend their homeland from invading Persians. The meeting provides an opportunity for guest stars to offer their own comic turns:

the king of Megalia (Ivo Garrani) is hampered by his Council of Thirty, the autocratic king of Megara, Parthenope (Enrico Maria Salerno), is regularly called to order by his mother, and the king of Sparta (Gian Maria Volonté dressed in something resembling a US flag), after a display of his spear-throwing ability involving a remarkably unhistorical map, refuses to fight outside his territory. What's more there's still tribute owed on the last war. Perhaps it's the Trojan War – certainly the whole event seems to be a comic re-enactment of the bad-tempered meeting at Sparta early in Robert Wise's *Helen of Troy* (1956). In these circumstances, there is nothing for it but for king Androcles to go it alone. At this point, Hercules rises from his leopard skin (leopard? what happened to the Nemean lion?) and solves the problem of who will sit on the throne during Androcles' absence by demolishing the seat, promising to build his king a better one when his ruler returns. Hercules' good-natured literal-mindedness over the throne is matched by a taste for domesticity. He now desires to settle down with family (Deianeira and Hyllus) and let others do the work for a change.

But this is a Hercules movie, not an Androcles one. So Hercules soon finds himself waking up from a drugged potion on a ship manned by galley-slaves and cut-purses that are all the great king of Thebes could enlist in his quest ('I fought against the senators, the sooth-sayers, the commanders of the army. Aren't you the one who is always saying that democracy …'). In no time at all, the crew mutiny and try to sail off leaving Hercules and Androcles stranded on an island. Hercules rouses himself from his sun-bathing to grab the anchor chain and, after a prayer to the gods to quiet the winds (the first of a number of prayers from our pious hero), hauls the desperately rowing crew back to land. From now on it is only three (Hercules, Androcles, and Timotheus) on the expedition – or rather four, since Hyllus is hiding below deck, worried that his father will be upset at him for breaking curfew. A massive storm arises, a stock effect not merely in peplums, but almost a requisite in epic tales from Homer's *Odyssey* onwards. Androcles is lost overboard and Hercules shipwrecked on an unknown island. There he discovers a maiden imprisoned in the rocks and in attempting to free her brings on himself the wrath of the spirit of the island, Proteus. Hercules' enemy constantly changes shape, allowing him to engage in combat with a mixture of fearsome creatures one after another, including a (rather tame) lion, a vulture (on a string), and a human-size lizard. Victory in this contest for the Greek champion not only rescues the princess Ismene, but also lifts the mists surrounding the nearby land – Atlantis.

The mythological now turns to science fiction.[72] Atlantis is ruled by Queen Antinea (cult favourite bad girl, Fay Spain, sporting a frightening bouffant), who is not in the least pleased to see her daughter return, since it has been prophesied that if Ismene survive her mother all Atlantis will be destroyed. But she does take a shine to Hercules, treating him to a

52

4. Hercules (Reg Park) is confronted by a group of identical, genetically manipulated Atlantidean super-warriors in *Hercules Conquers Atlantis* (1961).

lavish banquet and dancing girls (another topos in peplum movies, happily revived in 2004 in a sequence at the start of Petersen's *Troy*). The strongman, dressed in a dainty shawl, appears to have fallen for the evil woman's wiles, forgetting about his wife Deianeira and publicly becoming effeminised in appearance. But it appears that he has already seen the handiwork of Sylvia Lopez in *Hercules and the Queen of Lydia*, who turned her lovers into wax statues, and so, after feigning a drugged stupor, Hercules escapes and learns the secrets of Atlantis. The island possesses a stone created from the blood of Uranus that is now being used to create a race of supermen to conquer the world. Hercules liberates the unfortunates who have resisted this course in eugenics (including the drugged Androcles, not lost after all). They are freed from their role as slave labour, but Hercules is unable to prevent their premature revolt and massacre by the queen's super-strength warriors.[73] In order to save his loved ones, Hercules races the enemy in an eight-horse chariot through underground caves, then climbs up to the roof and creates a hole through which light may penetrate and destroy the stone which is the source of Atlantidean power. Having set this solar time bomb, Hercules races out, dives into the sea as the island explodes – a reprise of Steve Reeves' exploits at the close of *Gli ultimi giorni* – and rejoins the others (including Ismene, who has taken a liking to young Hyllus) as they sail off, literally, into the sunset.

The bad geography (does Hercules intend to take the Panama canal on his way home?) and the joke on king Androcles, who cannot remember any of this adventure, that it was really he who had saved Greece (would

53

anyone believe such a ridiculous story?) are signals to the viewers. If they had forgotten the narrative during the volcanic spectacular at the conclusion of the film, they are reminded that another tall tale is coming to an end. Cottafavi appears to have realised that the fairly straightforward approach to mythology had become stale within three years of the making of the first Italian Hercules film. Instead, he concentrates on spectacle, particularly in the Atlantis scenes, utilising brightly coloured, spacious sets and sunny sea vistas. Even the most depressing material, such as the depiction of the ulcerated victims of the Valley of the Weaklings, is associated with rapid action sequences in glorious outdoor locations. All the elements expected of a Hercules movie are presented, but in a tongue-in-cheek fashion that anticipates James Bond a year before the release of *Dr No*.[74] Not that Reg Park is Sean Connery, despite the film's conclusion with the destruction of the villain's secret lair. This Hercules is monogamous, with a teenage son to keep an eye on,[75] no longer a lion but a sleepy pussycat ready for retirement and only displaying his remarkable strength when something finally stirs him to superhuman effort.

Cottafavi's film might almost be regarded as the culmination of the peplum series, its successors condemned to ever more exotic locations and plots in order to provide some excitement for a jaded audience. However, another remarkable effort, creating a gothic effect from claustrophobic interiors and anomalous shades of lighting, was to follow almost immediately. Mario Bava had been working on the special effects for *Hercules Conquers Atlantis*[76] when the American International Pictures 1961 release of his first effort as sole director, *Black Sunday* (*La maschera del demonio*, 1960), became a box office success across the Atlantic. SpA's producer, Achille Piazzi, immediately took the opportunity to enlist Bava for another Hercules effort, scripted by the writer for *Hercules Conquers Atlantis*, Sandro Continenza, with help from Ducio Tessari. The frugal director completed the project in a mere three weeks, filming at Cinecittà and various sites regularly used in peplums that were mainly in or close to Rome (Cascate de Montegelato and Tor Caldara).[77]

Hercules at the Centre of the Earth (*Ercole al centro della terra*) opens on a sunlit day with a couple making love in a hay-barn, close to waterfalls and a pristine pond. Suddenly hidden assailants attack, throwing spears that just miss the man, who pushes his girlfriend to safety and calls for help. Hercules appears, picks up a hay-cart and demolishes the barn, routing the brigands, and saving his young friend, Theseus. It turns out that the Greek hero has been out of town and is on his way to Oechalia to marry Deianeira at long last. He is surprised by this recent outbreak of lawlessness in the area – just as the attackers are astonished to find that their target is none other than the invincible strongman. This scene comically plays on audience expectations: the handsome lover, played by George Ardisson, later to become the Italian equivalent of James Bond, Agent 3S3, is not Hercules himself, but his sidekick, the perpetually

5. Smoke and mirrors: Hercules regards an ethereal Deianeira in *Hercules at the Centre of the Earth* (1961).

amorous Theseus. The tale turns out to be a *prequel* to his conquest of Atlantis, beginning with a scene that appears to be a pastoral paradise (surely alluding to Constable's *Hay Wain*, 1821), but one into which a snake has slithered. The next, internal scene, colour-coded in blacks and reds, reveals the mastermind to be king Lyco (Christopher Lee, fresh from his Hammer Horror roles as the Prince of Darkness). Not only does Lyco dispose of his henchmen after their failures by sudden impalement, but, rising vertically from her coffin, an insensible Deianeira appears clad in a white peplum that might easily be a shroud.

This introductory sequence encapsulates the almost Manichaean cinematic style Bava applies to *Hercules at the Centre of the Earth*: sunny outdoor locations promise humour and love; dark indoor scenes, lit by filtered, carefully directed spotlights, often in bizarre shades of orange, turquoise, and violet, and frequently enhanced by dry ice mists create ominous foreboding. Having spent nearly twenty years as cinematographer and set designer, Bava seems to strip the role of Hercules to that of an almost primordial upholder of what is good, making him the pivot of the film, but always in reaction to others. This makes a virtue of what is normally considered the weakness of the various screen Hercules, their limited acting abilities. The lighting in particular focuses the viewer's attention on the excesses of the spectacle, including the impressive musculature of the hero. Perhaps most remarkably, this is achieved with a set that comprises little more than four columns and a wall with a double door, reassembled in various configurations to create numerous interiors and even a beachside temple in the final scene.

As the film proceeds, Hercules arrives in Oechalia (the same vaguely Mycenaean outdoor sets as used by Cottafavi for Atlantis) to discover his intended bride in a coma. Consulting the Sybil, a marvellously Eastern-looking priestess wearing a mask once used by a nightclub performer in Fellini's *La dolce vita*, Hercules learns that he must travel beyond the Garden of the Hesperides to retrieve the living stone which shines in the depths of Hades. In the company of Theseus and a vertically challenged Telemachus (the comic replacement for the dwarf Timotheus in *Hercules Conquers Atlantis*), he seeks the magic ship of Sounis. The latter is a version of the bandit Sinis who used to tie his victims to two bent trees so that they were torn apart when the trees were released – a fate he himself suffered at the hands of Theseus.[78] In Bava's film, Sounis is going to tear Telemachus in two by harnessing him to two sets of horses ('Seems he knew his wife far too well') when Hercules comes to the rescue, enabling a typical display of strength as he restrains both teams at once. Sailing off on what soon becomes a (red) wine-dark sea, the team reaches the land of the Hesperides, women, as they state, 'condemned by the gods to live in darkness'. The Golden Apple, required to enter – and leave – Hades (a substitute for the Golden Bough of Vergil's *Aeneid*) must be fetched by Hercules alone from high in a gnarled sacred tree. Unable to climb to collect it because of lightning and showers of fire, Hercules takes a giant rock and hurls it into the tree to bring his prize down. The spell is now broken and the Hesperides reveal that Theseus and Telemachus are about to be killed, having been taken to rest on the beds of Procrustes.[79] In the nick of time, Hercules arrives to battle this rock monster, hurling him against the cave wall, burying him and opening up the path to Hades in the process. On the way to find the sacred stone, Hercules and Theseus encounter the trap of a Siren and vines that bleed (perhaps based on the tale of Polydorus in *Aeneid* 3). Hercules creates a rope from the vines to climb across a pit of lava to retrieve the stone, but Theseus falls in and is believed lost. In fact, he has passed through the fire and encounters a beautiful girl whom he smuggles onto the ship for the journey back. On his return, the magic stone revives Deianeira, but Oechalia is cursed by fire and pestilence, the result of Theseus taking from Hades the lady who is now revealed to be Pluto's favourite daughter, Persephone.

It hardly need be said that this (as the stories from the ancient world were already) is a farrago of mythological events. For instance, Theseus is said to have assisted his friend Pirithous in attempting to snatch Persephone, the *wife* of Pluto, and as a result was trapped in the Under-world until rescued by Hercules. The shape-shifting temptress, the souls of the damned in the vines, and the fiery lava are more appropriate to a Christian Hell than to classical depictions of the underworld. The pestilence that greets Hercules on his return is modelled on the myth of the scorching of the earth by Pluto after Persephone, whom he had kidnapped, had returned to the world of the living. This plague only ceased when Persephone returned to Hades. In Bava's version, Hercules must journey once more to the oracle to discover what had caused the disasters around him (allowing Lyco in the meantime the opportunity to kidnap Deianeira) and comes to blows with Theseus over his beloved. It is Persephone herself who makes the choice to return, having first drugged Theseus so that he would forget their relationship. The next scene comes from an altogether different genre. Hercules, discovering Deianeira missing from the palace, pursues Lyco through his underground world and prevents him from sacrificing the princess during an eclipse of the moon. He fights off swarms of the undead by throwing giant stone grave markers at them, and Lyco, trapped underneath one, in true vampiric fashion burns up when the light of the moon returns. Hercules and Deianeira are reunited at the film's end on a sunlit beach, where Theseus, a little dazed, recognises the woman he had been with in the very first scene, approaching with Telemachus. Back to his normal womanising self, he snatches her from her fiancé and runs off happily.

The underlying plot of *Hercules at the Centre of the Earth* is banal. The monogamous love of Hercules for Deianeira conquers all, while Lyco, in his desire to be all-powerful and immortal, and even Theseus, desirous of that which he cannot permanently attain, the girlfriends of others or the daughter of the Lord of Hades, will always be thwarted. Yet the treatment of this story as a chance to create pure cinematic magic seems too close to artistry, to a rejection of the kitsch sensibility that underlies much of the Hercules mythology. A hero who is associated with the open air – for instance, posed as a modern Olympic victor between Castor and Pollux, the bronze and silver medal winners, in a shot from *The Labours of Hercules,* where Hercules is schooling the youth of Iolcus in throwing the javelin and discus – is disconcerting when placed in enclosed spaces, battling not with regular mythological terrors, but with the dead themselves.[80] Bava would continue his exploration of eros and thanatos in other genres (for instance, the gothic *The Whip and the Body* (*La frustra e il corpo*, 1963), also starring Christopher Lee), but only Riccardo Freda's *Maciste in Hell* (*Maciste all'inferno*, 1962)[81] trod a similar path in the peplum tradition. Despite some interesting scenarios and effective use of the normally unimpressive Kirk Morris,[82] the appearance of a loincloth-clad muscleman in seventeenth-century Scotland and a mythological hero in a mainly Christian Hell are rather odd. Indeed, only one significant Hercules film followed *Hercules at the Centre of the Earth*,[83] Francisci's *Hercules, Samson, and Ulysses* (*Ercole sfida Sansone*, 1963), involving an all-star cast of mythological strongmen. Such grand reunions, while popular with fans – witness the pleasures of Godzilla meeting once again with Mothra, Ghidorah, Gigan and the rest of the crew in *Godzilla, Final Wars* (2004) – indicate that the camp element has taken over. It would be more than thirty years before Hercules in the shape of Kevin Sorbo once again strode beneath the earth.[84]

A much more detailed study of peplum films would be valuable, since I have hardly touched on 'historical' examples, such as the Tourneur/Bava effort, *The Giant of Marathon* (1959), Corbucci's *Romulus and Remus* (1961), or Cottafavi's *Messalina* and *Legions of Cleopatra* (both 1960). The Classicist has little to add on such efforts except to note the remarkable freedom enjoyed by the scriptwriters in varying from traditional accounts, just as the Hercules peplums happily rewrote mythology and other muscleman efforts (starring Maciste, Ursus, Goliath, and the rest) plundered from adventure tales both from the past (e.g. pirate adventures or tales of the Tartars) and the future (the bizarre *Goliath and the Vampires* (*Maciste contro il vampiro,* 1961) or *Hercules against the Moon Men* (*Maciste e la regina di Sama,* 1964)).

This is peplum

The interim definition of 'peplum' derived from Siclier and Aziza can now be revised to 'an exotic action drama in a technologically limited setting, involving a clear conflict between good and evil characters'. There need not be a specific requirement for a past setting, as even science fiction elements can be incorporated so long as the protagonist(s) achieve victory through personal worth and effort. The requirement of exoticism excludes realism and the attribution of psychological motives to its characters. In the absence of realism, the peplum cannot be 'political' in any meaningful sense.

What appear to be restrictions on the scriptwriter are in fact the consequence of specific conditions in the Italian film industry of the 1950s and 60s. Budgetary considerations required most filming to be done in Roman studios, recycling sets and props, while location shooting was restricted to a few sites, such as the seaside at Tor Caldara, which as a result became familiar elements of the staging. The need for the heroes in such films to triumph by personal effort excluded any actor who was not athletic[85] and obviously encouraged the choice of body-builders for such roles. Their adversaries could be more varied: a scarred Broderick Crawford as king Eurystheus (*Revenge of Hercules*), Christopher Lee as Lord of the Underworld, and the memorable women of the peplums, such as Gianna Maria Canale, Fay Spain, and Belinda Lee (*Messalina*), whose powers of seduction might unman the hero. Within this system, there were likely to be multiple scriptwriters, since even if one individual had outlined a storyline, compromises and changes would need to be made in response to the resources available and opportunities that might suddenly arise.[86] The directors would often be as anonymous as all the other members of the production team working on a project; hence, they can rarely be regarded as *auteurs*.

3. The Peplum and Other Animals

That they are able to leave their mark on this material is a sign of Bava's and Cottafavi's abilities. Bava could take the various elements (including Reg Park)[87] which he had been granted and create a remarkable set of illusions. The lack of clarity in the storyline of *Hercules at the Centre of the Earth* only enhances the film's dreamlike atmosphere. Cottafavi instead looks to create a carnival atmosphere that confuses the simple male/ active female/ passive dichotomy. In his *Legions of Cleopatra,* the queen leaves her palace at night to dance incognito in the local tavern, creating chaos wherever she goes. This may be a variant on tales of a disguised male tyrant brawling in town such as are associated with Nero, but here the tone is mischievous rather than malicious. Cottafavi's regular association of dwarfs with the strongmen in his films, together with the exotic dancers, offers a wry hint that the audience is in the end merely watching a circus performance.

In their ability to recycle material, the peplums should thus not be viewed teleologically as a development of filmed historical dramas but as a reversion in a pseudo-historical guise to pre-cinematic popular entertainment. Either because the permutations were becoming exhausted or due to the broader financial and even artistic opportunities of filming westerns in Spain, by the mid-1960s the almost industrial production of peplums in Italy had ceased. Particular storylines may be revived – indeed *Hercules* and *Xena* frequently revel in similarly serving up a farrago of elements derived from different times and places. But the closest modern analogies are the national film styles represented by the melodramas of Hong Kong and Bollywood. Hercules may return to the screen, but not as a symbol of foreign physical excess (even Italian musclemen were given American stage names) in the service of the Italian film industry of the 1960s.

4

The *Odyssey*, High and Low

After the mutant form of the ancient world we have seen in the peplum, the prospect of tracing versions of the *Odyssey* comes as a relief. After all, the Homeric epics are not only the beginning of Western literature but also represent a cultural point of origin. The Classical Greeks held regular recitation contests for the *Iliad* and *Odyssey*. Alexander the Great mourned the lack of a Homer to celebrate his exploits and consciously sought to imitate Achilles when he visited Troy. The Augustan era geographer Strabo still defended the poet's geographical knowledge despite more modern investigations of the Mediterranean.[1] Most significantly, Vergil's *Aeneid* provided his Roman audience with a nationalist recreation of both Homeric epics when he recounted the fate of the surviving Trojans. In short, the reputation of Homer has always been substantially higher in the upper echelons of society than that of Hercules, who was best reclaimed from his plebeian popularity by turning his labours into allegories of public service. Greater faithfulness to the source material is to be expected in any retelling of Homer. As a consequence, changes both substantial and subtle will indicate shifts of focus by the filmmakers and permit us to read their films as evidence for cultural history at specific times and places.

Filmmakers and viewers have generally found the Trojan War part of the epic cycle, particularly events not directly narrated by Homer such as the rape of Helen and the Wooden Horse, more attractive than the stories of journeys home that include the *Odyssey*. Early silent depictions of individual scenes of the siege of Troy exist, such as Pastrone's 35-minute *Fall of Troy* (*La caduta di Troia* 1910), and the German *Helena* (dir. Manfred Noa, 1924) is the first clear entry in the Trojan War blockbuster tradition. At 204 minutes it certainly had the requisite length, although its Wagnerian style was far removed from the bright Mediterranean settings of later recreations. Robert Wise's 1956 *Helen of Troy* was a major contributor to the rise of the peplum genre, both through its repopularisation of the mythological subject matter among English-speaking audiences and through the employment of an Italian crew and the injection of funds into Cinecittà. The film's stars, Jacques Sernas and Rossana Podestà, went on to have lengthy careers in Italian sword-and-sandal films.[2] Muscleman versions of the epic cycle followed, including *The Fury of Achilles* (*L'ira di Achille*, dir. Marino Girolami, 1962, with Gordon Mitchell as Achilles), a fairly faithful, but dull retelling of the *Iliad*, and Steve Reeves as Aeneas in *The Trojan Horse* (*La Guerra di Troia*, dir. Giorgio Ferroni, 1961) and, having now escaped to Italy, in *The Avenger* (*La legenda di Enea,* dir. Giorgio Rivalta, 1962). Particularly noteworthy as an odd derivative of Euripides' *Helen*, rather than being based on epic, is *The Lion of Thebes (Il leone di Tebe,* dir. Giorgio Ferone, 1962), recounting Helen's adventures in Egypt when being brought home by Menelaus. Foreshadowing the abrupt, if unHomeric, end of Menelaus at Hector's hands in Petersen's *Troy*, Helen's unpleasant husband meets a deserved bad end, leaving the beauty in the hands of the heroic Arion (Mark Forrest).

An HBO version of *Helen of Troy* (2003) preceded Wolfgang Petersen's 2004 blockbuster, but fails (among other reasons) by neglecting Aristotle's admonition that basing a plot on a single character does not provide a story with unity.[3] While the *Iliad* tells of the anger of Achilles at having his prize Briseis taken from him and the *Odyssey* is focussed on its hero's return, *Helen* recounts the multiple stories from her childhood to the sack of Troy. In Petersen's *Troy*, as in Homer's *Iliad*, the personalities of the doomed Achilles (Brad Pitt) and a surprisingly family-oriented Hector (Eric Bana) overshadow the other characters, including Paris (Orlando Bloom) and Helen (Diane Kruger). The conclusion, with a callow youth named Aeneas taking on the mantle of Troy and the worldly-wise Odysseus saying farewell to the age of heroes, suggests sequels for future filmmakers.

Various light-hearted versions of the tale of the rape of Helen also exist, including Alexander Korda's *Private Life of Helen of Troy* (1927 – only partially preserved) and Jean Renoir's depiction of the power of love over the military in *Paris Does Strange Things* (*Elena et les hommes,* 1956). The latter stars Ingrid Bergman, whose elopement from Hollywood to be in Italy with Roberto Rossellini in 1950 had recently created a scandal worthy of the Spartan princess. There is even a parody of the conclusion of the Trojan War in an early series of *Dr Who* (*The Mythmakers,* 1965), now lost but for a taped soundtrack.[4]

While less popular than the Trojan War, the return of Odysseus from Troy is perhaps more cinematic in form. As the original road movie – or better still, to use German terminology, *Wasserstrasse* – the *Odyssey* may be seen as the ancestor of John Ford's *The Searchers* (1956)[5] or as offering an epic grandeur by lending its title to films as diverse as *2001: A Space Odyssey* (dir. Stanley Kubrick, 1968) or *The Navigator: a Medieval Odyssey* (dir. Vincent Ward, 1988). In this chapter, I start by considering two direct retellings of the epic, the 1954 Kirk Douglas vehicle, *Ulysses* (dir. Mario Camerini), and the 1968 RAI-De Laurentiis television production *L'Odissea* directed by Franco Rossi, with Mario Bava responsible for the Polyphemus episode. Then follow two adventures that show the universality of the story. *The Return of Ringo* (*Il ritorno di Ringo,* dir. Duccio Tessari, 1965) presents the *Odyssey* in an Italian western setting, concentrating on the story of the hero's return in disguise after his home has been taken over by outsiders (in this case, the Mexican Fuentes brothers and their gang). By contrast, the Coen brothers' comic version (*O Brother, Where Art Thou?*, 2000) focuses more on the picaresque journey of its hero and his chain gang comrades within a Depression-era southern US setting. The last two films considered are not direct retellings of the *Odyssey*, but use the epic and its themes to provide a contrast with a much less heroic modern world. While Godard's *Contempt* (*Le Mépris*, 1964) uses the story of Odysseus as a means of contemplating sexual politics, by placing the filming of the *Odyssey* as film within film, it also comments on artistic politics as well, illustrating the tension between the peplum and the art film or, perhaps better, between the (European) intellectual tradition and (American) commercial cinema. Godard's postmodernism can be fruitfully contrasted with Theo Angelopoulos' modernist films that situate mythology not in a lost Classical Greek past but as part of the continuing story of the Greek nation. In the post-Cold War era, the road movie becomes a means to consider the nature of boundaries and their dissolution, of return to homes real and imagined, and the passage through history that continues but without signposts. *Odysseus' Gaze* (1995) is replete with allusions to the journey and features a tragic homecoming set in Sarajevo during the Bosnian civil war. The film looks nostalgically back toward an original undivided Greek gaze and the cinema of the brothers Manakias, while itself recording the dissolution of a common Balkan heritage through the twentieth century that culminated in the collapse of Yugoslavia.

Filming the epic

Anyone filming the *Odyssey* faces the usual difficulties of adapting a written (or more accurately oral) form to a visual medium. For instance, a fixed portrait of individuals or presentation of scenes may well differ from that envisioned by individual readers. It will also be necessary to abridge complex narratives to create a story that can be told in a mere 90 minutes. In Homer, Odysseus' return to deal with the suitors in his palace is constantly retarded by his narration of his earlier adventures to the Phaeacians in the palace on Scheria, which in turn sometimes involves even more deeply embedded tales. For cinema, a direct recounting of events after the capture of Troy – showing the sequence of adventures which leaves the hero as the sole survivor of the Ithacan contingent that took part in the Trojan War – is likely to provide far too lengthy a build-up to the action sequence that concludes the story.[6] On the other hand, a sequence of flash-backs that mirrors the Homeric narrative may confuse or, worse, bore an audience that is looking forward to the tale's rousing climax.[7]

Dialogue and staging also involve major decisions. English language versions of tales set in the past commonly display sub-Shakespearean dialogue, since the Bard's history plays are the closest analogy to Greek high cultural forms, such as epic poetry or tragedy. However, archaic phrasing creates a barrier between the viewer and the events portrayed, as well as failing to represent the fluency of the Homeric story-telling tradition. The use of colloquial idiom, on the other hand, may lack epic gravity or even suggest a comic undercutting of the high style (particularly noticeable in English language dubbing of Italian sword-and-sandal films). The recreation of authentic ancient buildings was likely to be too expensive prior to the turn of the millennium, when powerful computers allowed the incorporation of now ubiquitous CGI effects. But the use of purely theatrical scenery for palaces, typically involving Minoan, Doric, or Corinthian columns (commonly suggesting the exotic, practical or even militaristic, and aesthetic culture of the societies that have erected them) accompanied by complementary wall paintings and art objects, although sometimes visually striking, reduces the sense of historical realism and at worst creates a bizarre pastiche.[8] In costuming the very use of the term 'peplum' indicates a common tradition of indeterminate Greco-Roman clothing that functions for all eras, from the Bronze Age (e.g. the Homeric epics) to Late Antiquity (e.g. the life of Theodora, the emperor Justinian's wife). *Ulysses* (1954) tends to use standard theatrical settings and techniques. *L'Odissea* (1968), perhaps in deliberate contrast, creates an unfamiliar atmosphere in its retelling – although this may be achieved by traditional techniques not usually employed in film adaptations, such as the use of Odysseus' maids as a Greek tragic chorus.

In 1911, Francesco Bertolini produced a substantial *Odissea* that began with Odysseus' departure to Troy, then portrayed the sack of the city and most of his adventures on his return voyage. The film is particularly interesting for its early use of special effects, including superimposition to provide a giant Polyphemus threatening Odysseus and his crew.[9] The 1954 *Ulysses* was able to exploit technical advances in the intervening years, most obviously sound and colour film (a Technicolor consultant is listed in the credits) although it was not filmed in the widescreen that came to be associated with screen spectaculars of the 1950s and 1960s.[10] Its screen-writing credits list no less than seven contributors (excluding the original story from Homer), most notably future peplum stalwart Ennio De Concini, Hollwood star screenwriter Ben Hecht, and Oxford educated 'expert' Hugh Gray.[11] Usually having multiple writers suggests the need to doctor a dodgy script,[12] but in this case it is just as likely that an original Italian script (adjusted by the director) has been given a light polish by outsiders after a major star (Kirk Douglas) was contracted to play the lead role. Given the length of the film (95 minutes),[13] considerable cuts were made to the story. Penelope and Telemachus are reduced to minor roles, and the Lotus Eaters, Scylla and Charybdis, the Laestrygonians, and the Cattle of the Sun disappear. Calypso is syncretised with Circe, who offers Odysseus immortality if he will stay with her, and the *nekyia* (Odysseus' meeting with the dead) takes place on Circe's island rather than at the edge of Ocean.

4. The Odyssey, High and Low

The opening scene shows Penelope pining for her husband and the unseemly behaviour of the suitors in Odysseus' palace on Ithaca, who are condemned by Penelope for 'taking advantage of a lonely and frightened woman'. As the stage has now been set at Ithaca by this depiction of a damsel in distress, the shipwreck of Odysseus (Kirk Douglas) on the island of Scheria and his discovery by Nausicaa (Rossana Podestà) immediately follows. This is not the Homeric crafty survivor who needs the Phaeacians to help him return, yet is initially reluctant to reveal his identity. Rather, through a trope perhaps taken from film noir, Odysseus has suffered a traumatic complete loss of memory and only the gradual revelation of his nobility and manly talents, such as his skill in wrestling, indicates that he must be someone of note. The Phaeacians accept him as a future husband for Nausicaa, but as he wanders alone on the island shore, Odysseus begins to remember in flashback the incidents that brought him there. Changes in certain episodes, such as the song of the Sirens, altered in the film from an account of the war at Troy promised in Homer's poem to an impersonation of the voices of Penelope and Telemachus calling for husband and father, stress the hero's desire to be reunited with his family. The sorceress Circe assumes the form of Penelope (both are played by Silvana Mangano)[14] and beguiles the hero into staying with her, while his men sail off and are shipwrecked. Odysseus may tarry with a single enchantress,[15] yet he comes to his senses as a good family man should. It is of his own free will, not through divine intervention, that he builds his raft to try to sail home and is shipwrecked on Scheria. Such a retelling of Odysseus' adventures, it need hardly be stressed, is quite different from the Homeric hero's desire to reclaim wife *and* patrimony. Once the groom has recovered his memory, a bigamous wedding will not do. Nausicaa is disappointed, but the Phaeacians graciously provide the man they now recognise as the great Greek hero with transport home to Ithaca.

The temptations of straying from fidelity are further stressed with the delayed arrival, a third of the way into the drama, of Antinoos, played by the guest star, Anthony Quinn. Unlike the Homeric leader of the suitors who is merely an Ithacan noble, Quinn's character is a king in his own right, riding in on his chariot and making quite an impression with his equestrian skills. He immediately invades Penelope's private quarters and declares himself ready to turn out the ill-mannered guests and restore order in Ithaca. In short, the sort of tall, dark and handsome man for whom a lonely and frightened widow might fall. But he also later reveals himself to be the arch-villain, intending to eliminate Penelope's son the day after his wedding (a variation of the ambush set by the suitors in *Odyssey* 4, which Telemachus escapes in Book 15) despite having promised his prospective bride that no one will lay hands on the youth. Tempted by the possibility of at least saving her son's life, the queen is ready to submit. However a beggar appears and advises her to pick her spouse by setting the same competition that had led to the selection of her first husband. Twelve axe heads are set in a row and the man who can string the bow that had been Odysseus' and fire an arrow through their sockets will be the victor. All the suitors fail to string the bow, even Antinoos who comes closest to success, but the beggar (Odysseus in disguise) succeeds with ease. He then proceeds to take bloody revenge on the suitors, assisted in his efforts by his son. After a comparatively brief struggle that hardly matches modern standards of action choreography or violence (except for an implied axe-slaying), Odysseus has reclaimed his kingdom and wife and can be expected to live happily ever after.

The 1954 film eliminates many minor characters. For instance, Eumaios the swineherd disappears, although the old dog Argos is retained for his sentimental recognition of his master after so many years. The fate of other figures after the final battle is simply ignored: Melantho and the other serving girls simply disappear from the screen, rather than suffer an ignoble death as in *Odyssey* 22, and no mention is made of the suitors' relatives. Entire themes are cut: there is no extended testing of the identity of the long absent husband by his wife, an epic trope which by inversion forms the basis of *The Return of Martin Guerre* (dir. Daniel Vigne, 1982) and its remake, *Sommersby* (dir. Jon Amiel, 1993). Nor is there any need in this film for Odysseus to assure himself of his wife's fidelity, whereas in the *Odyssey* the infidelity of Clytemnestra and her murderous welcome of Agamemnon are recalled to warn the hero against excessive trust and, as it turns out, to provide a contrast with Penelope's behaviour. The reasons are obvious: the audience knows perfectly well that Kirk Douglas, even dressed as a beggar, is the real thing, and doubting the virtue of Penelope, given the romantic tone of this version which requires Odysseus' unquestioning love, would simply be churlish. In the *Odyssey* (21.311-19), Penelope asks the suitors to allow the beggar's request to attempt to string the bow, since he at least has no intention of taking her with him on his wanderings. In *Ulysses,* Odysseus presents the ironic comment when he asks the queen not to fear having to marry such a poor man, since he is in fact married already. This variation is once again in line with the emphasis on the male protagonist (and 'star') and his monogamous desires, reinforcing the characterisation of a faithful but passive Penelope, hardly Homer's cautious and circumspect (*periphrôn*) heroine, well-matched with her cunning (*polymêtis*) spouse. In this film, men go off on adventures in distant lands and the women remain faithful at home, awaiting their return. It is an old patriarchal melodrama, given new impetus by the European adventures in exploration and, more significantly for the film's international audience, by the exposure to new lands and customs of soldiers serving overseas in and after the Second World War.

4. The Odyssey, High and Low

A modernist Odyssey

Ulysses can easily be seen as a proto-peplum. It has non-Italian stars as male leads (Douglas, Quinn) and stunningly attractive Italian actresses who either were already stars (Mangano) or soon would be (Podestà). Costuming is also typical for the genre: men in short tunics, women in full-length peplums.[16] The Phaeacians are marked as strikingly different in their non-Hellenic garb, as befits peaceful islanders who wish for no contact with the outside world.[17] Scenes are shot on the lot at Cinecittà or, for sea scenes, off Anzio using a combined oar-and-sail galley-style vessel that will be familiar to viewers of later mythological films such as *The Labours of Hercules* (1958), *The Giants of Thessaly (The Argonauts)* (1960), or *Hercules Conquers Atlantis* (1961). As an adventure film *Ulysses* is a far cry from the gloom of Italian neo-realism, harking back instead to earlier Hollywood efforts in the genre. Indeed, the last scene of the film might easily have been translated from some version of the Robin Hood legend, as the bowman storms the banquet hall of his enemies[18] and triumphs over numerous opponents to save Maid Marian.

By contrast, Franco Rossi's 1968 television mini-series, *L'Odissea*, seems crafted not from the theatrical tradition that leads through *Ulysses* to the peplum tradition, but from European modernism. Its costumes appear to have been specifically made for the series, not taken from the rack. Clothing is woven wool and generally limited to shades of grey, brown, and black.[19] Odysseus' raft is simply timbers roped together over which the sea breaks, with a makeshift mast, and when he accidentally allows the sail to drag in the water, it quickly becomes saturated and its weight nearly submerges the entire vessel. The first view of Ithaca provided to the viewer is of a truly rocky beach, extending up to some rather unimpressive stone dwellings.[20] The grandeur does not, then, lie in the spectacle, but rather in the tale that is told through the actions of its characters. The omnipresent narrator is both Homer, the voice sometimes duplicated by Phemios the singer of tales at Ithaca[21] or a tragic chorus of servant girls, and the camera that records the events. Even the divine apparatus, stripped away in other retellings of Homeric material such as *Helen of Troy* or *Troy*, is preserved. No cottonwool Olympia is presented as in *Jason and the Argonauts* (1963), where baroque scenery mirrors the second-hand Hellenistic sensibilities of Apollonius of Rhodes in remarkably appropriate fashion. *L'Odissea*'s deities are not visible in a conventional sense, but are disembodied voices that can only be comprehended behind their conventional marble images.

The tone is serious throughout the series without the comic undercutting of heroic pretensions that is a regular motif of peplum films. In particular, certain motifs reveal the ability of cinematic technique to highlight and refresh epic themes. Most audiences would recognise the suitors' violation of the laws of hospitality as one of the major themes in the *Odyssey*, but Rossi's version highlights the importance of commensality throughout the poem. For instance, after showing the suitors' physically seizing sheep for their feasts (in contrast to the productive shearing of the animals and spinning of their wool by the loyal servants), Rossi presents a scene of ritual procession, the purification of a garlanded beast, and ceremonial sacrifice by Nestor at Pylos. The montage of striking images makes it clear both to Telemachus, who is about to land and seek information about his father, and to the viewers that the anarchy of Ithaca has been left far behind. This assumption is reinforced when Nestor welcomes Telemachus to his feast on the shore and subsequently tells of his last sighting of Odysseus. Likewise, when Odysseus arrives at their court, the Phaeacians gracefully receive him as a supplicant and offer him food. Their metal utensils conspicuously contrast with the earthenware used in Ithacan scenes, but even more striking is the depiction of the hero dining alone. Such a description appears in *Odyssey* 7.167-77, but Rossi's staging – Odysseus seated on a level below the enthroned Phaeacians – stresses his separation, physically and socially. When he returns to Ithaca, his first meal in his guise of beggar is with the swineherd Eumaios, who displays simple hospitality to a stranger that is in no way repeated by the banqueting suitors.

While food and drink reveal the social bonds and stratification of society, the most famous example of this theme is depicted in negative terms. The Cyclops appears to be providing a ready table to Odysseus and his companions when they enter his cave and find cheese and milk in abundance. But instead they will provide the monster with his meal of raw meat, in violation of divine laws of hospitality. Only Odysseus' cunning gift of drink, in the form of extra-strength wine, can accomplish Polyphemus' undoing, as the Greeks are able to blind him as he lies in a drunken stupor.

There are dangers in other potions too: Circe's cups have the ability to turn men into swine (Odysseus is fortunately rendered immune by the herb moly) and Helen, who is portrayed sporting remarkable Egyptian eye-liner, can reduce the sorrow of the past for herself, her husband Menelaos, and their guest Telemachus by adding a drug to their drinks. Perhaps the most remarkable expansion of the Homeric text is the portrayal of the court of Aeolus, king of the winds. The blessed life of Aeolus and his family is briefly described in the *Odyssey* (10.9-11: 'innumerable foodstuffs are set out before them; the palace is filled with the smell of food and echoes with the sounds of woodwinds'); in the modern version the poem's humour is stressed in a bizarre scene of small children playing Aeolian tunes, while the monarch and his puffed-up family feast continually on a cold buffet. Excellent, if odd hosts, who much appreciate his tales of the Trojan War, they send Odysseus off after sealing up all contrary winds in a oxhide bag. What in the *Odyssey* is a brief episode to confirm the hostility of the gods to the hero's return, in *L'Odissea* is used to display Odysseus' lack of self-awareness (he swears, rather unconvincingly, to

6. Montage from *L'Odissea* (1968): Telemachus arrives at the shore of Pylos, where Nestor is sacrificing: (a) Procession along beach seen from Telemachus' ship; (b) Garlanded sacrificial ox in close-up; (c) View of procession having passed through ceremonial arch; (d) Nestor purifies his hands in water provided by attendants; (e) Attendants fetch sacrificial ox; (f) Close-up of axe-head against sky; (g) Procession leaves sacrifice site; (h) Reverse shot of Telemachus' ship landing on beach now stained with blood from the sacrifice.

Aeolus that he is not being pursued by the anger of any divinity) and his gradual loss of esteem in the eyes of his companions. This disharmony, which leads to his men opening the bag of wind on their journey home, is intensified during his stay with Circe (contrary to the Homeric version, the sailors, once returned from the animal shapes into which they have been turned by the sorceress, stay well away from her powers). This becomes a complete rift after his starving companions decide to eat the sacred Cattle of the Sun. The result is the destruction of Odysseus' ship, the drowning of his men, and his subsequent eight-year stay on Ogygia with the nymph Calypso.

One can easily multiply examples of scenes of eating and drinking. For instance, Odysseus' narration of the decision to kill the Cattle of the Sun is immediately followed by an image of legs of beef roasting. But the consumption of food is actually occurring on Scheria and the generous banqueting as the hero tells his tale is set in contrast with the illicit feasting of his comrades. In the *nekyia* episode, where Odysseus summons up the spirits of the dead from Hades, the weakness of the dead is portrayed by their dismal thirst for the blood of the black ram that has been sacrificed. Visual indicators of food and drink are thus constantly used to reinforce narrative themes.

If this were all, Rossi's version of the *Odyssey* might merely be praised for its skilful depiction of Homeric motifs. Yet another mythological pattern has also been teased out of the epic text. The story of the hero's humiliation, loss of trust among his supporters, and struggle once more to claim his rightful place in his society forms an easily recognisable typology in many periods. Viewers of *Buffy the Vampire Slayer*, for example, will recall this exact story arc in Seasons 6 and 7 when Buffy is resurrected after her self-sacrificing death at the end of Season 5. Unfortunately, unlike the Athenian audiences at tragic performance who, according to Aristotle (*Poetics* 13) found pleasure in pitying heroes at their lowest ebb, modern viewers tend to find the hero's fall unsettling, as ratings and negative viewer responses to these seasons made clear. Rossi stresses the hero's humiliation by including an incident that is often omitted: Odysseus' brawl with Iros, who regards the newcomer as a threat to his status as resident beggar at the palace on Ithaca. In Homer, Odysseus wins the fight and admonishes his unconscious opponent: 'Now sit here and ward off the pigs and dogs and don't try to be king of mendicants and beggars, when you are so pitiful, or something even worse may happen to you' (*Od.* 18.105-8). Bekim Fehmiu's character, however, shows compassion for Iros as a human being: 'Don't try to be king of the beggars any more: a wretch is simply a wretch.' The slight change, stressing the pitiful democracy of poverty, is significant. Given the general message in *Ulysses* that the good and bad receive their just desserts, these are not lines that could be expected from the mouth of Kirk Douglas' Odysseus.

Comparison between the 1954 and 1968 versions of the *Odyssey* is instructive. Kirk Douglas' character returns in disguise to Ithaca and settles his score with the suitors, recovering his bride and returning Ithaca to a peaceful state. This ending would be familiar to audiences brought up on Hollywood westerns, where the protagonist's task is to defeat the villains and allow normal life to continue. However, the Vietnam War and the querying of the post-war settlement throughout by the student movements of 1968 had dented any optimism about Americanism as the way of the future. The peplums' simple morality had been replaced by the more cynical mood of the Italian western.

Rossi's Odysseus shows himself capable of extreme anger, for instance when challenged by Euryalos the Phaeacian and again by Iros, yet on both occasions also exercises self-control.[22] His revenge on the suitors is, however, carried out mercilessly and leaves him physically exhausted. Realising that the relatives of the suitors will be bound to avenge their kinsmen, he orders all in the palace to give the impression of a wedding feast to explain why the menfolk have not returned home. This buys him time to spend the night with Penelope (who responds to his earlier unwillingness to reveal his identity to her by testing his knowledge of the architecture of their marriage bed) and to visit his father Laertes the next day. In the meantime, the bodies of the suitors are carried through the town in a funeral procession. The framing of this shot, set against the background of the harbour, to indicate the social effect of the slaughter, would do Theo Angelopoulos proud.[23] Even more than Homer, Rossi stresses that at this point Odysseus has still not been integrated back into his community. Whereas in *Odyssey* 24 a brief confrontation between the families of the suitors and Odysseus' clan ends when Mentor brokers peace between the two factions, in *L'Odissea* Mentor initially suggests that Odysseus should pay compensation for the dead to end the feud. While the families of the suitors hesitate, Odysseus advances to fight. Only at the last moment does he place his arms in the ground and accept peace. The end of the *Odyssey* (24.533-48) where the relatives of those killed throw away their arms in terror and Odysseus, who is ready to pursue them, is halted by Athena, may be the origin of this depiction. In Rossi's version, however, peace is not imposed by further violence, but by a readiness of all to accept its necessity. Restoration, not retribution, is the order of the day.

Even though Rossi keeps close to the Homeric text, his Odysseus is in the end a far cry from the traditional egotistic epic hero. The underlying themes of *L'Odissea* reveal European humanism, rather than Classical aristocratic values.[24] It is significant that Rossi's Odysseus listens to the song of the Sirens not for his own pleasure but in order to falsify the prophecy that no one may hear their singing without dying.[25] Man need not be bound by Fate, but has the opportunity to shape his own destiny. There is no necessity for Odysseus to return to Ithaca alone after the deaths of his crewmates, despite Circe's warnings. If the sailors ultimately succumb to the temptation of killing the Cattle of the Sun and so seal their fate, this is a choice they have made. Perhaps the most significant theme in *L'Odissea* is the transformation of Odysseus from self-centred epic hero to popular leader.[26] This Marxist reading of history derived from analysis of ancient societies may seem irrelevant in a modern, post-Cold War, global society, yet it strikingly reflects the influence of Greek literature on European humanism.

Of course, *L'Odissea* would not have been such a major television event in Europe if its production values had not been so high.[27] American studio funding that had supported the Italian film industry through the 1950s and early 1960s, ranging from blockbusters such as *Helen of Troy* or *Ben Hur* to joint ventures such as *Ulysses* or even the AIP-funded Hercules films, had now been largely withdrawn. The financial disaster of *Cleopatra* in 1963 made the large Hollywood studios wary of investing in large-scale productions, particularly overseas where financial control was uncertain, while distributors such as Joe E. Levine were becoming interested in moving into more prestigious American-based efforts. Dino De Laurentiis was now able to use European investment and exploit favourable conditions within the Italian film industry for a major television production. Large numbers of films (perhaps as many as 300 per year) were still being made, but, aside from the work of internationally famous *auteurs* such as Visconti, Antonioni, and Fellini, much of the production was in short-lived styles (*filoni*), first westerns replacing the peplum genre, then *gialli* (crime thrillers), while a number of horror films were produced throughout the period. Experienced directors, often used to working with limited budgets, became available for television studios wishing to show that they too could produce work of cultural value and so compete with the cinemas. Vittorio Cottafavi, for instance, produced well-regarded historical dramas for Radiotelevisione Italiana (RAI), including Euripides' *Trojan Women* (*Le Troiane*, 1967), Molière's *Don Juan* (*Don Giovanni*, 1967), and Conrad's *Under Western Eyes* (*Con gli occhi dell' occidente*, 1979). Franco Rossi had already established himself as a scriptwriter and director of note with *Friends for Life* (*Amici per la pelle* 1955), but his version of the *Odyssey* launched a career as a skilful adapter of classical material for television that included *The Aeneid* (*L'Eneide,* 311 minutes, 1971) and *Quo vadis?* (360 minutes, 1985, with Klaus Maria Brandauer as Nero and Frederick Forrest as Petronius).

In the English language, television adaptations of stories set in the ancient world have had mixed success. The BBC television adaptation of Robert Graves' *I, Claudius* (dir. Herbert Wise, 1976) that was so successful for the American Public Broadcasting System set the tone for drama of the upper classes presented as Roman history.[28] A sign of its influence is David Chase's choice of the name Livia for the patriarch of that equally dysfunctional American family, *The Sopranos*. The recent *Rome* mini-series (2005-7) also shows its descent from the *I, Claudius* model, providing sex and violence to the American cousins as English costume drama (what is sometimes caustically referred to as 'master race theatre').[29] By contrast, Andrei Konchalovsky's *Odyssey* (1997), described in the All Movie Guide as 'a fun-filled adaptation of Homer's most famous epic poem', and the John Kent Harrison directed *Helen of Troy*, both made for HBO, suffer from restricted length (both are under three hours long). Rather than 'bringing culture to the masses', they may be thought of as adapting their stories to modern tastes for rapid editing and relentless activity. While, as Richard Burt has shown, it is very much possible to 'dumb down' Shakespeare to a point where the vacuousness becomes interesting in itself,[30] in the twenty-first century it seems difficult to unbind Homer's epics from literate culture. Despite detectable Homeric influences on *Buffy*,[31] an *Iliad* set in a high school is unlikely to appear and 'Young Odysseus', the prequel, doesn't sound like an idea that is likely to attract producers. Even the Coen brothers' version of the *Odyssey* can exist only in the context of another obsolete form, the chain gang film. This perhaps offers hope: apparently irretrievably non-modern, epic can be adapted with some ease to other film genres depicting an imaginary past, as our next example will show.

Duccio Tessari's *The Return of Ringo*

While Sergio Leone could label John Ford as the 'Homer of the Seventh Cavalry and of friendships between men ...',[32] an Italian director with experience in the peplum tradition was the first to exploit fully the myth of the hero's return in a western context. Duccio Tessari has already been mentioned as one of the scriptwriters for *Gli ultimi giorni di Pompeii* (1959 – also assistant director) as well as for Cottafavi's and Bava's Hercules films of 1961. He had since earned director's credits for a semi-comic peplum *My Son, the Hero* (*Arrivano i titani* 1961), which starred a previously unknown actor, Giuliano Gemma, as the weakest (and thus, necessarily the most cunning) of the Titans, sent to liberate Crete from the tyranny of Cadmos. In 1965, following the new trend for Italian westerns to be filmed in Spain, Tessari had written and directed *A Pistol for Ringo*, also starring Gemma under the alias Montgomery Wood. The success of this feature led to the recall of much of the cast in *The Return of Ringo*, the story of a Civil War soldier, Montgomery Brown, returning in disguise to his hometown of Mimbres as the Mexican peasant, Ringo.

In part, the film draws on the tradition of the 'man with no name' who arrives in a town divided between Mexican and American criminal factions and then plays them off against one another – Sergio Leone had popularised this plot in *Fistful of Dollars* (1964) and it soon reached its pinnacle in Sergio Corbucci's *Django* (1966).[33] There are also elements borrowed from more traditional American westerns, such as the alcoholic town sheriff, who needs to regain his self-esteem and stand up to the villains, and Rosita, the saloon girl of dubious loyalty, who *à la* Marlene

Dietrich is also capable of providing a musical interlude.[34] The latter is played by the vivacious Nieves Navarro, who as Susan Scott would later be a significant star in Italian thrillers (*gialli*). Her fortune-telling through the cards may also hark back to Dietrich (in her role as madam in Orson Welles' *Touch of Evil*, 1958), but also suggests that she plays a part similar to Circe in the *Odyssey* – part temptress, part guide. The story of the liberation of the hero's town from the Fuentes brothers and their gang when the locals find a leader in Captain Brown may also come from the American western. However the plan of Don Francisco 'Paco' Fuentes (the elegantly evil Jorge Martin) to force Hally Brown, the wife of the hero, to marry him now her husband is assumed dead, is a plot element that clearly derives from the *Odyssey*. Since Montgomery Brown has merely been away fighting in the Civil War, not adventuring for twenty years, there is no Telemachus to aid his father's return. Instead his small daughter whom he has never seen is being kept hostage by the Mexicans and he must rescue her during the final battle.

Some aspects of the Odyssean story are integral to the plot. Initially, no one recognises the homeless peasant being humiliated by the Mexican bandits. He, in turn, is uncertain of the loyalty of his wife when he sees her driving in a carriage with Paco Fuentes. In a striking variation, 'Ringo' the indigent stranger is welcomed not by the swineherd Eumaios, but by the equally lowly town florist, Myosotis ('Forget-Me-Not' – and, as Miosotis, usually a female name).[35] That the florist is kept busy in Mimbres making wreaths is a blackly comedic variation on the coffin-maker in *Fistful of Dollars*. The intended wedding between Paco and Hally is particularly striking visually. The wedding party's passage through windswept and deserted streets to the church is intercut with scenes of the townsfolk arming themselves, and Hally arrives in widow's black rather than a wedding dress. Something is amiss in the church as well, since four coffins have been placed there, framing the bride and groom during the service. At the very moment that the priest is about to complete the ceremony, the church doors blow open. 'Sono tornato', 'I am back', is repeated three times by the silhouetted figure in full cavalry regalia, clutching a rifle, before he disappears into the cloud of dust swirling outside. Here is Odysseus, transformed in a flash from beggar to the avenger at the threshold, scattering his arrows at his feet before striking down the suitors. The coffins hold the bodies of Paco's men, killed by Ringo, announcing his vengeance to come.

Many of the faults of *The Return of Ringo* can be found in generic Hollywood westerns of the 1950s. Scenes of shooting regularly feature nameless stuntmen falling off roofs into wagons of hay or reeling back into horse troughs. As nameless victims of the hero's skill with a gun, their origin may be seen in the countless Trojans and Greeks who fall to Achilles or Hector. More worrisome is the implied racism in the portrayal of Mexicans (mainly Spanish actors) mistreating white Americans. Tessari's

俺は帰って来た！
血に飢えたコルトに
復讐の弾をこめて
俺は帰って来た
陰謀うずまく無頼の町へ

7. 'I have returned.' In *The Return of Ringo* (1965), the ragged peasant metamorphoses into Captain Montgomery Brown in full military uniform standing at the door of the church where Paco Fuentes is about to marry his wife.

American western is thus a throwback, in contrast to Leone's *Fistful of Dollars* where Americans and Mexicans are equally despicable. In later westerns, such as Damiano Damiani's *Quien Sabe?* (aka *Bullet for the General*, 1966) or Sergio Sollima's *Big Gundown* (1967) the political implications of a genre in which white northerners exploit uneducated Mexicans are made clear. It is difficult not to feel that *The Return of Ringo* belongs to a world of simpler ethical values, where the despised Mexican peasant, Ringo, may metamorphose into a Union army captain. Thus the film lacks epic grandeur, but by borrowing from the stock of Western story-telling through its Odyssean themes, it is capable of entertaining and sometimes even of capturing the imagination of its audience.[36]

Hard times in the Cyclops' cave

The brothers Ethan and Joel Coen have established a reputation for exploitation of film genres, often to black comic effect.[37] Film noir is a particular favourite (*Blood Simple*, 1984; *The Big Lebowski*, 1998; *The Man Who Wasn't There*, 2001) along with gangster and police procedural narratives (*Miller's Crossing*, 1990; *Fargo*, 1996). Much of the pleasure of their output, then, is in the recognition of period styles that have been given a modern makeover: *The Hudsucker Proxy* (1994) is clearly a screwball comedy, *The Ladykillers* (2004) an update of the classic Ealing crime caper from 1955. A frequent inspiration is the work of Preston Sturges, whose screenwriter seeking a subject in *Sullivan's Travels* (1941) is darkly mirrored in *Barton Fink* (1991) and whose intended title for a socially realistic film is re-used in *Oh Brother, Where Art Thou?* (2000). Sturges' hero had intended to write about the lives of struggling working men in a Depression-era drama and discovered from harsh experience in a chain gang that the best cinema he might offer would be a comedy that would lighten their sufferings. This self-reflexive narrative (*Sullivan's Travels* is itself the comedy that the screenwriter finally discovers he has been seeking all along) is partially recreated by the Coen brothers' tale of Depression-era escapees from a chain gang. *Oh Brother* also re-enacts the *Odyssey*'s archetypal adventures of heroes seeking to return to their homes. Social questions that might once have been treated as high drama (the injustices of the peculiar penal institution of chained work gangs depicted in *Cool Hand Luke*, 1967) have been transformed into elements of story-telling as familiar and dated as the tales of brave Ulysses. The American tradition of neo-Classical nomenclature that lives on in Homer J. Simpson is mocked in the follies and foibles of Ulysses Everett McGill, Odysseus as con man and dandy.[38]

Comparisons may as easily obfuscate as elucidate. The Soggy Bottom Boys' rendition of 'Man of Constant Sorrow' conveys a permanent farewell to the singer's home, promising instead another end to the journey: 'I'll meet you on God's golden shore'.[39] Such a message of Christian hope is a far cry from Odysseus' desire for his return home (*nostos*) and his characteristic endurance (*polytlas*).[40] It is, however, very much in line with the Depression-era sociology of the film.[41] In fact the Classical sub-text seems mainly to derive from the 1954 Kirk Douglas *Ulysses* rather than reflect any high literary values. The introductory title, quoting the opening lines of the epic, creates a deliberate misconception of adaptation of highbrow entertainment ('based on the *Odyssey*') that is as reliable as the claim that *Fargo* (1996) is based on real events. In fact, comic misinterpretation dominates. The Sirens as washing-girls (perhaps a nod to Nausicaa's laundry duties when discovering Odysseus on the shore of Scheria) combine female allurement to destruction with Circe's ability to transform men, here under the influence of moonshine, if not into swine, then at least into toads. That (Ulysses) Everett's companion Pete is found not to have been transformed after all completes the comic undercutting of the well-known story. There are, however, indications that other sources (*Cliff's Notes* or *Classics Illustrated* no. 81?) have been consulted: the Palace of the Aeolus is alluded to in the call sign of the radio station where the Soggy Mountain Boys get their big break (WEZY), the Cattle of the Sun by the cows machine-gunned by George 'Babyface' Nelson.

All this appears to be good, simple fun. As might be expected, things get much blacker with the appearance of the Coen brothers' favourite psycho-path, the giant John Goodman as a one-eyed bible salesman, Big Dan Teague. Although he does not literally eat Odysseus' men, he certainly feasts off the naïvety of Everett and Delmar, concluding the salesman's lesson that you must 'recognise who you're dealing with' by applying the bough of a tree to the heads of both and then taking up 'Pete' in toad form and crushing him in his hand.

In the 1954 *Ulysses*, the Polyphemus episode illustrates how a cunning Greek may overcome the rustic Cyclops by plying him with alcohol. Folktale elements are to the fore as Polyphemus is portrayed more as the stupid giant of Jack and the Beanstalk than Homer's terrible monster. The wine is not the extra strong brew that Odysseus has brought with him to offer to his host, but grapes crushed on the spot (which miraculously produce alcohol rather than grape juice). The rapid dance of Greeks treading grapes intensifies as Polyphemus consumes more and more wine and only slows down as the Cyclops starts to lapse into a drunken stupor – all accompanied by appropriate music. After the blinding of the monster, Odysseus plays a game of blind-man's-buff, pretending to be hiding behind the rock that blocks the cave door. He thus induces the giant to remove the stone and let him and his crew escape with Polyphemus' sheep. As the Greeks depart, Odysseus taunts his host: 'Goodbye Polyphemus, you drunken son of Neptune. Enjoy your wine and remember the stringy Greeks and the dance they danced in your cave. ... Roar on, you drunken Cyclops, roar on.' The depiction of drunkenness as a sin along with the quaint Mediterranean methods of wine-making suggest that in Kirk Douglas' film the story has been recrafted through the American puritani-cal tradition into a simple morality tale.

The Coen brothers reverse this portrayal by setting events not in a cave but outside in an idyllic country landscape where Everett and Delmar picnic under a shady tree and by having their Cyclops, the craftiest of Bible salesmen ('And what do I sell? The Truth! Ever' blessed word of it, from Genesee on down to Revelations!'), teach his rustic guests a lesson they should not forget.

Big Dan Teague reappears in another scene, labelled 'Defeating the Cyclops' in the DVD edition. Here Everett and his men attempt to rescue their friend, the black musician Tommy Johnson, from a Ku Klux Klan lynching (the rally is depicted as a Busby Berkeley song and dance number). When discovered by Teague, now dressed as a klansman (and needing only one hole in his hood for his good eye), Everett hurls the standard he is carrying high into the air and it descends towards the Cyclops' eye. The audience's expectations of the blinding of the monster are defeated when he catches the flag at the last moment, a comic relief of tension that permits a reprise as Everett cuts the wire stay of the burning KKK cross which now falls on Teague and the assembled klansmen. The escape of the protagonists in the resulting confusion requires no depiction.

The story of Polyphemus need not be comic, as comparison between *Ulysses* and *L'Odissea* shows. Eugen Schüfften, most famous for his work on Fritz Lang's *Metropolis* (1926) had provided the special effects for the 1954 film, but flaws in his use of scale and props reduce the fantasy effect.[42] When in 1968 Mario Bava made the episode as featured director for Rossi's *L'Odissea*,[43] he was working with a script closer to the Homeric story and given twice as much time (approximately 30 minutes instead of the 15 for the episode in *Ulysses*). His Polyphemus is no stupid giant, but a true monster who dashes out the brains of Ulysses' men and fishes them out of hiding with his fingers before feasting on them. Bava's characteristic use of chiaroscuro lighting intensifies the dread of the Greeks trapped within the cave for two days, drawing lots to undertake the terrifying task of offering their captor the extra-strength wine they had brought as a present for a more generous host. The beam that is thrust into the Cyclops' eye gleams red-hot and produces a satisfying sizzle (a retelling close to *Odyssey* 9.371-94: cf. 379: *diephaineto d'ainôs* 'it glowed incandescent'). The tension is maintained when Polyphemus calls on the other Cyclops to help him take revenge on his tormentors, a danger which is luckily avoided by Odysseus' ruse of styling himself as 'No Man'. The Greeks finally make their escape literally through the fingers of the monster, strapped to his sheep. The Homeric story of the abject, one-eyed outsider who does not welcome the visit of strangers is thus revealed to be the precursor to modern horror stories.

The change of tone in *Oh Brother, Where Art Thou?* is simple to explain. The Coens are exploiting a time-honoured story, but, by placing it in another temporal setting (the Depression-era South), they can treat serious social concerns (racial prejudice and violence) by mocking the upholders of discredited values. As noted, it is likely that they had already detected comic opportunities in Kirk Douglas' version of the *Odyssey*, particularly in the Cyclops episode. While Rossi's Odysseus shows his courage and leadership abilities by rescuing his men after bringing them into the most hideous danger, Ulysses Everett McGill's actions regularly display total incompetence. In the twenty-first century the Western public often views its national leaders and their politics as being as disreputable as the Depression-era charlatans portrayed by the Coens. In such circumstances, appeals to heroic values are seen as fraudulent – better to muddle through than trust appeals to authority.

4. The Odyssey, High and Low

In such a fashion, the grandiosity of the epic has morphed into the comic mode of bathos for the general audience.

Jean-Luc Godard's *Contempt*

I have suggested that the tales of the past now resonate with the general public only through strongly altered recreations (e.g. the HBO *Odyssey*) or as performed in other guises (*The Return of Ringo* was a period piece for its day, while the Coens deliberately created their Odyssey as a Depression-era drama). Yet Homer's work is also important to a minority who recognise its place in Western cultural history and appreciate even radical reassessment of its value. To illustrate this, I have chosen as my final examples two films that can be regarded as 'art-house' cinema, appealing to a limited audience who have been educated in the history of film as well as literature: Godard's *Contempt* and Angelopoulos' *Ulysses' Gaze*. While Godard explores the history of cinema through a film about the filming of one of Western literature's seminal works, Angelopoulos explores modern Balkan history through a recreation of an Odysseus' journeys in a story of a filmmaker searching for a seminal film. While Godard is post-modern in style and Angelopoulos resolutely upholds the tradition of Murnau, Dreyer and Welles, I hope to show that both reflect a national cinema of the time in their creations.

In 1954, the Italian novelist Alberto Moravia published *Il Disprezzo* (*Contempt*), the story of a writer whose desire to gain employment with a film producer to script light comedies leads his wife suddenly to reject him. The novel in part reflects Moravia's own stormy relations with his wife, Elsa Morante, but it also portrays the anxieties of Italian intellectuals in the post-war period, wishing to avoid conformity but also forced by economic necessity to make their way in a capitalist system. The demands for a higher standard of living imposed on the writer protagonist by his ex-typist wife may also be seen as indicative of the demands on the Italian bourgeoisie from a newly emancipated working class. While the latter's desire for a better life is seen as justified, it is impossible for the intellectuals to fulfil these material demands without betraying their idealism, thus leaving both parties feeling aggrieved. Moravia's protagonist, Riccardo Molteni, despises his career as scriptwriter, forming ideas that can only be realised by others, a mere nursemaid to projects that the director mothers, and forced in the process to work with people who are his inferiors in culture and breeding. His self-loathing is particularly expressed in his opinion that 'the mechanical, stereotyped way in which scripts are fabricated strongly resembles a kind of rape of the intelligence, having its origin in determination and interest rather than in any sort of attraction or sympathy'.[44] The strain of working as an artisan rather than artist is intensified when his producer, Battista, announces that he wishes his next project to be a break with post-war Italian neo-realism, a depressing genre with limited commercial appeal. Instead he would be producing a version of the *Odyssey*, which he sees as the Mediterranean equivalent of big-budget American Bible epics. Nausicaa and her maids would appear as bathing beauties observed secretly by Ulysses; Polyphemus would be another version of King Kong; and for Circe, the model would be Antinea in *Atlantis*. In effect, this would be a regression to the non-realistic style of *Cabiria* and other early Italian spectacular films.[45] By contrast, the German director who would oversee the project, a director of *kolossals* with the suggestive name of Rheingold, a second-tier talent not in the same league as the Pabsts and Langs, seeks to internalise the story of Ulysses' travails on his return to Ithaca. Instead of a *spectacolare*, this will be the tale of a man who was afraid of returning to a wife who did not love him yet could not stay away. As Molteni immediately recognises, this is the dark drama of modern man, not sunlit adventures at the dawn of man's fantasies.[46] The play between possible scripts and actual life is intensified when at Battista's villa on Capri, where the filming is about to begin, Molteni sees the producer attempt to kiss his wife. Has she betrayed him or has he pimped his Muse to the brutalities of Capital? Following Rheingold's interpretation of Ulysses having lost Penelope's love by allowing gifts from a suitor and winning it back by slaying Antinoos on his return, Molteni seeks to 'kill' Battista by refusing to work on his script. The outcome, however, refutes the modernist interpretation of the *Odyssey*: this gesture does nothing to change Emilia's contempt and she leaves for Rome in the company of the producer, not as his lover but as an ex-wife. Moravia solves the problem of the object of desire's future by having Emilia die in a road accident, turning her into an eternal version of the goddess she appeared to be in life, from whom Molteni may seek forgiveness and contemplate as his personal 'image of consolation and beauty'.

Moravia views film as a low art form and particularly rejects modern psychologising approaches, the dark work of northerners and Anglophones that will drain the vitality of Mediterranean humanism. One can only imagine how he would have reacted to Pasolini's *Oedipus Rex* (1967) or *Medea* (1969). At the same time, Moravia despises the vulgarity of Battista's vision, apparently preferring something like Bertolini's 1911 *Odissea* to the popular entertainment of the Camerini film of 1954. Still, the book is the story of a possible film of a story, a chance to reflect on the art of writing and commercial necessities in the form of a bitter romance. It would seem to be ready material for Antonioni.

Instead, the screen adaptation (*Le Mépris* (*Contempt*)) came in 1963 from Jean-Luc Godard, resulting in a film about the making of a book into a film. The post-modernism of the project lies in the simultaneous struggle between Godard as both writer and director and the producers, Carlo Ponti and Joseph E. Levine. It is simplistic to attribute automatically the bad taste of Godard's cinematic producer Jeremy Prokosch (Jack Palance) – an American replacement for Moravia's Battista – to Levine and assume that the latter expected a peplum from his director. As already seen, Levine had made his name with recut versions of Steve Reeves' *Hercules* films marketed by Embassy Pictures, but he was also interested in being involved with more upmarket fare, as seen by his credits for *Zulu* (dir. Cy Enfield, 1964), *The Graduate* (dir. Mike Nichols, 1967), *The Producers* (dir. Mel Brooks, 1968), and even the thoroughly art-house *Lion in Winter* (dir. Anthony Harvey, 1968).

In some cases, external decisions led to creative explorations. The requirement to film in Technicolor and Cinemascope allowed Godard and cinematographer Raoul Coutard to exploit colour changes (notably in the bedroom scene between the scriptwriter and his wife, mirroring movements in male desire) and the wide screen (to maximise the distances between the estranged couple). When his producers demanded a scene featuring a naked Brigitte Bardot, Godard turned to Moravia's novel for inspiration, despite minimising its value as a source in interviews.[47] Moravia lingers on the surprising beauty of the various parts of Emilia;[48] Godard teasingly has his heroine ask her husband if he approves of each piece of her body, then reject his sexual advances. While the scene plays on the screen persona of Bardot as sex kitten, it also permits her to control that sexuality.

That Godard changes the Moltenis into Camille and Paul Javal perhaps simply results from choosing French rather than Italian actors for the lead roles. The replacement of the Italian producer Battista with Jerry Prokosch is a more deliberate indication of Godard's rejection of American capitalism. Yet Prokosch's sheer physicality is in the end more attractive than Paul Javal (Michel Piccoli)'s self-pitying claims to intellectual superiority.[49] More confusingly, instead of a poor man's Lang as the German director, Godard hires Fritz Lang himself. But this Lang is strongly conservative, rejecting wide-screen film as fit only for snakes and funerals and creating an *Odyssey* that is extraordinarily dated in style.[50] A reliable journeyman, he remains to finish the film after the death of the producer and the departure of the scriptwriter. Prokosch may be a barbarian ('Whenever I hear the word culture, I bring out my checkbook'),[51] but his view of the *Odyssey* as a domestic struggle between Odysseus and Penelope is cunningly designed to appeal to Paul Javal's sensibilities (and not far from Godard's own troubled relations with his wife and muse, Anna Karina).

Contempt is post-modern in its melange of self-contradictory elements. Thoroughly Aristotelian in its construction in three clear acts (at Cinecittà and Prokosch's house; in the Javal's apartment; on the island of Capri), it refers both to the past glories of German cinema (through Lang, whose exotic Indian epics of the late 1950s and *Thousand Eyes of Dr Mabuse* (1960) themselves quote the director's silent films) and the Hollywood of 1950s (particularly Vincente Minnelli's 1958 film *Some Came Running*). Yet intellectual fantasy (Paul Javal sees himself in the persona of Dean

Martin from the latter film) is undercut by the reality expressed by Camille ('You don't remind me of Dean Martin but of Martin and the ass'). The scriptwriter, in continual motion as Odysseus while Penelope remains a static point of reference, deserves his wife's contempt. He cannot kill Prokosch the suitor (despite having a gun available on Capri) and win back his wife's affections. The death of Camille with the producer (in Godard's film, but not in Moravia's novel) provides a substitute sacrifice. In cinema such a fate is common for the female betrayer, yet it is unusual in Godard, where *la belle dame* is often present at the killing of her lover (cf. the endings of *À bout de souffle*, 1960, or *Pierrot le Fou*, 1965). By contrast with Moravia, whose protagonist undergoes a strange fantasy with the image of Emilia in the grottoes of Capri around the time of her death in Battista's car, the reality of death is almost the last image of *Contempt*. The *Odyssey* can only exist as an image of the past. But in a striking self-contradiction the alienated intellectual in post-war Western society both rejects the concept of modernising the story and embraces the possibilities of its commercialisation. Only the death of the producer at the same time as that of the object of his desires – no romantic ghosts for Godard – creates a way out, providing both an end to Paul Javal's need to earn money to support his wife and to the project which would provide sufficient monetary return to fulfil his ambitions (at the cost of his wife's contempt and his own self-loathing). Liberation from capitalism and romanticism, as Godard reveals, is itself an impossible fantasy, the end of (the) film.[52]

Theo Angelopoulos and the internalising of myth

Godard perhaps suggests that by the mid-twentieth century the best film that could be made from the *Odyssey* that would satisfy both intellectual and commercial demands is one about the impossibility of such a project. Rossi's *L'Odissea* is undoubtedly an artistic success, but commercially it appears relatively unsuccessful and is now only available as an Italian DVD.[53] And even as an artistic success it is obscure, hardly visible in the shadow of *Ulysses*.[54]

Nonetheless, retellings of the Homeric epics in other guises have succeeded, as the films of Tessari and the Coen brothers show. These need not merely be 'vernacular' or popular movie-making. While Walter Hill's *The Warriors* (1979) implicitly creates a comparison – perhaps comic book in style – between Greek soldiers and New York gang members, the most Homeric of modern films dealing with war has been Terence Malick's *Thin Red Line* (1998). Without portraying spectacular battles, Malick captures the essence of violence through the individual soldier's experience. Yet while this may recall the *Iliad*, the director also undermines any classical precedent for glorifying war by having the modern Greek Captain Staros (Elias Kotias), who is unwilling to sacrifice his men for the glory of his commander, patronised by Lieutenant Colonel Tall (Nick Nolte) who quotes Homer (*'Eôs rhododaktylos* – rosy-fingered dawn. You're Greek, aren't you captain? Did you ever read Homer?'). The ability to understand ancient Greek, the mark of education and class, enables the West Point graduate to bully an outsider.[55] This is a twentieth-century *aristeia*, Tall proving his superiority not by personal deeds of valour, but by requiring their display by the foot soldiers.[56]

The contrast between the educated quotation of ancient Greek by those who are not ethnically Greek and the incomprehension of modern Greek speakers had already been used by Greek director Theo Angelopoulos in *Megalexandros* (1980). At a soirée in Athens on New Year's Eve 1899, some English businessmen and their wives are introduced to a Greek dignitary. The leader of the English group greets him with *'Ti tênikade aphixai, ô Kritôn?'*[57] To the look of incomprehension from his host he responds with a scornful 'He doesn't understand!' Shortly afterwards, the party makes its way to the Temple of Poseidon at Sounion to watch the dawn on the first day of the twentieth century and as the sun rises, the same Englishman begins to recite the first choral ode from Sophocles' *Antigone* (100-5): *'aktis aeliou, to kalliston heptapylôi phanen Thêbai tôn proterôn phaos, ephanthês pot', ô chryseas hameras blepharon, Dircaiôn hyper rheethrôn molousa, ton leukaspin Argothen ekbanta phôta ...'* ('Light of the sun, showing itself finer than any before to seven-gated Thebes, you have appeared at last, the eye of the golden day, passing over Dirce's stream, driving away the white-shielded men from Argos ...').[58] At this point, he stops and steps back, as very slowly a remarkable figure on horseback rides up the temple steps and into the frame. This is Megalexandros, the Great Alexander, a brigand and folk hero who takes the English hostage and, after releasing the women, marches the men to a village in Greek Macedonia. The irony of a modern Greek cross between Robin Hood and Saint George the dragon-slayer capturing the tuxedoed (and hence, white-fronted) industrialists who have come merely to guarantee continuing access to coal deposits in Attica is underlined when there are negotiations between representatives of the Greek and English governments with Megalexandros and his men. The leader of the bedraggled hostages, seeing the hope of freedom, repeats the same Sophoclean words as before, only to be met this time by the English emissary's response: 'I do not understand.'[59] The negotiations are ended by rifle-fire, miscomprehension (increased by the arrival of a party of Italian anarchists) develops into tragedy, and by the film's end, both hostages and Megalexandros and his men are dead.

Megalexandros illustrates many of Angelopoulos' techniques. First he takes an historical event (the Dilessi murders of 1870, when three upper-class English tourists were taken prisoner at Marathon by brigands and killed when the Greek government refused an amnesty and attempted to rescue the prisoners by force), and then he changes the time and setting to include the developments of the twentieth century (the rise of Socialism in Anarchist and Communist forms, as well as the development of dictatorial rule, which might be Fascist or Stalinist). The English attempts at intervention in 1870 – contrary to the Greek constitution which specifically outlawed amnesty for criminals – foreshadow the intervention of General Scobie and his British troops to crush left-wing unrest in Athens in 1944-45. There is also a folkloric side to the story. The guide who brings tourists to the village styles Megalexandros 'Alexander the Great', then narrates marvellous tales of his mysterious birth and adoption. The local landowners had hired gunmen to murder this threat to their power, but instead only killed his bride at their marriage ceremony. Megalexandros himself then appears and poses on horseback in front of a mural of a dragon. He has now become the local legend.

Later, when he lies mortally wounded, the villagers who surround and attack their hated tyrant discover that no body can be found. Megalexandros is no longer flesh and blood, but simply an historical memory. The allegorical message is reinforced when government soldiers arrive soon after to find nothing where he had been but some blood stains and a marble bust. Another Alexander, the child of the bandit's daughter-in-law, survives and rides off, in a striking change in chronology, into a modern Athens. But the country and the burdens of history are coming to a city that is still in darkness – Sophocles' glorious light that shone on Thebes has still to appear.

References to ancient Greece are thus adumbrated rather than open in Angelopoulos' films. Megalexandros is *not* Alexander the Great, with all the political baggage attached to that figure. Or rather, he is Alexander but that fantastic figure as relayed by popular tale, the saviour of the weak who fought the Turks. He is also the dragon-slaying Alexander who appears in Karaghiozis' shadow puppet theatre, his role as the poor Greek hero emphasised through his outlandish costume (sword and cocked pistols, cape and long-plumed cavalry helmet and oversized shoes with pom-poms).[60]

Such folklore contrasts with the revived Classicism that royalist and conservative elements of Greek society have favoured since independence. These groups defined 'pure' Hellenism as an alliance of the Orthodox Church and Hellenophones (thus excluding problematic groups which might be labelled Turkish, Albanian, or Vlach) to achieve the Great Idea (*Megali Idea*), the reunification of all Greeks of the Eastern Mediterranean. Western films about Greek history often show traces of this ideology. Robert Rossen's *Alexander the Great* (1956) by listing HRH Prince Peter of Greece as technical adviser suggests a line of succession between the Macedonian and the Greek (or, maliciously, Bavarian) monarchies. In its closing credits *The 300 Spartans* (1962) offers special thanks for assistance to 'Their Majesties, the King and Queen of the Hellenes, the Greek government, and the Royal Hellenic Army' – further indication of royalist support for a national myth of warrior heroes prepared to die for the cause of liberty in the face of totalitarian Eastern threats.[61] At the same time, the Greek armed forces actively supported a doomed attempt by the American Edward Jay Epstein to film the *Iliad* in strong preference to an intended Russian-Greek production.[62] The effect was to marginalise the Greek Left. Branded as 'unpatriotic' for not supporting the semi-mystical idea of a reborn Hellas, they were also caught between a desire to support more contemporary popular traditions and their awareness of the importance of Classical literature for progressive thinkers such as Hegel, Marx and Engels.[63]

Angelopoulos, who began his career as one of a group of liberal film-makers opposing the Junta that ruled Greece from 1967 to 1974, has generally enjoyed more auspicious conditions in which to practise his craft. As a mere child at the end of the Second World War, he escaped the guilt endured by many of the 'redeemed' Left who 'repented' and were re-educated in the aftermath of the Greek Civil War. After the discrediting of the Right in the wake of the fall of the Colonels and the abolition of the monarchy, he could use the opportunity given to reconsider Greece's history. So, when Angelopoulos incorporates classical references in his films, their purpose is not to celebrate the past but to show the tragic themes innate in Greek culture. As living mythologies they need no artificial resurrection, unlike the Greek monarchy, propped up by Western powers who idealised a Classical Greece long past.[64] The Greek Civil War of 1946-49 is no longer portrayed as a struggle against a foreign, godless ideology (Communism) and non-Greeks, particularly Slavs, threatening the integrity of the Hellenic state. Instead it is seen as a fully indigenous struggle, pitting members of the same family against one another. Likewise, the participation of Britain and the United States in the conflict should not be seen as supporting Greek freedom, but as just one of a series of foreign interventions (including those of Italy and Germany) in modern Greece.

Angelopoulos' 2004 film *The Weeping Meadow* begins with the expulsion of Greeks from Odessa by the Red Army in 1919. It concludes in 1949 with the female protagonist Eleni, who first appeared as an orphan survivor of this diaspora, being taken by train along with other women to Thrace and arriving once more in the area of her village. But this is a bitter return: an army officer greets the passengers and announces: 'Your husbands, brothers, sons lie behind you on the field of honour.' On an island in the river, Eleni discovers the body of one of her two sons, Yannis, who has fallen serving in the Greek army. Later, the old village women tell her that the other son, Yorgis, who had been fighting for the guerrillas, lies in a burnt-out house in the lake on the other side of the military zone. Eleni crosses the military boundary of the embankment, atop which Yannis and Yorgis had last sadly met before the battle, and makes her way to the lake. The film ends with her grieving for both her sons, as well as for her husband who has died fighting in the American army in the Pacific War.

The depiction of the cruelties of civil war alludes to the classical story of Oedipus' sons, Eteocles and Polynices, and the Seven against Thebes. In particular, the isolation of the unburied Yorgis, contrasted with the hero's death of Yannis, and Eleni's dangerous journey to find his body recalls Antigone's defiance of the powers of the state in slipping past the Theban guards and burying her brother Polynices against Creon's decree. The pathos of the film's ending is heightened by other images that regularly occur in Angelopoulos' films: the flow of time expressed through the modern metaphor of the movement of trains and the visual depiction of the artificiality of geographical separation.[65]

Elsewhere, the director creates a similar fusion of classical past and present. In *Reconstruction* (*Anaparastasis*, 1970), a Greek *Gastarbeiter* returning to his Epirot village is murdered by his wife and lover. A scene of black-clad village women pursuing the wife after her arrest as if they were the Furies visually underlines the link between this strong if enigmatic character and the mythological Clytemnestra. In *The Travelling Players* (*O Thiasos*, 1976), a troupe of actors travels Greece between 1939 and 1952, attempting to put on a nineteenth-century pastoral drama, *Golpho the Shepherdess*,[66] but are continually interrupted by war. Only one member of the cast is specifically named, Orestes, the son of the director, but from this clue the audience can attribute names to the others: the mother, Clytemnestra, with her lover, Aegisthus, who later betray Agamemnon to the Germans; her daughters, Electra, the strong female character in the story, and the malleable Chrysothemis, who prostitutes herself and eventually marries an American soldier; her son, Orestes, and his friend Pylades. By the film's conclusion, Orestes, who has joined the resistance, has taken revenge for Agamemnon's death by killing Clytemnestra and Aegisthus (on stage – although the audience is appreciative, this results in yet another abortive attempt to perform *Golpho* and another deferral of pastoral utopia) and has himself been executed by the government forces, while Pylades as a detainee on a prison island has eventually agreed to renounce his beliefs and has been released, free but spiritually crippled.[67] The film ends with the troupe arriving at Aegion, the same scene that had appeared at the beginning, but now set not in 1952, but in 1939. Events are thus shown to recur cyclically, whether they are historical, such as the establishment of the Metaxas regime and the election of General Papagos' conservative regime in 1952, or the mythological familial tragedy of the Atreids.

In *Landscape in the Mist* (*Topo Stin Omichli*, 1988), the travelling players reappear within the story of two children, Voula and Alexander, who are trying to make their way to Germany where they believe their father is working. The players are still seeking a venue for their production of *Golpho*, but now decide to disband the company. Chrysothemis chooses whatever costumes best fit her role in the city (one thinks of her life as a good-time girl in *Travelling Players*), while a new, youthful Orestes takes on the role of the children's temporary guide on their journey in life. In this, the final film in what has been called Angelopoulos' 'trilogy of silence' (the others being *Voyage to Cythera* (*Taxidi Sta Kithira,* 1983) and *The Beekeeper* (*O Melissokomos,* 1986)), the struggles of the past are finally set aside. The utopian dreams of the older generation must also be abandoned in the face of a new, industrialised, but not necessarily caring society. It may be possible to guide the young some way on their path, but they are clearly embarking on a journey into unknown places. The ambiguous conclusion, after the children have crossed the border and find a sheltering tree in the fog, if not entirely pessimistic, certainly leaves the future undecided. One striking image illuminates the entire film: Orestes and the children suddenly stop when they see a giant, monumental hand (carried by an unseen helicopter) rising above the harbour of Thessaloniki and moving across the city. Although Angelopoulos himself has been reticent to explain this scene,[68] it is difficult not to link this image with Fellini's *La dolce vita* (1960). There the scene of a statue of Christ transported across the skies of Rome does not show a revival of interest in religion but rather its lack of effect in the modern world. The past, as exemplified in Angelopoulos' hand, does not point the way forward (the first finger is broken off) but simply exists to amaze. Attempts to recreate it in the modern world, such as *Days of '36* (1972)'s faux-Olympic ceremony – antiquity as staged by Leni Riefenstahl – rudely interrupted when government officials learn of that one of the parliamentary deputies has been taken hostage, are at best doomed, at worst risible.[69]

The *Odyssey* is a particularly frequent reference point for Angelopoulos, whose own films can often be regarded as 'road movies'.[70] Still he does not treat the theme of nostalgia, the desire to return to a home, in a simplistic fashion. In *Landscape in the Mist*, home is an imagined construct, equivalent to the tree which Orestes claims can be seen in the scrap of discarded film he picks up and gives to little Alexander. The film's ambiguous conclusion suggests that perhaps the children have by dint of imagination arrived at this goal. In *The Suspended Step of the Stork* (*To Meteoro Vima Tou Pelargou,* 1991), the journey is that of a television reporter seeking to discover a Greek politician who had vanished years ago. Yet while this Telemachus searches for his Odysseus, neither the possible father-figure nor 'Penelope' (the politician's wife) are willing to acknowledge the end of the journey.[71] The wife, when she meets the impoverished figure who might have been her husband (almost Odysseus as beggar), declares 'It's not him', yet remains in town until the mystery man disappears again across one of the nearby borders. At the same time, refugees from around the world are shown crossing their own territorial boundaries in search of a new home in Greece. In this new world of permeability, to cross the border, as a Greek army colonel states early in the film, holding his leg up over the line of demarcation between Greece and Albania, is to open up two possibilities: 'If I take one more step I will be somewhere else. Or die.'

'Then it was Destroyed by the Volcano'

Voyage to Cythera (1983) expresses the Odyssean themes in their clearest form. A director named Alexander is preparing a film about the return of a Greek exile after many years in the Soviet Union. As the film progresses, the director transforms into the son of the returning Odysseus-figure, Spyros. But ironically there is no magical island (Cythera, the home of Aphrodite) to which the characters may repair.[72] When Spyros comes back to his northern Greek village, his presence is as disruptive as that of Odysseus when he confronts the suitors in Ithaca. He alone refuses to permit the sale of the village's commonly held land for a new ski resort, shattering the hopes of the villagers who have ago long moved from the harsh uplands to the valleys below. While readily recalling the past (by using the secret whistles used by the insurgents to communicate with one another, performing a Ponti dance at the grave of a now dead comrade, and even by greeting his aged dog, Argos),[73] he is oblivious to the present. Even his friend Panyiotis describes him as a dead man, a ghost, condemned to death by military court four times many years ago. There are consequences for his actions (his daughter Voula accuses him of having always only thought of himself), just as for Odysseus' slaying of the suitors. The villagers complain to the local officials and Spyros is officially declared to be a displaced person, not a Greek national. Attempts to place him back on the Russian ship fail, as Spyros' only comment on the procedure is one he makes frequently: 'Rotten apple' (a rejection of the times, in contrast to the joyful folksong 'Forty Apples' he has sung earlier with Panyiotis). So the harbour officials set him on a barge and tow it out into international waters. As the dockworkers hold their annual festival, now dedicated to 'the old man out at sea', Spyros' wife ascends the stage and twice declares 'I want to be with him.' The two are next shown alone on the raft at daybreak: Katerina announces 'I'm ready' and Spyros casts off the anchor ropes. The film ends with them drifting away.

Voyage to Cythera is a statement by the director that he is 'out of step' (a phrase repeated by Alexander in the film). The past and its ideology is gone, but has not been replaced by anything more than the ability to reflect on it (the film within the film). Only old Katerina/ Penelope is willing to follow Spyros/ Odysseus in his continuing journey, but the intended endpoint is unknown. Odysseus cannot return to his adventures, as an insurgent (the *Iliadic* tale of Achilles) or as a traveller in foreign lands. He has a wife and children 'over there', i.e. in Russia, but the Circes, Calypsos and Nausicaas are in the past. All that is left is Penelope. And this leaves Alexander/ Telemachus/ Angelopoulos[74] alone, still in search of a father.

If *Voyage to Cythera, The Beekeeper* and *Landscape in the Mist* display disappointment with political and social developments after the restoration of democracy in Greece, Angelopoulos' films from the 1990s, which may be styled his 'trilogy of borders'[75] – *The Suspended Step of the Stork* (1991), *Ulysses' Gaze* (*To Vlemma Tou Odyssea*, 1995), and *Eternity and a Day* (*Mia Eoniotita Ke Mia Mera,* 1998) – allow a return to history. There is no longer an endpoint in modern Greece, because the permeability of borders since the collapse of the Soviet system means that the voyage continues. But this journey can also be viewed in terms of the movements of the Greek people since the re-establishment of their national identity in 1821. There is a thread of history from that time (represented by the Poet, Dionysios Solomos, collecting rare Greek words such as *xenitis* 'stranger/ one who is alienated', from the peasants in the 1820s) through to the displaced Albanian Greek boy who is rescued by the dying poet, Alexander, in *Eternity and a Day*. As the boy is last seen being smuggled off to another destination (Western Europe? America?), it is clear that the migrations of the Greek people (to America, Germany and Australia; from the Black Sea, the Balkans, and especially from Turkey in the 1920s) are a continuing story.

Angelopoulos' most extended use of the mythology of the Odyssean journey occurs in *Ulysses' Gaze*. A Greek American director, A. (Harvey Keitel), travels around the Balkans in search of three rolls of lost film made by the Manaki brothers at the start of the twentieth century. The story is of a quest for an original vision of life in this area at a time when boundaries were more porous (the film begins with the screening of the film of the Manaki brothers' 114-year-old grandmother spinning wool in the West Macedonian village of Avdela in 1905).[76] In the early 1990s, at the time of Angelopoulos' film, boundaries were once more opening up after the collapse of the Communist system in Eastern Europe, but the break-up of Yugoslavia also threatened a return to the Balkan Wars of the early twentieth century. The search takes the protagonist from Northern Greece to Albania, through Macedonia, Bulgaria and Romania, to Serbia, and finally to war-torn Sarajevo in Bosnia.[77]

Complicating the task of understanding the film are the connections between the gaze and the journey (through lands and through time). *Ulysses' Gaze* begins with a quotation from Plato's *Alcibiades*: 'And thus the soul too, if it wishes to know itself, will have to look into the soul' (*Alc.* 133b). This declaration of the necessity of introspection is, however, itself a reference to George Seferis' *Mythistorema* (1935). Poem 4 ('Argonauts') begins with the above Platonic quotation and adds 'the stranger and enemy, we've seen him in the mirror'.[78] This is not simple introspection, but the awareness of a divided soul.

Angelopoulos' recall of the never-ending voyage for knowledge in Seferis (who himself refers obliquely in his poem to the death of Elpenor in the *Odyssey*) may also prepare the viewer to recall the poem that comes before this. In Poem 3 (with the epigraph: *Remember the baths where you were murdered* – a line from Aeschylus, *Choephoroe* 491), the weight of past sorrows (Orestes recalling the murder of his father and his duty of revenge) is transformed into something monumental: 'I woke with this marble head in my hands; / it exhausts my elbows and I don't know where to put it down ...' The similarities to scenes already noted in *Megaloxan dros* (the transformation of Alexander into a marble bust) and *Landscape in the Mist* (the hand moving over Thessaloniki) are clear.[79] The past weighs heavily on Greece, and by quoting Seferis, Angelopoulos sets himself firmly in an earlier Greek liberal tradition.

But there is another allusion in *Ulyssses' Gaze*: after A. has boarded a train from Skopje to Bulgaria, he recalls being on Delos and watching an old olive tree suddenly topple to reveal underneath a head of Apollo.[80] As he walked on, he found 'a small secret place, the birthplace of Apollo according to tradition'. Attempts to photograph this with a polaroid camera simply resulted in a 'blank negative picture of the world, as if my glance wasn't working. ... I felt I was slipping into darkness.' As a result, A. grabs the chance to look for the missing three reels of the Manaki brothers film: 'The first film, perhaps, the first glance, a lost glance. A lost innocence. It turned into an obsession, as if they were my own work, my own first glance, lost long ago.'

The story acts as a classic piece of seduction: A. is speaking to the Macedonian film archivist, Kali, as the train slowly begins to leave the station and she is forced to walk, then run, then board the train and join the director in order to hear the tale of the incident on Delos. But it also recalls Seferis' Poem 3: 'I look at the eyes: neither open nor closed / I speak to the mouth which keeps trying to speak / I hold the cheeks which have broken through the skin. / That's all I'm able to do. / My hands disappear and come towards me / mutilated.' It is not the elusiveness of memory that is stressed, but the interchange of the gaze: A. cannot achieve Apollo's gaze by photographing the god, but only by discovering what the divinity saw, by gazing back into himself.

His despondency at his failure may also recall the ambiguous strip of film featured in *Landscape in the Mist*, with its potentially pessimistic undertones (is there a tree or is this mere wishful thinking?). Yet in *Ulysses' Gaze* the possibility of a journey to enlightenment has already been indicated: at Florina, the projection of A's latest film is accompanied by sound from external speakers for those who cannot enter the makeshift theatre. The audience hears the lost politician's words from *The Suspended Step of the Stork*, the unseen film being projected: 'We've crossed the border, but here we still are. How many borders do we have to cross before we reach home?' and the searching reporter's words later on the bridge between Greece and Albania: 'If I take just one step ... If I take just one step I'm elsewhere.' There is a choice: possibly to die,[81] but also to be somewhere else. To endure much and learn: 'he saw many cities of men and learnt their minds, and suffered many pains to his heart on the sea, struggling for his life (lit. *psychen*: 'soul') and the return home of his men' (*Od.* 1.3-5). A.'s friend Nikos in Belgrade repeats this theme: 'The first thing God created was the journey,[82] then came doubt and nostalgia.'

On the journey the voyager finds versions of Odysseus' female companions (all played by the Romanian actress, Maia Morgenstern). As he leaves

90

Florina ('In my end is my beginning'),[83] he sees a woman walking down the street. 'Do you remember the railway station? You were shivering in the rain. Like now. The wind was blowing hard. I was going away but I meant to come back soon. But then I got lost, wandering along strange roads. If I should but stretch out my hand I will touch you and time will be whole again. But something's holding me back. I wish I could tell you I've returned. But something's holding me back. The journey isn't over. Not yet.' The ghost is that of the Penelope whom A. had left after his military service, a dream he follows just like the three reels of film.

Later the Macedonian film archivist, Kali (Calypso), accompanies A. across the Macedonia-Bulgaria border where the director relives the arrest of Yannaki Manaki by Bulgarian troops and exile to Plovdiv in 1915. The Odyssean connection is made once more when A. announces that the exile used to come daily and stare at the Evros, a river that flows into the Aegean Sea. Kali does not understand: there is no river by the border town of Gyueshevo (the Maritsa/ Evros flows past Plovdiv well to the east), but also she cannot comprehend A's Odyssean nostalgia.[84] At their hotel in Constantia, A. like Odysseus, 'lies beside her of necessity ... unwillingly next to one willing' (*Od.* 5.154-5), and cries as he departs 'because I cannot love you'.

His Calypso sends him off, not on a roughly constructed raft, but on a barge that is carrying a colossal statue of Lenin to be shipped off to Germany. The scene of the loading of Lenin's head recalls the monumental hand in *Landscape in the Mist,* a wondrous sign that cannot easily be interpreted. As the barge makes its way up the Danube, the local inhabitants run down to the riverbank and make the sign of the cross at its passing. Lenin no longer points the way and, as the barge enters Serbian

8. *Ulysses' Gaze* (1995): the colossal statue of Lenin sails up the Danube on its barge.

territory, customs inquiries as to the presence of passengers are met by the reply: 'Niemand.' No Man has escaped the Cyclops' cave, but the journey continues.

Learning in Belgrade that the three rolls of film are now in Sarajevo, A. is brought along the Sava in a small boat by a local woman (thus re-enacting another woman's assistance to Yannaki in escaping from Philopoupolis along the Evros during the First World War). She feeds him, dresses him in new clothes, and entertains him in her bed (just as Circe had done with Odysseus) before sending him off to what might appear to be the place to summon ghosts from Hades – war-torn Sarajevo. But this landfall is also at Scheria, since A. is welcomed by the Jewish film archivist, Ivo Levy, and his daughter, Naomi (Nausicaa),[85] who provide one end to his journey, the development of the lost film ('The captive gaze set free at last at the end of the century'). Yet, as with the Phaeacians who are punished for their generosity in helping Odysseus return home, Levy and his family are killed by unseen assailants when the protecting fog over Sarajevo lifts. Devastated, A. returns to the ruined cinema to play the film:

> When I return it will be in another man's clothes, another man's name. My coming will be unexpected. If you look at me unbelieving and say 'You are not he', I will show you signs, and you will believe me. I will tell you about the lemon tree in your garden. The corner window that lets in the moonlight and then signs of a body, signs of love. And as we climb trembling to our old room, between one embrace and the next, between lovers' calls, I will tell you about the journey all the night long. And in all the nights to come, between one embrace and the next, between lovers' calls, the whole human adventure. The story that never ends.

The lines are Angelopoulos' own, drawing on the *Odyssey* and themes of return and resurrection as well as love poetry.[86] We do not see the developed film except as snowy images on the screen[87] and it is tempting again to make the link with the scrap of misted film of *Landscape in the Mist*. The journey to recover the film has ended for A., but his gaze is no longer at the film but at the audience. 'In my end is my beginning': the pessimism of reality (the war in Sarajevo which at the time of the making of *Ulysses' Gaze* was still continuing) is counterbalanced by the affirmation that the story of the journey itself may substitute for the loss. Homer through Seferis through modern cinema: the journey may take us back from the modern Balkans, from the stranger and the enemy in the mirror, to the original gaze of Apollo.[88]

Travelling on

There will certainly be further versions of the *Odyssey* in film and television, since the epic readily lends itself to both popular and art-house adaptations. For commercial cinema, the epic provides a straightforward tale in which the hero's adventures serve to retard the denouement of reclaiming home and family. At a deeper level, Odysseus' actions pose questions of the nature of successful leadership and social responsibility that may be explored by more adventurous filmmakers. Despite their resolutely uncommercial nature, especially in contrast with the classical Hollywood narrative, Angelopoulos' films represent a particular national response to the *Odyssey*, filtered as it is through more modern literary sources that resonate within Greek culture. However, the problems experienced by Angelopoulos with the production of *The Dust of Time*, the second part of his *Trilogy*,[89] show one of the difficulties of national cinema: government support for local film industries to produce commercially unattractive but culturally significant projects cannot be guaranteed. A large consortium of media companies financed *Hell* (*L'Enfer*, dir. Danis Tanovic, 2005), a French, Italian, Belgian, and Japanese production that retold the *Medea* based a scenario by Krzysztof Kieslowski, but the film may not have recovered its costs of production.[90] Broadcasting networks that have public interest requirements in their charters may be more amenable to such projects (cf. Danmarks Radio's support for Lars von Trier's 1988 *Medea*, based on a scenario by Carl Theodor Dreyer). Still the prestige of the past alone is insufficient. Films that appear to cater to minority interests (e.g. by appealing to an educated elite) cannot expect to enjoy the budgets of Hollywood blockbusters. However, by concentrating on their niche markets, they may thrive through modest financial returns and artistic prestige for sponsoring organisations.

An obvious danger is that depictions of the ancient world will be supported only where this past is seen as an essential part of the national culture. Yet in *The Thin Red Line* Malick performs the remarkable trick of both using the *Iliad* as a prestige marker for an American power elite and simultaneously indicating its modern resonances as a part of mankind's intellectual heritage. International film studios (once Hollywood companies, but now global corporations) will be always attracted to the best-known features of the past and seek to represent them through well-known narrative conventions (e.g. *Ulysses* or *Gladiator*). One might then expect Alexander the Great to be attractive as an almost universally known figure, and so his depiction in film and in television series is worth exploring. As will be seen in the next chapter, although directors may choose to follow their own vision of the Macedonian king, they soon discover that they have a multi-faceted subject, aspects of whom appeal to various, often opposing interest groups. So far this complexity has defeated attempts to create a globally acceptable portrait of Alexander.

5

Alexander the Hero

Alexander the Great occupies a special place in the pantheon of Western military leaders that includes the likes of Julius Caesar, Charlemagne and Napoleon. Unlike barbarians such as Attila, Genghis Khan or Tamerlane, agents of the destruction of more civilised empires, his reputation is built on his role in spreading Hellenic culture to an effete East. Of course, not all Asians have shared this Eurocentric judgement on his work – for instance, the Zoroastrian tradition portrays the Macedonian ruler as destroyer of Iranian civilisation and persecutor of the priestly class (the Magi).[1] Still, as indirectly responsible for the Hellenistic kingdoms that would generally be incorporated in the Roman Empire, Alexander has always been the inspiration for European imperialist enterprises, particularly modern colonising of the Indian subcontinent. To many modern Greeks, he is the embodiment of past greatness, although the topic of his actual ethnicity as the son of a Macedonian king and an Epirote princess readily leads to heated debates in the Balkans. In brief, he is a controversial figure (as he was in his own era) whose depiction varies not only according to the times during which he is portrayed and differences in national cinema, but also in response to historical and novelistic treatments of his reign.[2]

A synopsis of Alexander's career may be useful, especially for the highlights that scriptwriters will ignore at their peril. The son of Philip of Macedon and Olympias of Epirus, Alexander soon acquired a miraculous tradition around his birth that suggested that, like Hercules, he was actually the son of Zeus. His teachers included Aristotle, while the romantic tale of his finding and taming his warhorse Bucephalus illustrates the importance of his training in horsemanship in line with Macedonian military tradition. At the battle of Chaeronea (338 BC), the sixteen-year-old Alexander played a major role as commander of the cavalry in the victory over a combined Athenian and Theban force. The result was Macedonian hegemony over Greece and the readying of a campaign to invade the Asian territories of the Persian king. Although relations with his father were sometimes strained (for instance, after Philip married the niece of his army commander, Attalus), few ancient sources suggest that Alexander was personally involved in the assassination of Philip at Pella in 336.

Ascending to the throne of Macedon, Alexander immediately reacted to rebellion in the south by destroying Thebes, then resumed the invasion of Asia, defeating a Persian force at the Granicus (334). Advancing south, he defeated a major Persian army under king Darius III at the Battle of Issus (333) and proceeded on to Egypt, where, in the winter of 332/1, he paid a famous visit to the temple of Ammon at the oasis of Siwah. Turning north again, Alexander met Darius once more at Gaugamela (331), winning a crushing victory that left him in control of Mesopotamia. The pursuit of Darius through Iran led to the capture and destruction of the Persian capital, Persepolis (330), the death of the Persian monarch at the hands of his own subjects, and Alexander's assumption of the role of king of both Macedon and Persia.

The tensions that arose from such success can be seen in Alexander's execution of his cavalry commander Philotas and his father, the highly experienced general Parmenion (330). Lengthy campaigning in central Asia added to the strain, as can be seen by the drunken quarrel between Alexander and his commander Cleitus the Black that resulted in the latter's death (328). After a campaign in the Indus valley, which included a victory over the Indian king Porus at the Hydaspes (326), the Macedonian army mutinied at the Hyphasis river and forced their king to turn back. His return through the Gedrosian desert (modern Baluchistan) is described variously as inflicting great hardship on his army or as simply disastrous. Certainly the new ruler of Asia continued to have problems convincing his Greek and Macedonian troops that he was concerned for them, as seen by another mutiny at the river Opis (324). At his death at Babylon in 323, variously attributed to overdrinking, disease or poison, the problem of reconciling the various groups, particularly the Persian nobility and the Macedonian soldiers, still had not been overcome.

The history of Alexander abounds in battles on the grand scale and court intrigue, not to mention romantic elements. Alexander married Stateira, the daughter of Darius, as well as the Bactrian princess, Rhoxane,[3] and his relations with companions such as Hephaistion have a strong homoerotic component. Moreover both his father, Philip, and his mother, Olympias, were larger-than-life figures.

The difficulty of incorporating all this detail into a coherent story that can include Alexander's political and romantic exploits and be told within a reasonable running time makes it unsurprising that no attempt had been made to tell the tale before Robert Rossen scripted and directed *Alexander the Great* in 1956. The very choice of Richard Burton as Rossen's leading man invites comparison with the actor's previous role in an historical epic – as Marcellus Gallio, a Roman officer who becomes a Christian and dies a martyr, in *The Robe* (dir. Henry Koster, 1953). Rossen instead makes a clean break with the line of Hollywood films that portrayed the rise of Christianity and the fall of the pagan Roman Empire.[4] Free from the need to promote any overtly religious message, the director can revert to a personally favoured subject: the degree to which an individual is able to follow his own destiny within the social constraints of his society.

Rossen's script for *The Sea Wolf* (dir. Michael Curtiz, 1941) had emphasised the quasi-National Socialist aspects of 'Wolf' Larsen's personality, while the Academy Award-winning *All the King's Men* (script and dir. Rossen, 1949) offered a striking portrayal of the descent of populist Louisiana politician Willie Stark into demagoguery.[5] Such Marxist-derived critiques of the self-contradictions of capitalist society, however, attracted the attention of the House Committee on Un-American Activities and Hollywood studios blacklisted Rossen from 1951-3. In the end he bowed to the pressure, appeared before the Committee in 1953 and named others. This action saved his career, but, like Elia Kazan, among many former colleagues he had earned the reputation of being a 'stoolie'. *Alexander the Great* has greater significance, then, as his first Hollywood film after his 'atonement'.[6]

Alexander is a typical Rossen hero who uses his peculiar skills to gain reputation, power and wealth, but in the end discovers that such individualist struggle amid the corruption of surrounding society can only be destructive for those who love and trust him.[7] The conflict between Macedon and Persia also has wider resonance, recalling America's involvement with Europe in the First World War (rather than the moral certainties of the more recent war against the Axis powers) that also ushered in a new, dynamic force in world history. But victory is shown to be insufficient by itself. Unless a new, just society replaces the old, there will be no real change.[8] If the film begins with the voice of Richard Burton praising the heroic values of the *Iliad* ('It is men who endure toil and dare dangers who achieve glorious deeds. And it is a lovely thing to live with courage and die leaving behind an ever-lasting renown'),[9] by its conclusion the lesson to be learned is that it is 'not lands that must be conquered, but the hearts of men'.

When Alexander takes Roxane as his bride (a conflation with his marriage to both Stateira, Darius' daughter, and Parysatis at Susa in 324)[10] and simultaneously arranges the wedding of a large number of Macedonian officers to Persian noblewomen, he appears to be inaugurating a new era of toleration:

> To you, for peace I pray, that Macedonians and Persians and all the people of my empire will always be alike, not merely subjects, but people who will live and build together in harmony and unity of heart and mind. For we are all alike under God, and if God is the father, he is the father of all.

However, he immediately collapses and dies soon afterwards. His mission is incomplete, yet Alexander once again asserts his own claim to divinity based on the heroic code even on his deathbed ('You gods, have I not done enough in this short span of life to sit among you?').

The film thus concludes as tragedy, quoting Sophocles' famous words

'Wonders are many but none is more wonderful than man himself' (*Antigone* 332-3) as if it were a Shakespearean epilogue. If a belief in the unity of mankind is suggested by Alexander's speech at the wedding, this is undermined by his deathbed declaration that the succession should go 'to the strongest'. Early in the film, Parmenion had expressed his view of Macedon's mission to Philip in quasi-Fascist terms: 'I believe in the glory of Macedonia, in the kingdom, in the army which you forge with your will and your struggle and your belief that we are better and stronger and more fit to rule than anyone in Greece – even in Athens.' At its conclusion, because of Alexander's Nietzschean egocentrism nothing has been learned and the wars of succession will follow.

Rossen clearly constructs his film after the historical plays of Shakespeare, modelling his dialogue on Elizabethan verse and frequently introducing dialogues between leading characters. So Alexander is shown charming Demosthenes and Aeschines, the two greatest orators of Greece, while Barsine and Memnon debate the sense of Greeks fighting alongside Persians against the Macedonians.[11] Not only does this add weight to the characters, but it also imparts a sense of the continuous movement of history. The glories of Henry V at Agincourt were soon to be followed by the Wars of the Roses; the triumph of Alexander at Gaugamela will lead to the chaos of the age of the Diadochoi. Monarchy breeds moral uncertainty, a theme expressed in *Alexander the Great* through the internal feuds of the Macedonian royal family that occupy the first half of the film. By contrast with 'barbarian' Macedon, considerable sympathy is elicited for democratic Athens and its values.[12] All this debate leaves little time for the depiction of Alexander's wars of conquest. This may be a deliberate choice by Rossen or a consequence of the production costs of a lengthy epic: Issus and Gaugamela are conflated into one battle and the romantic side of Alexander's character concentrated on his relations with Barsine and Roxane (who, as Darius' daughter, replaces Stateira). After the climax of Gaugamela and Darius' death, the film concludes quite rapidly. Alexander has become the Persian king's heir. Uncertain of his very nationality, as seen by his adoption of Persian customs, he proclaims himself son of a god, no longer son of Philip, and treats his court with growing paranoia. The result is the deaths of Philotas and his father Parmenion and the killing of Cleitus which is now set during the Indian campaigns and given as the reason for Alexander's return from the East. The marriages at Susa and his death follow immediately.

While the film treats the last seven years of Alexander's life in a mere twenty minutes, this may not be due to financial expediency. Alexander has obtained all his desires after the final Persian defeat, but has no vision for the future except greater glory (for instance, being declared a living god) and further conquest. Even his proclamation of the unity of Persian and Greek (following the posthumous advice of Darius) seems to be the vision of an isolated autocrat, rather than the articulation of his subjects' desires. Rossen, despite his personal experiences, has adapted the critique of individualism that informed the writings of Jack London and other American Socialists of the first half of the twentieth century to the ancient world and thus made it universal. Although in the defeat of the Greek city-states and Persia a decadent older world had been forced to submit to a vigorous new power, Alexander's individual success had within it seeds of personal ruin. Glory is not enough.

Alexander in the twenty-first century

From the mid-1950s, films with a didactic religious message fell out of favour. The 1959 remake of *Ben Hur* removed the subtitle of the 1925 version, *A Tale of the Christ*.[13] A year later, the suggestion of a proto-Christian martyrdom at the conclusion of the story of Spartacus was balanced by the Exodus-like story of the slaves' desire to escape to a new land. This message was reinforced as the son of Russian Jewish immigrants, Kirk Douglas, played the leader of the rebellion.[14] By the time of Anthony Mann's *Fall of the Roman Empire* (1964), Rome was no longer portrayed as the Whore of Babylon and ally of Satan in the persecution of Christians, but, like the United States after the Second World War, as an international power seeking to maintain civilisation in the face of constant external threats.[15]

In the post-Cold War era, it might have appeared difficult to revive the ancient epic film as the moral tension between clear-cut forces of good and evil, defined in religious and political terms, had evaporated. Instead the new breed of Hollywood films set in the ancient world, beginning with *Gladiator* (2000) and *Troy* (2004), were based on a moral nostalgia: the worlds of Greece and Rome would be seen as offering codes of value lost in the modern West. *Gladiator* stressed 'Strength and Honour' and the agrarian values of times past before urban corruption had sapped the strength of Roman society.[16] This conservative vision of a rural paradise can even be seen in *300* (2006), where scenes of golden cornfields in Laconia reflect a simple, rural lifestyle in contrast to Persian luxury and decadence. These scenes and the subplot of the Spartan Queen's personal battle with corrupt politicians have been added to the story of masculine endurance that informs Frank Miller's graphic novel. Likewise, in *The Last Samurai* (dir. Edward Zwick, 2003), John Logan, who had adapted the script for *Gladiator,* transposed his protagonist from Antonine Rome to rural Japan in the Meiji era. His account of the Bushido system is deeply flawed in its attribution of the values of a caste to all Japanese society in the period prior to European influence. Indeed the film, which concludes with Tom Cruise lecturing the Japanese emperor on the virtues of Honour and Discipline, has commonly been disparaged as *Dances with Samurai*.[17]

Traditional family values are also emphasised in these treatments (unlike the 'boy-loving Athenians', Spartans for all their emphasis on the body beautiful are definitely not gay). *Troy* turns Achilles into a tragic hero, not through his choice between returning home and living a long life in obscurity or avenging his comrade Patroclus and dying young but famous, but because as the pre-eminent but lone warrior on the Greek side he is denied the happiness of family life enjoyed by his Trojan counterpart, Hector. While in the *Iliad* both heroes are obsessed with their fame, even to the exclusion of their own society's welfare, Brad Pitt in Petersen's version is closer to another doomed warrior, Alain Delon's Jef in Jean-Pierre Melville's *Le Samourai*, than he is to Homer's Achilles. Both embrace their desire for death, represented in female form (Briseis, Valérie the pianist) in a romantic mix of eros and thanatos that is hardly Homeric.

The character of Alexander the Great could be similarly updated. For instance, the American writer Rory Stewart in a review of a number of biographies of the king published to coincide with Stone's film lamented that present-day academics are placing too much stress on Alexander's egotism and destructiveness.[18] By contrast, ancient writers had 'grasped that Alexander's love of glory was a reflection of his Hellenic background and an essential part of his heroism' and that the Macedonian 'gave his life with a social fiction called "honour" for a fantasy called "heroism" '. As modern man cannot meet such standards, he ignores or belittles this part of the hero's character.

While no one doubts Alexander's concern for glory or his striving for honour – two rather concrete terms in Greek, since *kleos* indicates that people are celebrating one's deeds and *timê* is an evaluation of worth by action, such as the appropriate bestowal of gifts – heroism is a much more problematic concept. Does Stewart mean *aretê*, a concept of excellence proven by deeds, particularly ones of valour, or is he indirectly referring to Alexander's insistence on the recognition of his divinity?[19] The danger is that modern moral concepts may be slipped into ancient settings, such as the nationalistic motto *Blut und Ehre* (Blood and Honour) reflected in *Gladiator* by Maximus' watchword 'Strength and Honour'.[20] Alexander's own values are likely to have been anachronistic by the standards of most Greeks of his day: he was, after all, a monarch in a Hellenic world that had generally replaced this form of government long ago. But his very position as king over a coalition of northern tribes meant that his position was much closer to that of Agamemnon than to his wilful ally, Achilles.

To Oliver Stone's credit, in his depiction of Alexander he rejects copying the displays of machismo from Russell Crowe in *Gladiator* or Brad Pitt in *Troy*. Stone omits any account of Alexander's battles through Asia (thus, no Granicus, no Issus, nor the various sieges such as those of Halicarnassus and Tyre) to concentrate on the climactic conflict at Gaugamela, which he depicts through mixing historical detail with the fog of war. This battle also serves to divide the account of Alexander's life into two halves: his upbringing at Pella and relations with his parents, and then his relations with Macedonians and Persian subjects after victory.[21] So although both Rossen and Stone emphasise his specific Macedonian origin, Rossen treats Gaugamela as the climax of his heroism while Stone sees it as only the beginning of his quest to discover the world – and his own true self. This is a romantic depiction of Alexander, emphasising his *pothos*, his desire to advance to the ends of the earth if necessary to explore and achieve memorable deeds, a regular theme in Arrian's history. Stone uses the framing device of showing Alexander's companion, Ptolemy, in his old age dictating his account of Alexander to indicate that his version of events (Ptolemy as preserved by Arrian) is only one of many possible accounts.

The narrative is, however, confused by a desire to combine the mythological and the psychological. To Stone, Alexander is both the legendary king Arthur (a comparison he makes explicit on the commentary to the director's cut), thwarted in his global vision of uniting the world, and a man whose inner conflicts can be traced back to the family feuds between his father and mother. Myths, such as those of Oedipus killing his father and marrying his mother and of Medea murdering her children, are depicted as representing the hero's psychological scars from his upbringing. Although he may not be personally responsible for Philip's death, by killing his father's general, Parmenion, Alexander asserts the power of a younger generation who are now disposing of their father figures. The Bactrian princess Roxane attracts Alexander's attention because in her wild exoticness she shows a remarkable similarity to his mother. But her open contempt for her husband because of his continuing affection for Hephaistion also duplicates his mother's attitude to Philip and thus renews Alexander's childhood traumas.[22]

At the same time, the empathetic side of Alexander is brought to the fore. For instance the king visits and consoles his wounded men after Gaugamela (a scene that appears modelled on a similar visit by Russell Crowe to his soldiers after the battle with the Germans in *Gladiator*). But Stone wishes to avoid presenting Alexander's heroism as simply Stoic manliness and stresses his feminine side too as he tenderly comforts his parents or embraces his companions. Indeed, the depiction of Alexander's pan-sexuality has sometimes been blamed for the film's lack of success, particularly in the United States.[23] Perhaps – but the success of *Brokeback Mountain* (Ang Lee, 2005) is a strong counterargument. As likely an explanation is the audience's confusion at the multiple romances surrounding Alexander. His relationship to Hephaistion most clearly represents the Greek philosophic view of the ennobling power of love between aristocratic males (so stated by Aristotle at the beginning of the film), but is unusual in that the two are of similar age so the normal relationship between mentor and young protégé is absent. Alexander's attachment to the eunuch Bagoas is portrayed as a feminine romance following the novels of Mary Renault.[24] Finally, his attraction to and sexual relations with Roxane follow traditional Western male fantasies about the animalistic allure of Eastern women. Stone has spoken of Roxane as his equivalent of the Queen of the Amazons who visits the Macedonian king in the Alexander Romance. Given the completely different tone of each of these tales of the king's sexuality (not to mention his Oedipal fixation on his mother), it is understandable that the audience has difficulty identifying the type of story being told. It is not surprising that the marriages at Susa (historically including Alexander's double marriage) that are one of the highpoints of Rossen's film are omitted: Alexander as multiple bigamist would certainly deepen the confusion.

Perhaps this multiplicity of images, styles, and narratives is the real problem with Oliver Stone's depiction. Alexander means different things to different people at differing times in history – the film's art direction at one time recalls the chiaroscuro of Dutch painting (the crowd of courtiers at the death of the king), at another, Macedonian coinage (Alexander on a rearing Bucephalus attacking Porus' elephant apparently modelled on the famous silver decadrachms from late in his reign showing a rider attacking two men on an elephant). Burton's initial voiceover from the Rossen film ('to live with courage and die leaving behind an ever-lasting renown') is once again taken out of its Arrianic context (Alexander's futile appeal to his troops to go further). This time it represents his emotions at the Battle of the Hydaspes and would seem to announce a conclusion to his life in a moment of glory, struck down with his horse Bucephalus when turning the battle against the Indians. But the corpse recovers to return to Babylon and a world of conspiracy theories (did Roxane poison Hephaistion? are the Macedonians trying to poison Alexander?). A second ending is the actual death of Alexander and the chaos that immediately ensues.[25] Then, returning to the framing composition in Alexandria, an elderly Ptolemy concludes: 'The dreamers exhaust us. They must die before they kill us with their blasted dreams', only to change his mind and substitute 'The glory will always go to those who follow their visions.' While the two verdicts are a fine summary of the gulf between Alexander and his Macedonian subjects, the multiple conclusions are indicative of a portmanteau film that may expand or contract according to the director's vision (a 175-minute theatrical cut, a 167-minute director's cut, and, most recently, the 214-minute *Alexander Revisited*).

It is hard not to conclude that older epic narratives using the ancient world as a model or warning for modern times work best in conservative mode. Bringing in modern psychology, as Moravia had warned, undermines heroic codes. When Stone seeks a model in more modern epic film, such as David Lean's *Lawrence of Arabia* (1962), his liberalism is undermined by the orientalist fantasy of a Westerner discovering his sexuality in the East while providing leadership for the disorganised natives. Alexander is simply too closely linked to Western imperialism to offer anything more than a critical and, finally, pessimistic view of ancient history. Since present-day audiences readily draw parallels with modern ventures in the

Middle East, any positive treatment of the struggle between West and East that concludes with the victory of the former is likely to be even more offensive to many than the tale of the heroic defence of freedom in the face of barbarian hordes that is *300*. It is unlikely that a cinema that seeks to appeal to an international market can offer an Alexander that does not betray the contradictions of liberal aspirations and imperial ambitions.[26]

Alexander goes East

Although, in a post-imperialist world, Alexander can no longer function as an international symbol, the tale of the great king may still resonate locally. For instance, as the conqueror who turned to Asia, rather than concerning himself with the affairs of the barbarian West, he provides a nationalistic exemplar for contemporary Greek politicians. Greece need no longer be dependent on Western Europe and its often patronising philhel-lenism for its foreign policy, but may strike out on its own road in the Balkans and Eastern Mediterranean. Still, as shown by the conflict over the name of the (Former Yugoslav) Republic of Macedonia, Alexander and symbols such as the Vergina Sun also serve as a reminder of more modern conflicts, particularly the Balkan wars of the first half of the twentieth century. It is hardly surprising then that Theo Angelopoulos, whose films are infused with modern Greek history, carefully skirts the possible chauvinism surrounding king Alexander. While the name Alexander is commonly used of the protagonists in his films (indeed, in *Voyage to Cythera*, Alexander is literally the director's alter ego, played by Giulio Brogi, but dubbed by Angelopoulos himself), unlike Orestes, a name which recalls ancient Greek tragedy, it is not given any strong association with the past. Megalexandros is a modern folk legend, only tangentially linked to the ancient world at the film's conclusion, when a bloodstained bust is shown as the dictator's main historical legacy.[27]

Further east, on the Indian subcontinent, Alexander could be seen as the precursor to the British Raj. In Kipling's *The Man Who Would be King* (1888), two ex-soldiers make their way to the mythical 'Kafiristan' in central Asia. By spreading the word that they are the children of Sikander (and of the legendary Assyrian warrior queen, Semiramis),[28] the adventur-ers establish a kingdom, ruling over a fair-headed Aryan tribe. These are presumably the descendants of the Greek colonists left in the area by Alexander more than two millennia ago but now 'gone native'. In an amusing parody of British imperial organisation, the would-be rulers convince themselves that they have discovered Masonic signs among these savages and organise an entire country through a system of Masonic lodges. But when one of the god-devils tries to take a local girl to be his wife, they are recognised as human and the brilliant adventure ends in tragedy. As filmed in 1975 by John Huston with Michael Caine and Sean Connery in the lead roles, *The Man Who Would be King* is a successor to ripping yarns set in India such as *Gunga Din* (dir. George Stevens, 1939), an anachronistic lesson in white men – even poor white men – attempting to create civilisation amid Eastern superstition and cruelty, and a reminder of eventual punishment for *hybris*.

Well before Kipling, however, the historical Alexander's expedition to India had been romanticised by European dramatists (e.g. Racine's *Alexandre le Grand*, 1665). In particular, from the eighteenth century the conflict with Porus had become a popular subject for opera and stage performance after Pietro Metastasio composed his libretto, *Alessandro nell'Indie*. A complicated love triangle is resolved when the noble Greek ruler shows his magnanimity by forgiving the Indian king for his conspiracies and reunites him with his lover Cleophis.[29] The exotic themes were so attractive that numerous composers, including Haydn, Handel (in a version renamed *Poro, re dell'Indie*), and Hasse (*Cleophide*), were to provide operatic music for this treatment. Updated for nineteenth-century tastes, Giovanni Pacini's 1824 adaptation of *Alessandro nelle Indie* was a major success in its time and is still performed occasionally today.

It is hard not to regard Sohrab Modi's Urdu language feature *Sikandar* (1941) as an indigenous reply to the importation of the European myth of the benevolent despot into an Indian setting.[30] Alexander in Persia is enjoying the company of Roxane, but Aristotle reminds him that his first duty is to conquer the world. Hence Alexander leads his expedition to India. While some of the local kings agree to become his vassals, Porus resists and becomes the embodiment of the struggle for his nation's freedom. In the meantime, Roxane has made her way to India in disguise and through the traditions of the local fire festival establishes herself in a sister-brother relationship with Porus in order to protect her Greek lover. After Alexander crosses the Hydaspes by a stratagem and kills Porus' brother in a cavalry battle, all is ready for the epic battle between the two kings. But Roxane has gained from Porus a promise to spare her lover and although the Indian kills Alexander's horse and could slay Alexander, he desists and allows himself to be defeated. When taken prisoner, Porus' defiant denunciation of Greek treachery earns him his freedom. Although the Indians seem to have lost the battle, the response of Alexander's men who mutiny rather than face continued resistance shows the hollowness of the Greek victory. Alexander accepts that the omens will not allow him to advance further and, now joined by Roxane, turns back to his army's applause.

Sikandar includes elements of the Alexander Romance such as Alexander going in disguise to Porus to bring the declaration of war, as well as historical incidents such as the battle at the Hydaspes and the mutiny at the Hyphasis. There is also the romantic love triangle from European opera with Roxane substituting for Cleophis. Yet it is not Alexander who embodies clemency, but his opponent Porus. The Indian sees through Alexander's disguise when he first arrives at his palace, but in a deliberate

104

change from the Romance, where Alexander has to fight his way past Darius' men at Babylon, Porus graciously permits his prisoner to leave. While Aristotle expresses the Western belief in unlimited conquest and Alexander tries to put this into practice, Roxane, who concludes the film singing 'Life should be enjoyed with love', embodies the feminine values of the East and king Porus its honourable martial values.

Sikandar clearly has a nationalistic aim in its rejection of collaboration with a foreign conqueror (as portrayed in the film by the alliance of some minor dynasts such as Ambhi with Alexander) and its laudation of heroic Indian resistance. Modi turns the weapons of imperialism against the aggressor. Opera's orientalist fantasies are countered by the display of Indian nobility in the face of Western treachery and the incorporation of indigenous song-and-dance forms into the film. In addition to the three songs Roxane sings to celebrate her love for Alexander, each army displays its hopes and emotions – for instance, before the battle Porus' court sings of its hope for Indian freedom and afterwards celebrates a moral victory. Two Shakespearean actors (Prithviraj Kapoor as Alexander, Sohrab Modi as Porus) use their skills to engage in verbal duels after the style of Parsee theatre.[31] The spectacular battle-scenes, which included large numbers of elephants, were rated as more than equal to those in any foreign film. Not surprisingly, *Sikandar* was a box-office success on release.[32] But in the crisis of 1941-2, amid the National Congress' demands for independence and the advance of Japanese forces to the India-Burma border, when many Indian prisoners of war captured in the fall of Singapore had chosen to serve alongside the Japanese army, it is not surprising that the movie was in places banned from theatres catering to Indian troops. The message of national pride when faced by foreign invaders was so strong that the film could be revived forty years later to coincide with the Indian march into Goa. [33]

If non-Western cinema can turn the legend of Alexander back against European imperialists, another possibility also opens up: the appropriation of Alexander in areas outside his normal cultural setting. The Japanese animated television series *Reign: the Conqueror* (Japanese original title: *Arekusanda Senki*, 'The War Chronicles of Alexander', dir. Yoshinori Kanemori, 1999) offers a particularly interesting case study. Based on the novels of popular Japanese fantasy author Hiroshi Aramata, with screenplay by Sadayuki Murai,[34] its character designs were provided by the Korean-American Peter Chung, best known for his MTV series *Aeon Flux*, working in conjunction with the respected Japanese animation studio, Mad House. Much of the animation was actually drawn in Korea, a common practice at present for both American and Japanese productions. There was substantial Hong Kong investment in the enterprise since the series would soon be shown in the Asian region dubbed into Chinese. Most significantly, *Reign* marked the first venture by Korean industrial giant Samsung into animation, justified by the company as an investment in a developing global market.[35]

Since *Reign* was shown on the 'cartoon' networks of American television,[36] it presents an apparent paradox of a tale normally told in high status forms (historical writing, opera, epic film) recreated in what is generally regarded as a low status, adolescent medium. Yet within Japanese culture, animation has a rather different cachet to the children's entertainment associated in the West with Walt Disney Studios. The success of Miyazaki's Studio Ghibli films, generally aimed at a youthful market, has tended to reinforce this prejudice. However, the films of Katsuhiro Otomo (director of *Akira*, 1988; *Steamboy*, 2004), Mamoru Oshii (*Ghost in the Shell*, 1995; *Ghost in the Shell 2: Innocence*, 2004), and particularly Satoshi Kon (*Perfect Blue*, 1998; *Millennium Actress*, 2001; *Tokyo Godfathers,* 2003; *Paprika*, 2006) indicate that animation may also be created for adults too. While animation lends itself easily to fantasy styles, which can be portrayed at lower cost than required for the meld of CGI and live action on which modern epic features such as *Gladiator* or *Troy* depend, all cinematic genres can be accommodated. Since animation is one of the few areas where Japan can compete on more than equal terms with the might of the Hollywood studios, it has attracted considerable investment, both from Japanese sources and distributors in North America and Europe (particularly for the burgeoning DVD market). A localised version is often produced for each market, sometimes with marked differences between the dubbed version and the original Japanese soundtrack. In the case of *Reign* a particularly odd effect is the change of voice actors after Episode 4. In order to win support for an English language release, Peter Chung and his associates had themselves organised the dubbing of the first four episodes. When the American distribution company TokyoPop took over the series, it provided an English soundtrack for the rest of the series but never re-dubbed the early episodes.

But what is there about the Alexander myth that might interest an Asian audience? After all, reference to the Greek and Roman worlds is rare in Western animation. For instance, while a large number of films have been parodied over *The Simpsons'* long history, the ancient world appears only through frequent allusions to the 1959 version of *Ben Hur* and two episodes featuring the Trojan War cycle.[37] Akira and Godzilla make appearances;[38] Hercules, Cleopatra, Nero and Alexander do not. While Japanese animation because of its range of styles is much freer in introducing 'highbrow' cultural material, here too the few allusions to the ancient European world are striking. At the end of Miyazaki's *Castle of Cagliostro* (1979), the real treasure that Lupin the Third has been seeking on his comic adventures is revealed to be a new Pompeii, preserved over the centuries in the local lake. This homage to ancient Greco-Roman culture also anticipates the director's later ecological concerns as seen in *Nausicaa* (1984) or *Princess Mononoke* (1997). Within the extraordinarily intertextual television series, *Revolutionary Girl Utena* (1997), the fencing duel theme, 'Spira Mirabilis', contains an allusion to Scipio's dream in its lyrics. The reference is to Cicero's *Republic*, where Scipio Africanus (the Younger) has a dream in which he meets his father who reveals the nature of the heavens and the unending cycle of reincarnation of great spirits after noble deeds. Not only is this cycle part of nature (and so equivalent to the marvellous natural spiral of logarithmic growth, the *spira mirabilis*), but it also parallels the efforts of the magical schoolgirl heroine Utena at Ohtori ('Phoenix') Academy to break the recurrent cycle in which all at the school are trapped and advance to a higher stage of life. Finally, *The Appleseed*, a *manga* (graphic novel) by Masumune Shirow that has twice been animated, most recently in 2005, has characters with names from Greek mythology, such as Briareos, the Titanic, cyborg love interest of the heroine, or Athena, the wise leader of the bioroids. Yet while the latest movie offers impressive three-dimensional animation, the Classical nomenclature adds little depth to a fairly standard science fiction action flick.

Reign, then, is quite unusual within Japanese animation for its focus on Ancient Greek history. Of course, the series is not just referencing Western history, but recreating the story of one of the West's greatest conquerors. Hiroshi Aramata, the author of the original novels on which the series is based, in an interview to coincide with the launch of the series, has talked about his difficulty in finding a theme to unify his story. When, however, comparison with Nobunaga, the warlord who was instrumental in the unification of Japan in the late sixteenth century, came to mind, he realised that similar principles of destruction and re-creation offered a clear thread through the Alexander legend.[39] The theme appears in Western versions, for instance at the birth of Alexander and in the debate between Barsine and Memnon over where Greece should stand in the conflict between Macedon and Persia in Rossen's film. But it has greater resonance for Japan whose modern development has taken marked changes in direction, first as a consequence of the intervention of Commodore Perry with his Black Ships in the 1850s and then through the allied occupation led by Douglas MacArthur (1945-51).

In addition to the political, Aramata's account of Alexander stresses the cultural changes of the Hellenistic world, particularly in the areas of philosophy and mathematics.[40] The series also has a strong element of 'steam punk', so named after storylines that combine nineteenth-century technology and later scientific discoveries.[41] Phalanx formations unite to create strange new weapons and assassins fly along on primitive gliders. But the introduction of a strange element, the Platohedron, a solid body of terrifying power consisting of the four elements and the primary principle, within which are contained the laws of the entire universe, moves *Reign* from the realm of fantasy into science fiction. Only Alexander embodying the force of destruction in the heat of battle can attract the Platohedron back from chaos. Yet this event obviously imposes the risk of a nuclear-type destruction of all natural principles, a cataclysm that all around him fear. It hardly needs to be stated that such an apocalyptic event, seen also in animation such as *Akira* or *End of Evangelion* (dir. Hideaki Anno, 1997), reflects Japanese fears as the only nation to have suffered nuclear attack.

The burning of the Temple of Diana at Ephesus around the time of Alexander's birth appeared to the Magi as a portent of the destruction of Asia (Plutarch, *Alexander* 3.7). In *Reign* Alexander's boundless energy becomes a threat to the entire world and Pythagorean, Zoroastrian and Brahmin assassins attempt to kill him before disaster occurs. The mounting panic of his own courtiers as his campaigns draw them to the edge of the known world and even further into the Trap of Mirabilia in the Indus valley is an effective depiction of the divorce between monarch and courtiers during the eastern campaigns (and perhaps a sly comment on how the histories of Alexander generally collapse into bizarre fiction at this point). Alexander's brief response encapsulates his heroism: 'The prophecy cannot change Alexander.' Indeed, in making his way into the land of the dead and then meeting and battling the reflection of himself, Alexander shows that his destiny is to keep going – even if, in this case, it means a return from India to Babylon once more.

Peter Chung's elongated character designs for the series assist in turning the story of Alexander from a celebration of imperialism into a more universal tale. The Japanese trailers to a preliminary theatrical

9. Alexander and his companions, from the opening credits of *Reign: the Conqueror* (1999).

5. Alexander the Hero

10. An art deco fantasy of Babylon from *Reign: the Conqueror* (1999).

version distinguish Darius and his Persian forces by clear Turkic-Islamic stereotypes, but in the final version the two kings are virtual mirrors of one another. In contrast with the orientalising depiction of the pair on the famed Alexander mosaic from Pompeii, showing a frightened Darius fleeing from the charging Macedonian king, in *Reign* Darius is provided with an excuse for leaving the battle at Issus. At Gaugamela, his duel with Alexander is the climax of the conflict. Alexander, the unstoppable force, personally kills his rival, but in doing so he becomes himself the Great King and a God. While this syncopates historical events, it offers a dramatically satisfying treatment of a known occurrence: Alexander's propaganda that his predecessor at his deathbed had adopted him as the next Persian ruler.

The malevolent personality of Olympias, the Epirot witch, looms large early in the series, but this adds to the fantasy rather than providing an opportunity for Freudian psychology. Alexander's desire for posthumous fame is recalled in his notorious lament that, unlike Achilles, he had no Homer to portray his deeds. But the epic effect is undercut when the series' narrator slyly comments: 'Of course, we don't intend to be the one, either' (a line omitted in the English dub). Other traditional elements of the portrait of Alexander are usefully retained: his ability to see the opportunity and combine this with maximum speed (*kairos* and *tachos*) to obtain his objectives is underlined in his first intervention in battle at Chaeronea. His *pothos*, the desire to test the limits of the world, is graphically portrayed through his swimming pool at Pella, shaped like a map of the world, a visual reimagining of Plato's comparison of the Greeks in the Mediterranean to frogs around a pond.

Reign incorporates the fantastic and folkloric (the wonders of India), plots and paranoid delusions. Yet all these became part of the Alexander legend within his lifetime. Indeed *Reign* is relatively restrained in the use of such material. Roxanne discovers the identity of the foreign intruder at Babylon when she hears of Alexander's distinctive perfume, a detail that Plutarch includes as vouched for by Aristoxenus (*Alexander* 4.4). Yet Darius had already recognised the Macedonian by his penetrating gaze – again a part of the standard physiognomy.[42] In Pseudo-Callisthenes' *Alexander Romance* (2.13-15), Alexander goes to meet the Persian king, pretending to be his own herald and making a fighting escape when eventually recognised. As already noted, this tale is incorporated in *Sikandar*, but now to show Porus' mercy to the insolent foreigner. In *Reign* the episode takes a slightly different form: Alexander and his companions venture to Babylon to spy on Darius and incidentally meet Roxanne in a delightful Chinese ivory carving version of the Hanging Gardens. The adventure also reinforces Alexander's *pothos:* 'A new prospect creates power. To observe wonders creates the desire for the wonders within you.'

Some changes are minor, such as moving the meeting of Alexander with Diogenes the Cynic from Corinth to Athens. Others are for dramatic effect, as when an eclipse of the moon heralding the fall of Persia, an event that occurred some days before Gaugamela (Plutarch, *Alexander* 31.8), is shown as occurring during the battle. Sometimes, historical romance and the fantastic coexist. Alexander's trust in his doctor Philippus despite warnings of plots to poison him [Plutarch, *Alexander* 19] has its chronological setting changed from before the battle of Issus to become part of the conspiratorial confusion in the years after the conquest of the Persian Empire. The patient's raging fever as the cause of the burning of the Persian capital thus becomes an hallucinatory metaphor.

Reign has, to the best of my knowledge, attracted no comment from academics and there has been little discussion in the community of fans of Japanese animation, although the series seems to have been popular enough to have had repeated screenings on American television. Its very hybridity seems to confuse viewers: elongated, androgynous character designs are set against an art deco background that recalls the style of early American graphic novels. Certainly this is not the 'big eyes, small mouth' style that is so typical of Japanese animation. Rather than being the great philosopher of Rossen and Stone's films Aristotle has become an old-fashioned wizard with a warrior-niece Cassandra.[43] The voice of reason is instead the mendicant Diogenes (confusingly/ amusingly rendered in the American dub as Yoda the Jedi) ushering in Hellenistic philosophy.

5. Alexander the Hero

Viewers may decide for themselves whether they prefer the Babylon of this series or the nineteenth-century romantic image recreated in Oliver Stone's film. The depiction in Episode 8 of a futuristic cosmopolitan Alexandria that will arise after Alexander's death reveals a multicultural outlook that is hardly what Western audiences expect from a Japanese production. Aramata, the novelist on whose books *Reign* is based, is a noted collector of and expert on Japanese ideograms. His interest both in archaic and poetic forms and in the future possibilities of unexplored signs is reflected in the blend of history and fantasy of the series.[44] Perhaps the particularly Japanese concerns with the traditional and modern and melding of the indigenous and external limit *Reign*'s overall appeal.

Still, one image strikingly sums up the series' appeal. In the end of the opening sequence to each episode, amid images of global destruction, Alexander can be seen on his horse frozen like a statue, but slowly awakening to the world around him. The scene encapsulates defiance and determination, as if a sleeping giant is awakening (the very last image of *Reign*, after the end credits, similarly shows a dormant Alexander revived by a revolving Platohedron). It also begs comparison with a European source: Briullov's romantic depiction of the *Last Day of Pompeii* (1834, now in the State Russian Museum, St Petersburg), which shows Vesuvius erupting and its population fleeing as if from God's judgement. On the right of the picture, a rider on a rearing horse is facing rather than escaping from the volcano. Comparison of the two images in their contexts suggests that for the modern world remembrance of the ancient Greek and Roman worlds need not simply function as a warning, but suggests the possibility of fresh creation, locally and globally.

6

It's a Man's, Man's, Man's World' – except for Xena and Buffy

One traditional function of a concluding chapter is to point the way for the future. I hesitate to do so: after all, only a year ago Gideon Nisbet quite rightly quoted Thucydides *Peloponnesian War* 1.10 on how much more visually striking ancient Athens was than Sparta. Because it had ruins and Sparta did not, Athens had come to be identified with Greece.[1] Cultural history, unfortunately, does not stand still. By the end of 2006, *300* had provided Sparta with a truly fabulous set of civic buildings to match its military power – not to mention a bottomless pit into which to throw Persian envoys. Sparta is back in style. Other predictions may be less risky: while *The 300 Spartans* has been recreated as *300, Alexander the Great* as *Alexander*, it is hard to see the titles (or the clothing of their heroes) shrinking any further.[2] I think it is safe to suggest that the use of computer graphics will encourage more films about the ancient world, but I would not venture an opinion on their general appearance. *300* was a hybrid of muscleman peplum and 1960s Cold War historical epic, not so much a morale-booster for a modern Western military faced with underwhelming numbers of technologically backward enemies[3] as a celebration of a 'traditional' machismo that never existed outside John Wayne war movies. In brief, the danger exists that in the future Greece and Rome may not appear so much as Classical as 'retro'.[4]

Of course, cinema, like opera and the stage before, has always thrived on remakes and the updating of the past is a valuable indication of popular values in the present. But in international cinema will there be a simple choice between supercharged machismo remakes of the past, for instance the death and mayhem fun of *300*, and the reversal of gender expectations of *Xena* and *Buffy the Vampire Slayer*? *Xena* replaces the male warrior hero by a female princess from Hong Kong's Wuxia tradition, the Greek populace by a multiracial cast dressed in generic Eastern European garb (working to the strains of the Bulgarian State Television Female Choir), and the landscapes of Greece with lush New Zealand scenery. The series' exploitation of ethical and sexual ambiguity ('It's not easy proving you're a different person') made Lucy Lawless a heroine for several sub-communities of fans simultaneously. Yet *Xena* needed the presence of *Hercules* to provide its subversive subtext of same-sex female desire and Girl Power. The archetypes must be preserved in order for them to be rejected.

113

Still, the need to break from the past shows the continuing strength of the ancient world in the popular imagination. Comic treatments of Rome, from *Roman Scandals* (1933) through *Carry on Cleo* (1964) to the more recent *Asterix* films[5] have relied on stereotypes of the past that are still strong. Gladiator movies have returned to the menu and depictions of the historical manoeuvres of the Caesars seem never to have left the television screen.[6] Perhaps an unexpected sport will appear to show the power of Greek mythology. Just as Rian Johnson's *Brick* (2005) breathed new life in the Chandleresque detective story by clever adaptation to a high school setting, perhaps another scriptwriter and director can take the tale of Odysseus and place it in an unexpected setting. After all, it worked once for Duccio Tessari.

Nor should there be fear for the future of 'high' art treatments of the past. The emergence in the 1960s and 1970s of European cinematic transformations of Greek drama (e.g. in Pier Paolo Passolini's *Oedipus Rex* (1967), *Medea* (1969), and *Notes for an African Orestes* (1970); Michael Cacoyannis' *Electra* (1962), *Trojan Women* (1971), and *Iphigenia* (1977); and Liliana Cavani's *I cannibali* (1970), based on Sophocles' *Antigone*) is a phenomenon that deserves a major study in its own right. Yet the Japanese director Toshio Matsumoto's version of the Oedipus story (*Funeral Parade of Roses*, 1969) and Lars von Trier's 1988 television treatment of *Medea* (based on a treatment by Carl Theodor Dreyer) show that innovative re-imaginings of well-known myths are not bounded geographically or chronologically. In the meantime, we await the next two parts of Angelopoulos' history of twentieth-century Greece as Oedipus myth.

Finally, with the announcement that Roman Polanski will be directing a script by Robert Harris based on his best-selling novel, it is reassuring to see that Pompeii is scheduled to erupt once more.[7]

Notes

Introduction

1. Pomeroy 2005.
2. The visit to the British Museum in Campion's *The Portrait of a Lady* (1996) is perhaps the closest connection to the ancient world in these filmmakers' works.
3. Probably *Hercules, Off to Conquer Atlantis* would best catch the levity of the Italian title, but the short English title will suffice.
4. It is also helpful that Quentin Tarantino has frequently mentioned the Macaroni Western Bible set of Japanese reissues in recent interviews.

1. The Actress and the Playwright

1. Grobel 1984.
2. Ibid. 66.
3. This Petronius, whose remarkable suicide in AD 65 is brilliantly portrayed by the Roman historian Tacitus (*Annals* 16.18), is usually assumed to be the same as the author of the picaresque novel, *The Satyricon*. This identification has encouraged the dubious practice of taking the comic incidents of the novel as indicative of contemporary behaviour of the Roman upper classes.
4. Broadway play of 1900, produced by F.C. Whitney; opera of 1909 by Jean Nouges; French film of 1902, directed by Lucien Nonguet and Ferdinand Zecca.
5. Directed by Raoul Walsh and Mario Bava, the scriptwriters include Walsh, Michael Elkins, and peplum veteran, Ennio De Concini.
6. For a detailed analysis of these themes within the historical contexts of the films, see Wyke 1997, ch. 5 'Nero: Spectacles of Persecution and Excess' and ch. 6: 'Pompeii: Purging the Sins of the City'. On *Quo Vadis*, Cyrino 2005: 7-33.
7. Coleman 2005 presents a call for 'authenticity' in cinema, as opposed to accepted theatrical forms (e.g. the clothing in Classical films, derived from the nineteenth-century fantasies of Alma-Tadema and others); for Lane Fox, see http://www.archaeology.org/online/interviews/fox.html which includes some startling photographs of an Oxford Classicist in a funny hat.
8. Burt 1998.
9. Ghose 2000; Hedrick 2000.
10. For Mickey Spillane and the Classics, see Winkler 1985: 93-8. Spillane's concern for punctuation (he required 50,000 copies of *Kiss Me, Deadly* to be pulped for missing the comma and never forgave Robert Aldrich for his 1955 version, *Kiss Me Deadly* [Sutherland, 2006]) suggests disquieting bourgeois aspirations.
11. Bogan: pejorative Australasian slang for the unfashionably lower class.
12. Dumas' original version was serialised in the *Journal des Débats* 1844-6. That it was the third title to be published in Albert Kantner's *Classic Comics* series, begun in 1941, illustrates its popularity in the English-speaking world too. Its international appeal can be seen in the most recent screen versions: an English

language film of 2002 starring James Caviezel, a French television mini-series with Gérard Depardeiu in the title role (1998), and a Japanese animated series (*Gankutsuou*, 2004).

13. The considerable number of Classical references that require explanatory footnotes in Robin Buss' most recent Penguin Classics translation (1996) reinforce this impression.

14. For instance, the soliloquy of the transvestite pioneer, 'Sally' Jenko (played by Iggy Pop), describing Nero as persecutor of good Christians, in Jim Jarmusch's *Dead Man* (1995), or the terrified reference to Poppaea Sabina ('Nero jumped on her and squashed her like a bug') by Leo Bloom (Gene Wilder) when threatened by Max Bialystock (Zero Mostel) in Mel Brooks' *The Producers* (1968). Both represent comic reinterpretations of the stock Roman tyrant, sufficiently recognisable by the audience to be open to parody.

15. 'Caligula or Nero, those great treasure-seekers, those desirers of the impossible, would have lent their ears to the poor man and granted him the air he so desired, the room he valued so highly, and the liberty that he was offering to pay for so dearly.' The Latin phrase is probably a misquotation of Tacitus, *Annals* 15.42.2, where Nero is described as *incredibilium cupitor*, 'a man who desired all his life to achieve the unthinkable'.

16. When initially queried about this turn of affairs by Albert de Moncerf, Monte Cristo explains her fate by another allusion: 'How was it that Dionysius the Tyrant became a schoolmaster? The fortune of war, my dear viscount, – the caprice of fortune.' Not for the first time, Classical learning obfuscates: the reference to the fourth-century BC Syracusan ruler disguises the real truth that Haidee's fate was no chance, but the result of Albert's father's treachery to her father.

17. Richard Lester's *Three Musketeers* (1973) and *Four Musketeers* (1974) are two memorable cinematic treatments of Dumas' famous novel.

18. Compare the orientalising and Classical mix of Flaubert's *Salammbo* (1862), a novel set in North Africa during the rebellion of Carthage's mercenaries after the First Punic War.

2. Hymns to the Ancient World in (the) Buffyverse

1. Scoobies: an ironic reference to the children's animated television programme *Scooby-Doo*, where a group of teenagers solve supernatural mysteries by revealing them to be a cover used by some adult for nefarious purposes.

2. In fact, Tara has secrets about her background that she is hiding, revealed in Season 5, Episode 6 'Family'. Yet these very secrets turn out to be false beliefs implanted by the patriarchal system that dominates her family.

3. Willow, like the other members of the Scoobie Gang, is a high school outcast, rejected by the in-crowd around Cordelia Chase. She has already undergone the nightmare of finding herself suddenly appearing in the lead role of *Madame Butterfly* ('Nightmares', Season 1, Episode 10).

4. In standard Greek texts this would be printed as follows (the line divisions produced by Willow's calligraphy are marked /; the last two and a half lines have not been transcribed onto Tara's back):

ποικιλόθρον᾽ ἀθανά/τΑφρόδιτα,
παῖ Δί/ος δολόπλοκε,/ λίσσομαί σε,
μή μ᾽/ἄσαισι μήδ᾽ ὀνίαι/σι δάμνα,
πότνι/α, θῦμον,/
ἀλλὰ τυῖδ᾽ ἔλθ᾽, αἴ/ποτα κάτέρωτα/

τὰς ἔμας αὔδας/ἀίοισα πήλοι/
ἔκλυες, πάτρος [δὲ δόμον λίποισα
χρύσιον ἦλθες
ἄρμ' ὑπασδεύξαισα.]
(Text from D.L. Page, *Lyrica Graeca Selecta* (Oxford Classical Texts, 1968)).

5. Joss Whedon, in his commentary to 'Restless' on the DVD release, credits MacIntosh for researching the Sappho material.

6. Most easily accessible in translation at http://www.seikilos.com.ar/Pillow-Book/PillowBook_en.html.

7. In the *Hymn to Aphrodite*, the goddess responds: 'Who wrongs you, Sappho? If she flees, soon she will become pursuer. If she does not accept your gifts, she will give them. If she does not love you, soon she will love you, even against her will.'

8. For the comparative ratings success of each series, see http://en.wikipedia.org/wiki/Buffy_the_Vampire_Slayer; http://tviv.org/Charmed.

9. Hornick 2007 lists about 500 published books, dissertations, and articles and approximately the same number of unpublished conference papers. I note among these the work of the Roman social historian, Walter Scheidel (Rogers and Scheidel 2004); Bowman 2002, who offers a good summary of Joseph Campbell's scheme of the Hero's Journey, which appears to be reflected in Joss Whedon's development of his leading character throughout the series; Raval and Krimmer 2002; and the various papers presented at the Open University conference, 'Greeks and Romans in the Buffyverse', January 2004.

10. Season 7, Episode 15 'Get it Done' reveals the origin of the Slayer in a patriarchal ritual that created an uncontrolled force for destruction which in later generations was brought under the management of the Council of Watchers.

11. 'In every generation, there is a Chosen One. She alone will stand against the vampires, the demons, and the forces of darkness. She is the Slayer': voice-over introduction to Seasons 1 and 2. As *Buffy* progresses, other Slayers are introduced, complicating the depiction of the lone heroine.

12. Hence the coinage 'Buffyverse' to describe the isolated world of the heroine, as opposed to the geographically situated (if film noir tinged) version of Los Angeles of *Buffy's* spin-off, *Angel*.

13. Buffy Ste. Marie, the Canadian First Nations singer-songwriter, is the most famous bearer of the name and probably responsible for the brief popularity of the name (a derivative of Elizabeth) around 1970. The meaning 'having good muscle tone' is more recent gym culture argot.

14. In the 1992 film, Buffy receives a C+ on a geography test ('Excuse me for not knowing about El Salvador, like I'm ever going to Spain anyway'). But, although she is not on the academic level of her friend Willow, she receives an offer of study from the respectable Northwestern University, as well as from the University of California, Sunnydale (Season 3, Episode 19 'Choices'). Being geographically challenged is also a useful trait for a heroine who is unfortunately tied to her hometown throughout the series and can only travel the world once her mission is accomplished.

15. Giles' lecturing style and the use of old woodcuts to illustrate demons throughout the series suggest that the comic horror tones of the Danish film on witchcraft throughout the ages, *Häxan* (1922) are being recreated. Whedon's interest in and knowledge of silent horror films is perhaps best illustrated in the Emmy-nominated episode, *Hush* (Season 4, Episode 10). By depriving the characters of the ability to speak, he forces viewers to turn their attention to the mise-en-scène and its musical accompaniment.

16. Vukanović 1959. McClelland 2006 offers a wide-ranging study of fighters against vampires from medieval Eastern Europe to Buffy. The alternative vampire-killer, a highly educated Western figure (such as Van Helsing), is dimly reflected in *Buffy* through Watchers such as Giles and Wesley Wyndam-Pryce.

17. OVA: Original Video Animation – series made in Japan for direct to video release (particularly aimed at the discretionary income of anime fans before the economic bubble burst).

18. Blade, in Marvel Comics' 1970 series *Tomb of Dracula* and the movie series since 1998, is a false dhampir, since his mother was already pregnant when bitten by a vampire. Miyu is also featured in a nine-volume manga series, 1989-2001 (Horror Comics Special: Akita Shoten, Tokyo) and a 26-episode animated television series (dir. Toshiki Hirano, 1997). Later versions of the dhampir include Mamoru Oshii's creation, Saya, in the animation *Blood: The Last Vampire* (dir. Hiroki Kitakubo, 2000) and his novel (*Blood: The Last Vampire, Night of the Beasts*, English translation 2005).

19. The glories of consumer capitalism are parodied in Xander's memorialisation of the Mall: 'All those shops gone. The Gap, Starbucks, Toys "R" Us. Who will remember all those landmarks unless we tell the world about them?'

20. Initially, the two major collections were Kaveney 2001 (with mainly British contributors) and Wilcox and Lavery 2002 (predominantly American).

21. '10 Questions for Joss Whedon', Reader's Opinions, *New York Times*, 16 May 2003.

22. For instance, Riess 2004, Craigo-Snell 2006.

23. South 2003.

24. Mr Chips (full name, Charles Edward Chipping) is the Victorian and Edwardian protagonist of James Hilton's novel, *Goodbye, Mr Chips,* first published in 1934 and since adapted several times for film and television. His unexpected romance with the suffragist Katherine Ellis may be an inspiration for the technophobic (Rupert) Giles' relationship with the computer teacher, Jenny Calendar. It is probably not surprising that the Oxford Classicist, Richard Jenkyns (2002, in an acerbic review of Kaveney 2001), describes Giles as 'the most interesting character in the story', regarding his portrayal as a sign of traditional American anglophilia. Jenkyns, the author of *The Victorians and Greece* (Oxford, 1980), proceeds from the analysis of Aldous Huxley to show that southern California is really not like that at all, which rather suggests a stronger acquaintance with inter-war novels than with the generic traits of Universal's horror films.

25. Season 3, Episode 19 'Choices'.

26. See n. 13 above.

27. Yurick 2003: xxxvi.

28. The irony seems to have been lost on the Auckland, New Zealand, rugby league team, the Warriors, who have used sound bites from the film in their advertising. The portrayal of an heroic Pacific/Maori warrior spirit in terms of American gang culture may be taken to display the appropriation of non-indigenous models as resistance to the dominant, Pakeha or European culture. But in light of critiques such as Alan Duff's *Once Were Warriors* (1990; film, dir. Lee Tamahori, 1994), the implied nostalgia for a warrior past is deeply problematic.

29. See *Anabasis* 3.2.24 on appearing to be ready to settle in Persia as a means of encouraging the Great King to assist the passage of the Ten Thousand home; 6.4 for the possibility of setting up a Greek city at Calpe. See also Nussbaum 1997, Dalby 1992, Hornblower 2004.

30. The writer is surely thinking of the series *Classic Comics/Classics Illus-*

trated, although the *Anabasis,* for all its Boys' Own flavour of overwhelming odds and derring-do, never featured in this series.

31. Other versions include the 1923 silent film with Lon Chaney and the 1956 and 1982 films with Anthony Quinn and Anthony Hopkins in the title role.

32. *The Hero With a Thousand Faces* (Princeton: 1949) is commonly assumed to have influenced Whedon, although I know of no direct acknowledgement of this source.

33. The *Ars Almadel* is the fourth part of an anonymous seventeenth-century grimoire (handbook of black magic), *The Lesser Key of Solomon*, a manual for summoning various spirits, which is itself based on earlier Jewish and Moslem mystic texts.

34. It also provides the title for a series of Japanese live action horror films featuring a schoolgirl witch, probably indicative of cross-cultural borrowing from *Buffy* which itself is happy to display the influence of non-western film styles, such as Bollywood or Hong Kong action dramas.

35. First published in *Form* 1921 in the article 'The Black Arts' by J.F.C. Fuller.

36. For Sappho as an inspiration for feminists of the first half of the twentieth century, see Gubar 1996.

37. Waquet 2001, Goodrich 2003.

38. Waquet 2001: 103-5 gives a number of amusing examples of the appropriation of Latin into local languages. Particularly striking, as it involves the incorporation of Greek within the Latin mass, is the 'understanding' of Kyrie eleison as Kirri eleiz ('there are heaps of carts') in Breton. For the history of the use of Latin in the Catholic church since the Renaissance, see Waquet 2001: 41-77.

39. For instance the Japanese vampire/ demon hunter Miyu has a Western demon servant, Larva ('Ghost'), who, in turn, has an old friend, Lemures ('Ghosties' – the use of the plural is odd). In a different genre, the Sisyphean Wile E. Coyote has enjoyed a number of Latin descriptors, *caninus nervous rex* in particular having an especial appeal for Classicists.

40. David Chase's creation Livia in *The Sopranos* is another homage to the BBC drama, recalling in Tony Soprano's mother the equally poisonous wife of Augustus.

41. A further example: the Japanese anime *Noir* has as a repeated feature of its soundtrack a Latin hymn in techno style, 'Salva nos' ('Lord, preserve us'). One verse begins 'dona nobis pacem et dona eis requiem, locum inter ovas': 'Give us peace and give them rest, a place within the flock'. *Ovas* is clearly what is sung and is printed in the booklet that accompanies the soundtrack, but it is simply a mistake for *oves*. Does it actually make any difference? The words are derived from various versions of the Requiem Mass and recognition that this is somehow a prayer for the living and a lament for the dead (in the series, those who have made the mistake of attacking the protagonists) is sufficient. For a similar judgement on the highly idiosyncratic Latin libretto to Stravinsky's *Oedipus Rex* (1927), see Farrell 2001: 117-23.

42. My thanks to David Tulloch for pointing out this reference to me.

43. Perhaps Xander's newfound ability to recite any Latin at all should be seen as part of the topsy-turvy world of this episode where nerdish Jonathan has become a superhero and the regular cast, including Buffy, are merely his assistants.

44. 'Path of combination, time and space: hear me when I command!' I take *conoureus* to be a defining genitive, after Willow has failed in her attempts to open the portal by the path through time (*via temporis*) and the path through space (*via spatii*).

45. Farrell 2001: 6.

46. Vergil, *Aeneid* 6.851-3: *tu regere imperio populos, Romane, memento/ (hae tibi erunt artes), pacique imponere morem, / parcere subiectis et debellare superbos* ('But you, Romans, remember that you are ruling over the nations under your command (*those* are your skills), imposing order on peace, sparing those in your power and fighting the proud to the bitter end.')

47. Contrast the famous dictum of Dean Gaisford, Regius Professor of Greek at Oxford, 1811-55: 'The advantages of a Classical education are twofold: it enables us to look down with contempt on those who have not shared its advantages; and it also fits us for places of emolument, not only in this world but in the next.' In the Buffyverse this afterlife would most likely turn out to be a demonic dimension.

Waquet 2001: 28 rightly speaks of the 'royalty of Latin' prior to the First World War, which continued considerably longer in some countries. Thus while the Bolsheviks abolished Latin as part of the old education, the language was strongly promoted as part of the Fascist revival of Roman imperial style in Italy.

48. While Spike appears in modern times as a punk, as William (the Bloody) in the nineteenth century he clearly received sufficient upper-class education to be able to parody Caesar's famous terse report of his Zela campaign of 47 BC (*Veni vidi vici*: 'I came, I saw, I conquered'). The traditional account, originating in Plutarch, *Caesar* 50.4, records this famous quotation as deriving from a letter by Caesar to the Roman Senate. However, Suetonius (*Caesar* 37) locates the phrase less gloriously as appearing on a placard at Caesar's triumph over Pontus, an advertising slogan rather than a soundbite.

49. Latin's status as cultural capital also enabled it to function as a means of social mobility. So Waquet 2001: 16 notes that in France 'gaining access to Latin could be presented as a feminist victory'. Farrell 2001: 99, however, recounts Booker T. Washington's rejection of the study of Latin at the recently founded Howard University. Washington viewed such learning as a cunning attempt by the Whites to delay the Black man's emancipation by co-opting the elite of Afro-American society into the middle class. True freedom would instead only occur when Blacks took managerial positions in the everyday workforce.

3. The Peplum and Other Animals

1. Nisbet 2006: 48-50 on 'hunks in trunks'; for information on individual members of Mae West's revue (including Gordon Mitchell, Reg Lewis, and Mickey Hargitay, who all starred in various Italian Hercules, Goliath, and Samson films) see Walker 2007.

2. See below (*Le péplum. Qu'est-ce que c'est?*) for a discussion of the origin of the term and an attempted definition.

3. Plutarch, *Life of Crassus* 8-11 is our main primary source for Spartacus' rebellion; for a readable modern account that also discusses Spartacus in the modern imagination, see Urbainczyk 2004.

4. Hopkins and Beard 2005 offer a brief history of this, perhaps the most famous of Roman monuments.

5. For Giovagnoli's historical romance with its clear Garibaldian overtones of a struggle against the corruption of the church and state, see Wyke 1997: 37-41. In the novel, unlike Vidali's film, Spartacus is unwilling to compromise with the Roman government, despite his love for the matron Valeria.

6. The works of the five main authors (Chariton, Xenophon of Ephesus, Achilles Tatius, Longus, and Heliodorus) together with the surviving fragments of other novels are available in translation in Reardon 1989. Pseudo-Callisthenes' *Alexander Romance* (discussed in Chapter 5) is also included in this collection.

7. For instance, Nicola de Pirro had been appointed as film censor in the Fascist period and was not ousted until the student riots of 1968. In the post-war period films were much more likely to have difficulties with Italian censorship for political ideology than for sexuality or violence. For Freda's intentions: http://www.peplums.info/pep00front95.htm#05 (with bibliography).

8. Elley 1984: 112 indicates that in the extended version Spartacus has handed over his dagger to the pregnant Amytis to be preserved for his unborn son.

9. Canale's career spans the gamut of the peplum. Among her best-known roles are those of Theodora (*Theodora, Empress of Byzantium*, dir. Freda, 1954), Antea, the Queen of the Amazons (*The Labours of Hercules*, dir. Francisci, 1958), and Astra (*Maciste Against the Vampire*, dir. Gentilomo, screenplay Sergio Corbucci, 1962). Outside sword and sandal films, she is best remembered for her portrayal of Giselle du Grand in the Freda-Bava horror story, *The Devil's Commandment* (*I vampiri* 1956).

10. Cf. Wyke 1997: 49-56.

11. Contrast the attitude of Coleman 2005, who asks that 'the director and the producers recognize historical authenticity as one of their top priorities' (48), contrasting 'the manifold inaccuracies of the sword-and-sandals genre that has bred a snobbish contempt in educated cinemagoers' (49). Wyke 1997: 41-7 regards Vidali's film as celebrating the now-achieved unity of Italy instead of Giovagnoli's promotion of continuing struggle. The depiction of Spartacus in the 1913 version as populist strong man and unifying leader (he was played by the well-known body-builder Mario Guaita) thus becomes a remarkable exemplar for modern Italian politics.

12. Cf. Nisbet 2006: 52: 'endlessly mutating, the sixties *pepla* are a film historian's despair'. Typical of the prosopographical confusion is *Maciste, il gladiatore più forte del mondo* (*Maciste, the Most Powerful Gladiator in the World*, dir. Michele Lupo, 1962), known as *Colossus of the Arena* in the USA. For the French market, it was alternately titled *Maciste contre les géants, Morts dans l'arène* and (moving down-market in audience expectations?) *Orgies romaines*. Germany watched *Maciste – die gewaltigen Sieben* probably in an attempt to cash in on the success of *The Magnificent Seven* (*Die glorreichen Sieben*, 1960). Amusingly, Ursus ('the Bear') metamorphoses into an anthropophobic gorilla general in *Beneath the Planet of the Apes* (dir. Ted Post, 1970).

13. See Malamud and McGuire 2001.

14. Murray (2004) offers a lively account of Bulwer-Lytton's life and activities on the occasion of the bicentenary of his birth.

15. To avoid confusion, I have chosen to use *Last Days of Pompeii* for the Hollywood film of 1935, *Les derniers jours de Pompeii* for Moffa's 1950 joint French-Italian production, and the title *Gli ultimi giorni di Pompeii* for other Italian versions, in particular for the 1959 film.

16. As no version of Vidali's film for Pasquali Studios seems to survive (Wyke 1997: 209 n. 47), it is impossible to tell whether this was simply a film version of Enrico Petrella's opera *Ione* (1858). Wyke also notes that the earlier attribution of the Ambrosio Studios film to Mario Caserini is incorrect – the actual director was Rodolfi.

17. Wyke 1997: 147-82 ('Pompeii: Purging the Sins of the City').

18. Pilate is played by Basil Rathbono, who both offers a foil to Marcus'

Brooklynese accent and follows the Hollywood stereotype of oppressors being portrayed by suave Englishmen (cf. Sir Laurence Olivier as Crassus in *Spartacus*).

19. Wyke 1997: 182. For a detailed account of Freda's *Spartaco* and its celebration of Italian resistance to the Germans with an anti-Communist message, see Wyke 1997: 47-56. Siclier 1962: 32 indicates that Moffa was instructed to remake *Les dernières jours de Pompeii* with sets left over from *Fabiola* in order to recover production costs.

20. It was not released in the US until 1955 and then as *The Sins of Pompeii*, presumably because the explicit Christian message (and suggestion of debauchery) in the title was thought more likely to attract an American audience.

21. Although Bonnard is given first credit as director, the *Internet Movie Database* (*IMDb*) reports that he fell ill on the first day of shooting and Leone had to shoulder the main responsibility for the film. Leone himself (interview with Oreste De Fornari, 1983, in De Fornari 1984: 16) suggested that Bonnard had left the project since he preferred to direct the comedy *Gastone* (1960), starring Alberto Sordi and Vittorio De Sica, at Rome instead. Bonnard's name was probably retained on the credits because he was a well-known in the Italian film industry (born 1889, he had begun his career as a silent movie actor, including taking the lead role of Petronius in Caserini's *Nerone e Agrippina*, 1913), while Leone had only directed second unit work previously.

22. For De Concini's ability to work on multiple scripts simultaneously and his sometimes honorary signature on 'sandaloni' (sword and sandal films): Lucas 2007: 251.

23. Wyke 1997: 182, 'Pompeii as a signifier of pure spectacle and, eventually, theme park thrills'.

24. In an interview with Oreste De Fornari in 1983, Leone states that he had wanted a James Bond type or Scarlet Pimpernel ('*intelligente, spiritoso*') but found on arrival in Spain that the production company had contracted Steve Reeves, requiring the script to be rewritten around him within ten days (De Fornari 1984: 16). Reeves' reputation was at its peak after the success of Francisci's *Labours of Hercules* (1958). Mario Bava, who worked on this and many later peplums, credited the film as saving Italian cinema since its commercial success enabled continuous employment of cast and crew in local productions for years to come (Lucas 2007: 209).

25. A name said by D'Annunzio (Günsberg 2005: 218 n. 5) to be derived from one of the cult attributes of Hercules. *makiste*, 'the greatest', is a vocative form in Dorian Greek dialect of the superlative of the adjective *makros* (Liddell, Scott, Jones, *Greek Lexicon* sv. *mêkistos* – Günsberg 2005: 100 is mainly erroneous on this topic). I cannot, however, find any example of the use of this attribute for Heracles and suspect that D'Annunzio, as often, invented this explanation. A possibility that at least explains the aberrant form of the name is that it is simply a phonetic recreation of *magister* ('master').

26. Landy 1996: 35-7.

27. Günsberg 2005: 101-2, drawing on Ghigi 1977 and Dyer 1997.

28. For such a depiction of Spartacus in Freda's 1952 film, Wyke 1997: 54 and plate 3.3. In later Hercules films, the hero is often depicted towards the climax with blood on his chest from whiplashes, claws, or sword cuts. He is thus both semi-divine in his strength and mortal in his suffering.

29. *Time*, 24 February 1961 ('Joe Unchained').

30. The derivative processes of Supertotalscope (the Italian version of Cinema-Scope) and Eastmancolor (a colour film stock that did not require the three-strip process of Technicolor but was prone to rapid fading) are used in *Gli ultimi giorni di Pompeii* (1959).

31. *Ben Hur* (1956): 224 minutes; *Spartacus* (1960): 184 (restored: 198) minutes; *Cleopatra* (1963) 243 (director's cut: 320) minutes; *Fall of the Roman Empire* (1964): 188 minutes.

32. Unfortunately Reeves dislocated his shoulder filming this scene, an injury that was to plague him for the rest of his screen career (Lucas 2007: 251).

33. Bulwer-Lytton 1834: book 1, chapter 4 ('The temple of Isis. Its Priest. The Character of Arbaces Reveals Itself').

34. Leone's westerns, for instance, are hardly calls to political action, unlike Damiani's *A Bullet for the General* (*Quién Sabe?*, 1966), scripted by Franco Solinas, who also wrote the screenplay for Francesco Rosi's *Salvatore Giuliano* (1962) and Gille Pontecorvo's *Battle of Algiers* (1966), or Sollima's *Face to Face* (*Faccia à Faccia*, 1967). While *Duck You Sucker* (*Giù la testa*, 1971) is set in Mexico in the revolutionary period and has an ex-Irish rebel as one of the main protagonists, it offers no political solution other than 'keep your head down' (cf. Landy 1996: 56-7). This is not to say that there are no contemporary references in Leone's oeuvre: the corruption of American society through the connivance of politicians and labour officials with organised crime is a major theme of *Once Upon a Time in America* (1984).

35. The finest cinematic exposé of the murky links between anti-Communist politicians, the carabinieri, and the criminal organisations of Sicily, Francesco Rosi's *Salvatore Giuliano* (1962), appeared three years after Leone's film.

36. *The Last Days of Pompeii* 1834: book 5, chapter 11 ('Chapter the Last'). In fact, the name had been bestowed on the house in the later eighteenth century because it was opposite a tomb inscribed as belonging to Arrius Diomedes.

37. Ibid.

38. *Corpus Inscriptionum Latinarum* 4.3882 (= *Inscriptiones Latinae Selectae* 5145).

39. The reference to Nero as (adopted) son of Claudius dates this event to AD 51-54.

40. Cf. the stills and critical commentary by Nisbet 2006: 26-9.

41. Maximus' war-cry *Roma victor* is also difficult to excuse (even allowing for reduced linguistic competence because of his Spanish background): it should be *Roma victrix*.

42. Plutarch, *Moralia* 241f (*Sayings of the Spartan Women*).

43. Plutarch, *Moralia* 225c (*Sayings of the Spartans*). In *300* (2007), Leonidas more realistically rejects a call to lay down his arms with 'Come and get them' (a more accurate translation of the original *molôn labe*).

44. See Chapter 4 for the (frequently tainted) role of Classical Greece in modern Greek political thought.

45. For the misuse of the Greek alphabet to provide a hyper-Classical version of what are really Roman titles, see Nisbet 2006: 96. A recherché example: most of the writing in the Japanese animation *Last Exile* (2003) is in English but transliterated into Greek symbols. Occasionally documents or phrases used in the fantasy world of Prester from this series are (rather inaccurately) written in modern Greek. Close is good enough.

46. Season 2, Episode 20 *DEUS IMPEDITIO ESURITORI NULLUS* ('there is no god who can block the way of a hungry man') with its collection of nouns looks as if it might come from a handbook of Latin tags rather than being an attempt at Classical construction.

47. Leone was an uncredited second unit director on *Quo Vadis* (1951), *Helen of Troy* (1956), and *Ben Hur* (1959). Coming from a distinguished film-making family, he had also worked on prestigious Italian projects such as *The Bicycle Thief* (*Ladri di biciclette*, 1948) and *Fabiola* (1949), but during the 1950s he was mainly engaged with local B grade fare.

48. *The Colossus of Rhodes* seems to be responsible for introducing a new strong man when *Maciste against the Monsters* (*Maciste contro i mostri*, dir. Guido Malatesta, 1962) was released as *Colossus of the Stone Age* in the UK (*Fire Monsters Against the Son of Hercules* in the US) and *Maciste the Bravest Gladiator in the World* (*Maciste, il gladiatore piu forte del mondo*, dir. Michele Lupo, 1962) became *Colossus of the Arena* (USA). *La regina delle Amazoni* (dir. Vittorio Sala, 1960) became *Ursus im Reich von Amazonen* for its 1962 German release and *Colossus and the Amazon Queen* for the American market.

49. *Cahiers du cinéma* 131 (1962) 26-38. List of specialists: p. 34. Assembly line: p. 31.

50. Siclier 1962: 34 adds 'ou nouveaux Michel Zevaco', referring to the French historical novelist (1860-1918) who in 1917 turned his hand to cinema, scripting and directing *Déchéance*.

51. Already in 1956, Bava had provided the atmosphere for *I vampiri* as cinematographer and then successfully completed the film as director within the twelve days allowed by the producers when Freda was unable to finish the project. Bava's stylish 1960s horror efforts and *gialli* generally surpass Freda's work in these genres too.

52. Brian Sibley, *Peter Jackson* (Sydney/New York 2006) 33-5, 51-2. For *Buffy*'s allusions to Harryhausen, see Chapter 2.

53. Truffaut was a great admirer of Cottafavi's *Traviata 53* as a version of Dumas fils' *La Dame aux Camélias* (1953; http://www.mymovies.it/dizionario/biblio.asp?r=1659). Luc Moullet has written with great admiration about *The Vengeance of Hercules* (Moullet 1961) as well as having his film critic protagonist in his comedy *Les Sièges de l'Alcazar* (1989) prefer Cottafavi over Antonioni. *The Hundred Horsemen* (*I cento cavalieri*, 1964), set in medieval Spain, is generally regarded as Cottafavi's masterpiece, but with its Brechtian asides was a box office failure. Thereafter Cottafavi concentrated on television versions of literary classics, including Euripides *Trojan War* (*Le Troiane*, 1967: RAI), regarded by Bertrand Tavernier as 'magnifique' (in interview for the Editions Fabbri release of *Hercules Conquers Atlantis*).

54. Nisbet 2006: 25, referring to *Colossus*: 'it raids the sword-and-sandal toy-box indiscriminately, pulling out story-telling devices as ill-assorted as its set dressing.'

55. Frayling 2005: 59-63 provides an extensive list of Leone's 'citations' from earlier westerns (many presumably suggested by his story writers, Bernardo Bertolucci and Dario Argento).

56. Cammarota 1987: 209 places it fourth on takings of 840 million lire, just behind *The Labours of Hercules* (1958: 887 million) and *Hercules and the Queen of Lydia* (1959: 890 million). The top earner is Aldrich and Leone's *Sodom and Gomorrah* (1962) with 1,150 million in takings, perhaps evidence that commercial and artistic success are separate entities.

57. Siclier 1962: 29: 'people in France and elsewhere have expressed surprise [after the post-war development of Italian neo-realism] at seeing a return to the screen of "spectaculars", now labelled "films à peplums" ' (my translation). While the French Wikipedia entry (http://fr.wikipedia.org/wiki/Péplum) declares that *péplum* is 'undoubtedly a reference to *"The Robe"* (1953)', the cloak of that film bears no resemblance to any peplum.

58. Aziza 1998: 10-11 has traced the very first use of the term in print to Michel Mardore's review of Freda's *Giants of Thessaly* (1961) in *Les Cahiers du cinéma*, August 1961.

59. http://www.peplums.info/pep00arles.htm.

60. Aziza 1998: 11 who would like to use the unaccented form 'peplum', to be pronounced 'peplom' as in *homme*, in order to distinguish these films from the French term for woman's robe (*péple/peplum*). I have followed his suggestion here and also his use of the plural 'peplums'.

61. Koven 2006: 5-6.

62. 'Le film à grand spectacle': the term used by Siclier 1962 for 'films à antique' prior to the mid-1950s.

63. Solomon 2001 has separate chapters for 'Greek and Roman History', 'Greek and Roman Mythology', 'The Old Testament' and 'The New Testament and Tales of the Christ'. But 'Muscleman Epics' includes entries from all the above categories as well as strongman films not treated elsewhere.

64. Siclier 1962: 35.

65. For a defence of muscleman epics as entertainment, see Solomon 2001: 306-23, especially 322.

66. The linkage was not lost on the *New York Times* (September 23, 1939) in its description of the film as 'the most ambitious Italian production since Abyssinia'. It is hardly surprising that *Scipio Africanus* was awarded the Mussolini Cup for Best Italian Film in the Venice Film Festival of 1937.

67. See Chapter 5 for a full discussion.

68. Bava and *Ulysses* (probably restricted to the Circe episode): Lucas 2007: 138-40; *Labours of Hercules* and *Hercules and the Queen of Lydia* (lighting, special effects, photography, and a considerable amount of direction): ibid. 202-5, 235; *Giant of Marathon* (special effects, photography, and director of underwater and battle scenes after Jacques Tourneur abandoned the project): ibid. 273-7

69. Lucas 2007: 387.

70. 101 minutes in the French-Italian original (CFFP-SpA, 1961), to be distinguished from the recut and redubbed, with new soundtrack, *Hercules and the Captive Women* (93 minutes, Woolner Brothers 1963). The latter changes the credits and removes most of the barroom brawl over a dancing waitress that begins the movie, as well as much of the comically disunified Council of Greek Kings called to discuss the menace facing the nation. Tracing the changes in the various versions of peplum films is often worse than detecting the manuscript tradition of a particularly corrupt ancient text. For instance, *Goliath and the Dragon* (AIP, 1960) at 87 minutes length is not only cut down from the 98 minute *The Revenge of Hercules* (CFPP-Achille Piazzi Produzione) but features an inserted dragon section from an incomplete AIP film as well.

71. For the various incarnations of Hercules' *eromenos* (his 'boyfriend') Hylas, including Iolaus in *Hercules: the Legendary Journeys*, see Nisbet 2006: 60-4.

72. This section of the plot is very loosely based on Pierre Benoit's 1919 novel, *L'Atlantide* (filmed by G.W. Pabst in French, English, and German versions in 1932), in which two French officers in the Sahara are kidnapped and brought to the secret realm of the sexually voracious Queen Antinea.

73. As his given names (Vittorio Emmanuele Secundo) indicate, Cottafavi was born into a family of royalists and, as frequently noted, retains his suspicions regarding class revolt in this film.

74. Gérard Legrand, writing in *Positif* (portrayed as an anti-Cottafavi film journal in Moullet's *Les Sièges de l'Alcazar*) praises the film for its demystification of Atlantis, be it Plato's myth or Benoit's novel (Legrand 1961). He describes *Hercules Conquers Atlantis* as 'extremely beautiful' and 'the most balanced and elegant ... peplum I know', a remarkable description for a genre usually seen as cinematic opiate for the masses.

75. Park, born 1928, was in fact only 33 in 1961; Luciano Marin, whose birth date I have been unable to confirm, would appear from his film career to have been at least 20 years old by this time.

76. Lucas 2007: 381-7.

77. Tim Lucas, liner notes to *Hercules in the Haunted World* (Fantoma DVD, 2003), who also identifies the use of the spectacular Castellana grotto (near Bari and so involving some travel time) for the cave scenes. For detailed analysis of Bava's techniques in this film, see Lucas 2007: 389-410, esp. 397-9.

78. Ovid, *Metamorphoses* 7.440-7.

79. Another bandit traditionally killed by Theseus in his journey around the Saronic Gulf.

80. This contrast had already been exploited by Euripides in his drama, *Alcestis*. Hercules, arriving at Pherae in Thessaly, feasts and drinks to his heart's content in almost comic fashion, only to discover that his host has just lost his wife, Alcestis, to Death. He excuses himself and later returns, bringing a veiled woman back with him: Hercules has defeated Death himself and, by rescuing Alcestis, rewards Admetus for his hospitality.

81. Sharing little with the 1926 Italian silent film masterpiece (starring Bartolemeo Pagano and directed by Guido Brignone) except its title.

82. Adriano Bellini, a Venetian gondolier, rather cruelly described by Laurent Aknin (Aziza 1998: 116) as 'having a gentle face and staring gaze that indicated nothing other than unfathomable stupidity ... Only Freda knew how to use him by making Maciste an abstract, unspeaking character' (my translation).

83. *Hercules the Avenger* (*La sfida di giganti*, dir. Lucidi, 1965) marks the return of Reg Park to the title role. Unfortunately, it is substantially a cento of scenes taken from the two 1961 films of Cottafavi and Bava, cut into the story and redubbed.

84. *Hercules the Legendary Journeys: Hercules in the Underworld* (dir. Bill L. Norton, executive producer: Sam Raimi; USA television, 1994). The influence of zombie movies and the comedy-splatter genre in particular, intensified by the use of Richard Taylor's Weta Workshop for creatures and prosthetic effects, makes this version of the Underworld closer to Sam Raimi's *Evil Dead* series (*Evil Dead*, 1981; *Evil Dead II*, 1987; *Army of Darkness*, 1992) and early Peter Jackson features than to the classic Universal Studios horror films that inspired Bava. The latter was himself quite aware of the possible comedic elements of the horror genre, as his epilogue to *Black Sabbath* (*I tre volti della paura*, 1963) shows.

85. Giuliano Gemma (*Messalina; My Son, the Hero*) not only possessed a remarkably handsome visage but had been a boxer and stuntman before gaining starring roles in peplums and Italian westerns.

86. In his interviews included on the DVD releases of Sergio Martino's late 1960s and early 1970s *gialli*, Felix Gastaldi offers testimony to the comparative unimportance of the scriptwriter in the peplum period. Since crime thrillers required careful construction, the directors of the *giallo* form were fully appreciative of his efforts in this field. By contrast, Bava, given his background in staging, special effects, and photography, showed little interest in the script for *The Whip and the Body* (1963) except as a peg on which to hang gothic effects. Worse still, Riccardo Freda simply cut the last 15 minutes of Gastaldi's script for *The Horrible Dr Hichcock* (*Il horribile segreto del Dr Hichcock*, 1962), creating a horror 'masterpiece' whose moody atmosphere may even have been heightened by the narrative's curtailment.

87. Bava, preoccupied with lighting, special effects, and photography as well as directing duties, generally ignored his Hercules. By contrast, Park warmly remembers Cottafavi whose *Hercules Conquers Atlantis* is more character-driven (Lucas 2007: 385, 396).

4. The *Odyssey*, High and Low

1. Recitation at the Panathenaic Games begun by Hipparchus: Ps.-Plutarch, *Hipparchus* 228bc; Alexander at Troy: Plutarch, *Alexander* 15.7-9 (see also Chapter 5); Strabo, *Geographica* 1.1.3, etc.

2. Podestà had already appeared as Nausicaa in *Ulysses* (1954); future roles in films set in ancient times include Antea in *The Slave of Rome* (*La schiava di Roma*, dir. Sergio Grieco and Franco Prosperi, 1960), Fabiola in *Alone against Rome* (*Solo contra Roma*, dir. Luciano Ricci, 1962), and even Hera in the Lou Ferrigno vehicle, *Hercules* (dir. Luigi Cozzi, 1980). Lithuanian-born Sernas' lengthy career (he had already made some thirty French and Italian films before *Helen of Troy*) includes the roles of Laertes in *Aphrodite, Goddess of Love* (*La Venere di Cheronea*, dir. Fernando Cercio and Viktor Tourjansky, 1958, with Belinda Lee as Aphrodite), Mathos in Sergio Grieco's *Salambò* (1960), Gaius Vinicius in *The Conqueror of Corinth* (dir. Mario Costa, 1962), and a bizarre, Lawrence of Arabia-style Kurtik, leader of the Blue Men, in *Goliath and the Vampires* (*Maciste contro il vampiro*, dir. Giacomo Gentilomo, 1961).

3. Aristotle*, Poetics* 8.

4. *Xena*, Season 1, Episode 3 'Beware of Greeks Bearing Gifts' subverts the male fantasies of the genre by having the Xena ask Helen what *she* wants to do with her life.

5. Clauss 1999: 2-17.

6. Most seem to forget that Book 24 of the *Odyssey* depicts the consequences of Odysseus' slaughter of the suitors as the families of the dead are obliged to seek revenge by the laws of vendetta. Although peace is restored after further bloodshed, Teiresias has predicted that Odysseus must resume his journeys until he arrives at a land where an oar may be mistaken for a winnowing fan and only then return to die in old age in Ithaca (11.119-26, repeated by Odysseus to Penelope in 23.247-84).

7. The chronological approach is the choice of the HBO *Odyssey* (dir. Andrei Konchalovsky, 1998), although adventures needed to be cut to fit the three-hour format. The Italian film and television versions discussed in this chapter are examples of the second method, using Odysseus' stay among the Phaeacians as an opportunity to recall his adventures up to that point.

8. This does not prevent advertising for films claiming historical 'authenticity', most notoriously in Gig Young's promotions for *Helen of Troy* that not only claim the movie as the recreation of the world's 'most famous love story, Homer's *Iliad*', but also offer erroneous information on the archaeology of Troy and Bronze Age weaponry. Cf. Winkler 2007b. 208-9. For the role of the British Museum art advisor in *Troy* (2004), see Fitton 2007, especially 105-6.

9. Details of this 2584 ft (approx. an hour) film are from the British Film Institute site: http://ftvdb.bfi.org.uk/sift/title/300031?view=synopsis. A restored version (missing some lost scenes) has recently been shown in various festivals.

10. The screening ratio is 1.66:1 against Cinemascope's 2.35:1.

11. De Concini, although heavily associated with the peplum tradition, was highly adaptable, winning a screenplay Oscar for the comedy *Divorce, Italian Style* (dir. Pietro Germi, 1961) and providing the script for Mario Bava's Italian horror success *Black Sunday* (*La maschera del demonio,* 1961) under the pseudonym Vasily Petrov. Apart from numerous notable screenwriting credits, Ben Hecht had regularly doctored scripts such as *Gone with the Wind*. Hugh Gray, who is credited as 'historical advisor' for *Quo Vadis* (dir. Mervyn LeRoy, 1951), would two years later be one of the screenwriters for *Helen of Troy* (1956). Other screenwriting credits go to Franco Brusati (director and screen-writer for *Pane e ciocolata,* 1972), Ivo Perilli, Irwin Shaw (author of the war novel, *The Young Lions,* filmed by Edward Dmytryk in 1958), and the director, Mario Camerini.

12. Cf. the various versions of the script of *Gladiator* (2000) discussed by Solomon 2005 and Lowe 2004, who offers important corrections regarding the original draft by David Franzoni, the clichéd expansion of Franzoni's second version by John Logan, and the final synthesis, with particular emphasis on character development, by William Nicholson that became the filmed version.

13. Both the Italian and English language DVDs are this length, which suggests that reports of longer versions are in error.

14. Star of *Bitter Rice* (*Riso amaro,* dir. Giuseppe di Santis, 1949) and wife of producer, Dino De Laurentiis.

15. Circe is perhaps modelled on the ghostly Lady Wakasa who seduces the married potter in Mizoguchi's *Ugetsu monogatari* (1953), which had recently been awarded the Silver Lion at the Venice Film Festival. Other aspects, such as Odysseus bathing in a bath with lilies floating on the surface, or dressed in fine robes, admiring himself in a mirror, suggest influences from the tale of the Lotus Eaters and Hercules under the power of Omphale (soon to be filmed in *Hercules and the Queen of Lydia,* 1959).

16. Short tunics for the female leads seem to have begun with Iole (Sylva Koscina) in *The Labours of Hercules* (1958) whose dress appears styled after Diana the Huntress and thus makes her an athletic counterpart to Hercules.

17. The headdress of Queen Arete is modelled on that of the Iberian *Lady of Elx* (fourth century BC). Other Phaeacian nobles seem to be dressed in a mixture of Iberian (cf. the *Lady of Cerro de los Santos*), medieval Italian and Minoan style.

18. In an odd inversion of cutting the ropes of the drawbridge, Kirk Douglas slashes the supports that hold down the door to the banqueting hall, thus impris-oning the suitors in the palace.

19. The Phaeacians are exceptional in wearing linen and even satin. Their costumes thus emphasise their alien presence in an Homeric Dark Age world.

20. Many of the external shots were filmed in Yugoslavia as part of the joint venture between Italian (Dino De Laurentiis cinematografica/RAI), German (Bavaria Film TV), and Yugoslav (Jadran film) companies. The series thus seems to mark the beginning of European, rather than national, television productions (Lucas 2007: 763).

21. Phemios appeals to Odysseus to spare his life, both because of his innocence and because he will be able to immortalise the deeds of the hero. *Od.* 22.343-53 only hints at this latter suggestion.

22. In Homer, Odysseus does not kill Iros in order not to alert the suitors to his strength. In Rossi's version, he shows compassion by recognising when his opponent is down and does not pursue him further; likewise, when on Scheria Euryalos in cowardly fashion hurls a spear at Odysseus after being defeated in a sword contest (a change from the Homeric wrestling match, presumably designed to foreshadow but vary from the later fight), Odysseus refrains from killing his opponent, at least in part because of the shame this would bring on his host.

23. Rossi's cinematographer, Aldo Giordani, appears from his credits to have been a journeyman worker (his best known efforts being the Trinity comic westerns). It therefore seems reasonable to attribute scenes such as this procession and the equally striking cremation of Elpenor on Circe's island with its parade of oars to the imagination of Rossi. Angelopoulos, whose work will be discussed later in this chapter, regularly incorporates in his films stately images of processions, such as funerals and weddings, indicating the impact of such events on the community in a similar manner to Rossi's.

24. For a reading of the *Odyssey* as a reactionary, aristocratic text, see Clark 1989. Contrast Rutherford 1986, tracing the hero's development from adventurer to conscious agent of his destiny.

25. This varies from Circe's advice that no one who hears them unwarned (*aidreiêi*) will escape (12.41) but that with adequate precautions Odysseus may hear the song and survive.

26. In *Ulysses*, Odysseus kills the suitors with the help of Telemachus; household servants are rarely seen assisting. In *L'Odissea*, Eumaios the swineherd and Philoitios the cowherd are given prominent roles in the fighting (as they are too in *Od.* 22.265-91), but the treacherous goatherd Melanthios is omitted. In effect, the massacre becomes a popular uprising against a decadent aristocracy.

27. The scriptwriters include Vittorio Bonicelli (*Garden of the Finzi-Continis*, 1970) and Fabio Carpi (*Homer: Portrait of the Artist as an Old Man (Nel profundo paese staniero)*, 1997). Rossi was also able to use actors such as Irene Pappas (Penelope); Bekim Fehmiu (Odysseus), who was a major star in Yugoslavia; Scilla Gabel, once a Sophia Loren look-alike and stand-in, but now, after plastic surgery, enjoying her own career (Helen); Juliette Mayniel (Circe); model Barbara Bach in her first screen role (Nausicaa); and even peplum stalwart, Mimmo Palmara, as Achilles. Polyphemus is played by Canadian strongman Samson Burke, perhaps best known for the lead role in *Three Stooges meet Hercules* (1962). The soundtrack is by Carlo Rustichelli, possibly the best known Italian film music composer, before Ennio Morricone. All this suggests the large investment that the European studios had made in the production.

28. Wyke 2002: 383; Joshel 2001.

29. The insertion of the common soldiers Vorenus and Pullo as major figures within the drama, however, harks back more to peplum heroes (such as Cottafavi's Curridius in *The Legions of Cleopatra*).

30. Burt 1998.

31. Bowman 2002.

32. Leone 1983: 167.

33. For information on *The Return of Ringo*, particularly in its Italian western context, see Hughes 2004: 29-39.

34. Ennio Morricone seems to have deliberately chosen a traditional Hollywood style for his music in this film, particularly by contrast with his well-known themes for Leone's and Corbucci's westerns.

35. Played by Pajarito ('little bird'), the stage name of Manuel Muñiz.

36. *The Return of Ringo* is not the only meeting between the Italian western and Western literature: *That Dirty Story of the West (Quella storia sporca nel West,* aka *Johnny Hamlet,* dir. Enzo Castellari, 1968) reminds the viewer that the stock revenge theme had already been popular in Shakespearian England.

37. On the Coens and their films, see Bergen 2000.

38. While 'con man' represents Odysseus *polytropos* ('cunning', 'shifty'), 'dandy' self-deprecatingly mocks the star attributes of the actor playing the role, George Clooney. For other Homeric names in the film, cf. Menelaus ('Pass the biscuits, Pappy') O'Daniel, governor of Mississipi and his political rival, Homer Stokes.

39. In 1913, Richard Burnett, a blind Kentuckian fiddler, provided the earliest known version entitled 'Farewell Song', but when interviewed by Charles Wolfe ('Man of Constant Sorrow – Richard Burnett's Story', *Old Time Music* 10 (Autumn 1973) 8) was unsure whether he was the composer or had learnt it from someone else.

40. Rutherford 1986: 148-9 imports Christian ideology by defining *polytlas* as 'the man of sorrows' in addition to the more Classical explanation as one 'who suffers yet finds the inner strength and wisdom to endure despite all his trials'. Everett McGill is actually much closer to Odysseus *polymechanos*, 'constant deviser of all sorts of schemes'.

41. Rob Content, Tim Kreider, Boyd White, review of *Oh Brother, Where Art Thou?* in *Film Quarterly* 55 (2001) 41-8.

42. Lucas 2007: 140.

43. Lucas 2007: 762-75, esp. 771-4.

44. *Contempt* 39.

45. *Contempt* 86: 'Fundamentally … Battista's taste was still that of the Italian producers of the time of D'Annunzio.' D'Annunzio was credited with writing the intertitles for *Cabiria,* although his actual participation in the film has been questioned. The incidents that Battista suggests might fit the peplum style as it later developed – for instance, Antinea appears in Cottafavi's *Hercules Conquers Atlantis.*

46. *Contempt* 144; 191: 'In Rheingold's interpretation … everything was debased to the level of a modern play, full of moralizings and psychologizings.'

47. 'A nice, vulgar read for a train journey' quoted in Phillip Lopate, *Totally, Tenderly, Tragically* (New York 1998), reprinted as the liner notes for the Criterion DVD of *Contempt* (2002).

48. *Contempt* 27: 'She had not, as I have already said, a really beautiful figure; and yet she appeared to have.'

49. Cruelly, in the film Javal is shown as having moved on to scriptwriting from the literary heights of the detective novel and to have been responsible for the box office success *Toto vs. Hercules.* His lack of inspiration is underlined by his desire to gain ideas from viewing other movies, earning the contemptuous reply from his wife: 'Use your own ideas instead of stealing them from everyone else.'

50. Prokosch claims that the *Odysssey* needs a German director, since Schliemann discovered Troy. Yet he clearly prefers scenes of naked starlets splashing in the waves more than Lang's static shots of Greek divine statues (a voyeurism treated ironically by Godard when he later shows a naked Bardot swimming at Capri). Still Lang, for all his depiction of gods as garden statuary, may be right in suggesting that man creates gods: Rossi effectively uses shots of Classical Greek statues and voice-overs to express divine conversation in his *Odissea*. Prokosch, by contrast, can only appreciate Greek culture by re-enacting the statue of the Discobolos, using a can of movie film as his discus.

51. The significance of this variation on a *bon mot* attributed to Goering (actually from a play by Hanns Johst) is not lost on Lang. However, the director, who had fled Nazi Germany, attributes the original use of the phrase to the Italian Fascists, with the suggestion that in Italy wealth is now replacing the revolver as the source of unbridled power.

52. Both a return to the quotation from Louis Lumière inscribed in the screening room in Cinecittà – 'Cinema is an invention without a future' – and a validation of Lang's verdict on the killing of the suitors: 'Death is no conclusion.'

53. The abbreviated film version distributed by Paramount (*The Adventures of Ulysses*) was never given a theatrical release in North America (Lucas 2007: 775).

54. Only Winkler 2007e: 46-7 shows awareness of Rossi's version and its remarkable virtues.

55. Staros is based on the Jewish captain Stein, a similar outsider in James Jones' 1962 novel. The change of ethnicity permits a generic Homeric connection rather than the novel's Wasp vs. non-Anglo Saxon conflict.

56. Tall makes his point clearer: 'Now, goddamit. The Admiral got up at dawn for this.' Cf. Winkler 2000: 204-6. A later Homeric reference is Private Dale's cruel declaration to a captured Japanese soldier that he will die, 'devoured by scavenging birds', echoing the opening of the *Iliad*, where the wrath of Achilles is described as sending many noble souls of heroes to Hades, but leaving their bodies to be devoured by dogs and all kind of birds (1.1-5). In addition, Dale's extraction of the gold teeth of a dead soldier may be seen as equivalent to the Homeric stripping the fallen of their armour and possessions.

57. The first line of Plato's *Crito*: 'Why have you come here at this time, Crito?'

58. The text of the last two lines is uncertain: Angelopoulos' script retains the manuscript text, while Jebb restores the metre by amending to *phôta ekbanta*.

59. 'The tourists in *O Megalexandros* are innocents, especially Lord Lancaster, who was related to Queen Victoria. He's an innocent, Byronic type, in love with Greece; but he is outside the responsibilities of power and has no real weight politically.' (Angelopoulos interviewed by Mitchell 1980 in Fainaru 2001: 29). Lord *Muncaster*, who was not in fact related to Queen Victoria, was released; the most prominent of those kidnapped and murdered was the English-born, Athenian-domiciled lawyer Edward Lloyd. It is hardly surprising, however, to discover that Angelopoulos is not historically accurate – he films dramas, not documentaries.

60. Cf. Myrsiades 1975.

61. *The 300 Spartans* concludes with an epilogue recording the Greek successes at Salamis and Plataea: 'But it was more than a victory for Greece, it was a stirring example for free people throughout the world.' At this point, the film displays not the 1955 monument to Thermopylae, but a more universal monument to fallen Greek soldiers in Athens, the Tomb of the Unknown Soldier in front of Parliament Buildings in Constitution (Syntagma) Square. Note also the credit for a military advisor (Major Cleanthis Damianos) along with an historical advisor (Paul Nord, *aka* Nikos Laides).

62. An hilarious account of the producer's complete lack of experience and the general incompetence of the production can be found at http://www.edwardjayepstein.com/Iliad2.htm and subsequent links. Roger Corman was also shooting his shoe-string *Atlas* (1960) on location in Greece at this time, originally with Greek financial backing, involving Greeks in cast and crew, and certainly with enough official assistance to use ancient sites as backdrops (Nisbet 2006: 13-15).

63. Hamilakis 2002 and Van Steen 2005 offer excellent studies of this dilemma. Prometheus and Antigone, as tragic characters who defied authority, were particularly popular subjects for dramatic productions on the Greek prison islands.

64. The Parthenon marbles are a striking example of the clash between Western European and Greek values. While the British Museum claims that it is protecting sculptures that form part of the Western heritage, the Greek government continues to press for their return as inseparable from their geographical origin.

65. A train shunts through Thessaloniki repeatedly in *The Weeping Meadow* marking the passage of time; the wedding across the river that is the boundary between Greece and Albania is perhaps the most striking scene in *The Suspended Step of the Stork* (1991).

66. A Greek version of Romeo and Juliet, written by Spyridon Peresiades in 1894 and also the subject of the first Greek feature film (1914, now lost).

67. The director Takos Mouzenidis had already linked Orestes and Pylades with the EAM resistance (both to the Axis occupiers and the returning Royalists) by dressing the two in peasant-style dark jackets over white shirt and trousers for the Epidaurus performance of 1969. Supporters of the colonels in the National Theatre ensured that these costumes were replaced (Van Steen 2001: 158-60).

68. 'I couldn't really tell you the significance of the hand pulled out of Thessaloniki harbour' (interview with Toubiana and Strauss 1988, in Fainaru 2001: 63).

69. *The Travelling Players* begins with a sequence which changes the temporal location from 1952 to 1939: speakers announce that Metaxas and Goebbels are about to visit on their way to Olympia. The connection between an empty reverence from antiquity and fascism is thus once again emphasised.

70. 'Yes, but with a difference. Usually, in road movies, the characters roam from one place to another without a definite purpose. In my films, these journeys always have a goal.' (Angelopoulos interviewed by Fainaru in 1999 in Fainaru 2001: 136).

71. For the Homeric and post-Homeric (e.g. Dante's) depictions of Odysseus' travels in *Suspended Step*, see Horton 1997a: 162-3, 172-4.

72. Angelopoulos is presumably thinking of Baudelaire's thoroughly disillusioned 'Voyage to Cythera' (in *Flowers of Evil*, 1857).

73. If Homer's Argos is at least twenty years old, Spyros' dog would need to be over thirty years old, having survived from the end of the Civil War in 1949 to the amnesty granted by the Greek government in 1981. Rather, Spyros is creating his own imaginary country, as does the old man in Seferis' 'Return of the Exile' (1938, from *Logbook I,* Athens 1940).

74. Alexander's office is shown as decorated with posters for Angelopoulos' films, making the connection quite explicit.

75. The classification is Angelopoulos' own: see Schulz 1999 in Fainaru 2001: 117.

76. The choice of the Manaki brothers is significant not only because they were pioneers of film in the region, but also because they reflect the political changes of the early twentieth century. Vlachs (speakers of Aromanian, rather than Greek or Slavic languages) born in the Ottoman Empire, they set up a studio and then a cinema in Monastir (modern Bitola, Republic of Macedonia) which was incorporated into Serbia after 1912, although it was under Bulgarian occupation during the First and Second World Wars (Yanaki Manaki was exiled to Plovdiv/Philipopolis in Bulgaria in 1916). Yanaki (Greek: Yannis Manakias) died in Thessaloniki in 1954, his younger brother Milton (Greek: Miltiades) in Bitola in 1964. Their films were originally mainly deposited in the Yugoslav State Archive but transferred to the Cinémathèque of the Yugoslav Socialist Republic of Macedonia in 1978. Other material exists in the Romanian Film Archive. In short, their life and works are a *Balkan* story, rather than corresponding to a single nationalist narrative.

77. Since filming in a battle zone was obviously out of the question, the relevant scenes were shot in Mostar (Bosnia) and Vukovar (Krajina/Croatia): Angelopoulos interviewed by Andrew Horton, 1995, in Horton 1997b: 103.

78. George Seferis, *Collected Poems*, trans. Edmund Keelley and Phillip Sherrard, rev. edn (Princeton, NJ 1995) 6.

79. Horton 1997a: 35.

80. Discussed in Winkler 2005b: 396-8.

81. Death is itself a journey as the opening scene of the film indicates: in 1954 Yanaki Manaki collapses while photographing a blue ship sailing from Thessaloniki harbour. This is almost certainly another Odyssean reference: 'Death will come to me from the sea, perfectly gentle in this fashion, and it will slay me bowed down by sleek old age' (*Od.* 23.281-3).

82. Angelopoulos (Horton 1997b: 107) attributes this to Seferis. I am grateful for the director's response: 'My phrase, "the first thing God created is the journey" is a personal variation of the Seferis verse.' The Seferis allusion is to 'Stratis Thalassinos Among the Agapanthi', written in South Africa in 1942 (published in *Logbook II*, Alexandria 1944) whose final stanza begins: 'The first thing God made is love / then comes blood / and the thirst for blood ... The first thing God made is the long journey; / the house there is waiting / with its blue smoke / with its aged dog / waiting for the homecoming so that it can die' (trans. Edmund Keeley and Philip Sherrard). The reference to Argos recalls the scene discussed above in *Voyage to Cythera*.

83. Quoting T.S. Eliot, last line of *East Coker* (London, 1940), Number Two of the *Four Quartets* (London, 1943). In Sarajevo, the film archivist Ivo Levy recites Rainer Maria Rilke's 'Ich lebe mein Leben' (1899; published as *Das Stundenbuch, Von mönchischen Leben* 2, 1905) to signal his desire to complete his work on the undeveloped films even in the face of death.

84. *Od.* 5.156-8: 'Every day sitting on the stones at the water's edge / And shivering his heart with tears and groans and suffering (*algesi*) / He looked out over the barren sea while shedding tears.' A.'s personal nostalgia also takes him to Costantia, city of his childhood, to experience once again the New Year's festivities from 1945 until his family's emigration to Greece in 1950.

85. Horton (1997a: 194) interprets Naomi's statement that she will wait for A. after they dance in Sarajevo as transformation into Penelope, but his refusal to declare that he will return suggests that she remains the potential bride, Nausicaa, not Odysseus' wife. More ambiguous is her first meeting with A. where she declares 'I'm looking for my father. ... Your face looks familiar as if I'd known you for years. ... Tell him I waited for him. Tell him we're expecting him.' This suggests Naomi is also playing the role of Telemachus at this point.

86. Theo Angelopoulos has confirmed by e-mail correspondence that he composed the monologue: 'The text however does cite Homer indirectly, using hypothetical dialogue ("when I return") in the famous Ulysses-Penelope meeting after the return of Ulysses to Ithaca.' In an interview with Andrew Horton in 1995 (Horton 1997b: 107), the director indicates that he was interested in poetry and its composition long before he became a filmmaker. In particular he cites the influence of Cavafy, Seferis, Odysseus Elytis, Eliot, and Rilke, the poetry of at least three of whom features in *Odysseus' Gaze*.

87. A three-minute sequence showing Odysseus making his way out of the sea, staring at the camera and asking at what land he has arrived (an atopic Odyssey) was filmed by Angelopoulos using a Lumière camera for his segment of *Lumière et compagnie* (1995).

88. Winkler (2005b) 398-400 has a similar reading of this final scene.

89. http://grhomeboy.wordpress.com/2007/02/16/a-celebrated-director-is-left-out-in-the-cold/; *Variety* (June 19, 2007) reports that Filmstiftung, the German film funding organisation, has since awarded the project $1,000,000.

90. *Variety* (12 September 2005) suggests that it would achieve only modest art-house success in France and abroad.

5. Alexander the Hero

1. *Book of Arda Wiraz* 1-7.

2. Perhaps the most influential study in modern times is Tarn 1948, suggesting that Alexander had risen above national concerns to promoting the ideal of a unity of mankind in his kingdom. Bosworth 1988 offers an acerbic antidote to this view. There are numerous other biographies, including that by the consultant to the Oliver Stone film, Robin Lane Fox (Lane Fox 1973). Novels include Mary Renault's *Fire from Heaven* (1969), *The Persian Boy* (1972), and *Funeral Games* (1981); and Valerio Massimo Manfredi's trilogy: *Il figlio del sogno* (1998; English translation: *Child of a Dream*, 2001); *Le sabbie di Amon* (1998; *Sands of Ammon*, 2001); *Il confine del mondo* (1998; *Ends of the Earth*, 2001). There is an extensive listing of Alexander novels in Reames 2007.

3. Spelled in this chapter according to the usage of each production's credits (Rhoxane/Roxane/Roxanne).

4. Cf. *The Last Days of Pompeii* (1935) discussed in Chapter 3; *The Sign of the Cross* (dir. Cecil B. DeMille, 1932; re-released in 1944); *Quo Vadis* (dir. Mervyn LeRoy, 1951).

5. Both are based on well-known novels by Jack London and Robert Penn Warren: London provided a critique of the Nietzschean superman, while Warren's subject was closely modelled on Louisiana governor, Huey Long. Rossen (originally Rosen) because of his Jewish extraction was particularly sensitive to the racist aspects of London's social Darwinism, as were his producers, the Warner brothers: Tony Williams, 'From Novel to Film' in Fumento and Williams 1998: xxi-xxv.

6. Rossen had in the meantime directed *Mambo* (1954) in Italy for Dino De Laurentiis. Although the scriptwriters were mainly Italian (including Ennio De Concini), the story of a shopgirl trying to escape her surroundings and the strong gay subtext (yet another variation on the theme of 'passing' as something one is not that Rossen frequently explored, e.g. in *They Came to Cordura*, 1959) are likely to have appealed to the director.

7. Cf. Eddie the hustler's inability to save the crippled girl in *The Hustler* (1961) and Vincent's sexual jealousy in *Lilith* (1964); Casty 1966.

8. Contrast Rossen's statement to the House Un-American Activities Committee, 7 May 1953, which is remarkable for its denial of his own values: 'I don't think after two years of thinking, that *any one individual can ever indulge himself in the luxury of individual morality* or pit it against what I feel today very strongly is the security and safety of this nation' (my emphasis).

9. Alexander's fine words to his mutinous troops at the Hyphasis (Arrian,

Anabasis of Alexander 5.26.4); his weary soldiers did not share his heroic code and would have preferred an inglorious death in old age back in their homeland.

10. Plutarch, *Alexander* 70. Bosworth 1988: 156-7 points out that this did not imply a fusion of the Iranian and Macedonian aristocracies, since the Persian male officers in Alexander's court were left out of the process.

11. Cf. Nisbet 2006: 93-5, who admires the literate script (100) but finds it too up-market, 'a self-regardingly "clever" film that prefers to tell (and ideally to lecture) than to show' (96).

12. Demosthenes is portrayed as if he were Churchill, ready to shed men and blood in defence of Athens, while Aeschines is the Chamberlain-like appeaser, echoing Philip's praise for the blessings of peace as city after city falls into Macedonian hands.

13. Cf. Winkler 2001 on the depiction of Rome as anti-Semitic.

14. Crucifixion: Winkler 2007c: 183-7 and Urbainczyk 2004: 107-9; Kirk Douglas and Zionism: Winkler 2007c: 166-8.

15. Winkler 1995.

16. Cf. Pomeroy 2005.

17. For trenchant Japanese criticism of the samurai system, see Masaki Kobayashi's *Harakiri* (aka *Seppuku*, 1962) or, more recently, Yôji Yamada's *The Twilight Samurai* (*Tasogare Seibei*, 2002). On the film's erasure of Japanese treatment of its own indigenous Ainu in this period, see Medak-Saltzman 2006.

18. *Guardian*, 8 January 2005.

19. For a brief summary of this topic see Bosworth 1988: 278-90.

20. Pomeroy 2005: 112.

21. The director's cut of the DVD version reduces this binary narrative by showing more of Alexander's life in Macedon in flashbacks during the story after Gaugamela at the risk of reducing narrative clarity.

22. Stone's own tense relationship with his demanding Jewish father and Catholic French-Canadian mother is well documented (e.g. Kagan 2000: 13-16).

23. *Guardian*, 6 January 2005, quoting Oliver Stone at the UK premiere as suggesting that the lack of box-office takings in the US was due to 'raging fundamentalism in morality'. On reactions to Alexander's homosexuality, see Nisbet 2006: 120-3.

24. See n. 2 above. Stone acknowledges the influence of Renault in his commentary on the director's cut.

25. The line 'to the strongest' is preserved from Rossen's film, but there is no explanation why some interpret this as 'to Craterus'. As seen in the examples from *The 300 Spartans* discussed in Chapter 3, ancient Greek does not travel well: *tôi kraterôi* / *Kraterôi* is a linguistic ambiguity ('to the stronger' / 'to Craterus'), but requires knowledge of the language to be appreciated.

26. One may only speculate what the Australian director Baz Luhrmann might have achieved in bringing Valerio Massimo Manfredi's novels onto the screen. Luhrmann's statement that 'Alexander was the first recorded cult of personality' (http://news.bbc.co.uk/2/hi/entertainment/2149048.stm) and his employment of Ted Tally (*Silence of the Lambs*) to produce the screenplay might suggest above all an interesting emphasis on Alexander's *image*.

27. Other Alexanders include a six-year-old child on a journey to find his father in a mythical Germany (*Landscape in a Mist*) and the dying poet of *Eternity and a Day* (which begins with his mother inviting Alexander as a child to 'go to the Island and go diving to look at the ancient city')

28. Fans of Xena have seen traces of Alexander in her depiction and in her progress from Greece through Asia and Egypt: Gregory Swenson, 'Alexander the Great: Blueprint for Xena?' (http://whoosh.org/issue4/richan.html). Perhaps Semiramis should be considered as a stronger female role model for a modern heroine.

29. Don Neville, 'Alessandro nell'Indie', *Grove Music Online* ed. L. Macy (http://www.grovemusic.com).

30. There is a detailed synopsis of the film at:
http://www.pothos.org/alexander.asp?paraID=72&keyword_id=19&title=Sikander%20(1941

31. Ashish Rajadhyaksha, Paul Willeman, *Encyclopedia of Indian Cinema*[2] (Oxford 1999) s.v. Sikandar. The Shakespearean style of *Sikandar*, already seen in Rossen's script, may be as much due to Modi's experience managing a theatre company that staged Shakespeare in Urdu (Sanjit Narwekar, *Directory of Indian Film-makers and Films* (Westport, CT 1994) s.v. Modi, Sohrab Merwanjee) as to the epic form of the film.

32. http://boxofficeindia.com/40-49.htm

33. Information obtained from 'Upperstall.com – a Better View of Indian Cinema' (http://www.upperstall.com/films/sikander.html).

34. Later scriptwriter for such thoughtful animation projects as *Perfect Blue* (1998), *Millennium Actress* (2001), *Kino's Journey* (TV series, 2003 – which includes two episodes set around a gladiatorial contest in a Roman-style colosseum), and *Steamboy* (2004).

35. Samsung representative's remarks at a news conference for the launch of the series (included as an extra on the first DVD of the series).

36. The Adult Swim section of the Cartoon Network in the USA and Australasia and Bravo in the UK, generally playing after 10 pm nightly.

37. Ben Hur: 'Days of Thunder', Season 3, Episode 9; 'A Star is Burns', 6.18; 'City of New York vs Homer Simpson', 9.1; 'Simpsons Bible Stories', 10.18; 'Little Big Mom', 11.10. Trojan horse: 'Lemon of Troy', 6.24; *Odyssey*: 'Tales from the Public Domain', 13.8.

38. Akira: 'When Flanders Failed', 3.3; 'Children of a Lesser Clod', 12.20. Godzilla: 'Treehouse of Horror VI', 3.7; 'Canine Mutiny', 8.20; 'Mayored to the Mob', 10.9; 'Thirty Minutes over Tokyo', 10.23.

39. Cf. Diogenes' words in *Reign,* Episode 5: 'The devil king of destruction can be a great king of creation'.

40. The meeting in Babylon of Alexander, readying his forces to invade Arabia (that is, at the point where the historical Alexander took ill and died), with the young Euclid, who is in possession of the Platohedron, makes this clear. Once again, a new world succeeds the old.

41. Cf. Otomo's *Steamboy*, in which the discovery of 'heavy water' allows a remarkable increase in steam power, for instance sufficient for powered flight.

42. Plutarch, *Alexander* 4.2, from observation of Lysippus' statues of the king.

43. One wonders if the name Cassandra is inspired by the rumour (Arrian *Anabasis* 7.27.1) that Aristotle and the Macedonian Cassander were responsible for poisoning the king. Aristotle's nephew, Callisthenes, did accompany Alexander, but as court historian, before coming to a bad end.

44. Interview of Hiroshi Aramata by Ken Sakamura, *Tronware* 66 (2000) 14-21; English translation:
http://tronweb.super-nova.co.jp/aramatainterview_tw66.html.

6. 'It's a Man's, Man's, Man's World' – except for Buffy and Xena

1. Nisbet 2006: vii-viii.

2. Of course, I may be embarrassed by the appearance of *Alex* and *30*. And, one day, heroic nudity could come back into fashion.

3. Cf. Jonathan Denby's review (*New Yorker*, 2 April 2007): ' "300" is a political fable that uneasily engages the current moment.'

4. Paul Arendt reviewing *300* for the BBC, 27 March 2007 (http://www.bbc.co.uk/films/2007/03/19/300_2007_review.shtml): 'taken on its own terms – as Greek myth meets Looney Tunes – it's kind of a masterpiece.' This seems to me to undervalue the mythological content of Looney Tunes (Wile E. Coyote as existential Sisyphus) and its political import as well (Chuck Jones' *Duck Dodgers in the 24½th Century* (1953) not only introduces Marvin the Martian as the prototype Roman, but, through the ruinous conclusion to his conflict with Daffy Duck, reminds the viewer of the doctrine of mutual assured destruction that restrained the two superpowers at the time it was made).

5. *Asterix and Obelix vs. Caesar* (1999); *Asterix and Obelix: Mission Cleopatra* (2002).

6. E.g. Italian-based, internationally funded television mini-series *Imperium*: *Augustus* (dir. Roger Young, 2001), *Julius Caesar* (dir. Uli Edel, 2002) and *Imperium*: *Nero* (dir. Paul Marcus, 2004).

7. *Variety*, 1 February 2007.

Filmography

Films and television series discussed in some detail in this book.

Alexander the Great, dir., script: Robert Rossen (USA 1956: United Artists)
    runtime: 136 min
Alexander, dir. Oliver Stone (2004; director's cut DVD 2005; Alexander Revisited
    DVD 2007: Warner Bros)
    script: Oliver Stone, Christopher Kyle, Laeta Kalogridis
    runtime: 173 min (165 director's cut; 220 extended cut)
Buffy the Vampire Slayer, dir. Fran Kuzui (USA 1992: Twentieth Century Fox)
    script: Joss Whedon
    runtime: 86 minutes
Buffy the Vampire Slayer, directors include: Joss Whedon, James A. Contner,
    David Solomon, David Grossman, Michael Gershman, Seth Green (USA
    1997-2003: Twentieth Century Fox Television)
    script writers include: Joss Whedon, Marti Noxon, Jane Espenson, David
    Furey, Douglas Petrie
    runtime: 144 episodes
Cabiria, dir. Giovanni Pastrone (Italy 1914: Itala Film)
    script: Giovanni Pastrone, Gabriele D'Annunzio
    runtime: 181 minutes (2006 restoration)
Contempt (*Le Mépris*), dir. Jean-Luc Godard (France/Italy 1963: Compagnia Cine-
    matografica Champion, Les Films Concordia, Rome Paris Films)
    script: Jean-Luc Godard
    runtime: 103 minutes
Gli ultimi giorni di Pompeii (*Last Days of Pompeii*), dir. Mario Bonnard, Sergio
    Leone (Italy 1959: Cinematografica Associati)
    script: Sergio Corbucci, Ennio De Concini, Luigi Emmanuele, Sergio Leone,
    Duccio Tessari
    runtime: 100 minutes
Hercules and the Queen of Lydia (*Ercole e la regina di Lidia*; US: *Hercules
    Unchained*), dir. Pietro Francisci, (uncredited) Mario Bava (Italy 1959:
    Galatea Film, Lux Compagnie)
    script: Ennio De Concini, Pietro Francisci
    runtime: 105 minutes
Hercules at the Centre of the Earth (*Ercole al centro della terra*), dir. Mario Bava
    (Italy 1961: SpA Cinematografica)
    script: Mario Bava, Alessandro Continenza, Franco Prosperi, Duccio Tessari
    runtime: 91 minutes (*Hercules in the Haunted World*: 81 minutes)
Hercules Conquers Atlantis (*Ercole alla conquista di Atlantide*), dir. Vittorio
    Cottafavi (Italy 1961: SpA Cinematografica)
    script: Alessandro Continenza, Vittorio Cottafavi, Duccio Tessari
    runtime: 101 minutes (*Hercules and the Captive Women*: 93 minutes)

Filmography

The Labours of Hercules (*Le fatiche di Ercole*; US: *Hercules*), dir. Pietro Francisci (Italy 1958: Galatea Film, Oscar Film, Lux Compagnie)
script: Ennio De Concini, Pietro Francisci, Gaio Frattini
runtime: 107 minutes

Landscape in the Mist (*Topio stin Omichli*), dir. Theo Angelopoulos (Greece 1988: Basic Cinematografica)
script: Theo Angelopoulos, with Tonino Guerra, Thanassis Valtinos
runtime: 126 minutes

Last Days of Pompeii, dir. Ernest B. Schoedsack (USA 1935: RKO Radio Pictures)
script: Ruth Rose, from story by James Ashmore Creelman and Melville Baker
runtime: 96 minutes

Megalexandros, dir. Theo Angelopoulos (Greece 1980: Greek Film Centre)
script: Theo Angelopoulos, with Petros Markaris
runtime: 165 minutes

L'Odissea (*Odyssey*), dir. Franco Rossi, Mario Bava, Piero Schivazappa (Italy/Yugoslavia/France/Germany 1968: Dino De Laurentiis Cinematografica; RAI; Jadran Film: ORT; Bavaria Film TV)
script: Franco Rossi, Giampero Bona, Vittorio Bonicelli, Fabio Carpi, Luciano Condignola, Mario Prosperi, Renzo Russo
runtime: 640 minutes (8 episodes)

Oh Brother, Where Art Thou? dir. Joel and Ethan Coen (USA 2000: Touchstone Pictures)
script: Joel and Ethan Coen
runtime: 107 minutes

Reign: the Conqueror (*Arekusanda Senki*), dir. Yoshinori Kanemori (Japan 1999: Mad House) English language version 2003: TokyoPop
script: Sadayuki Murai from novels by Hiroshi Aramata; character designs: Peter Chung
runtime: *c.* 300 min (13 episodes)

The Return of Ringo (*Il ritorno di Ringo*), dir. Duccio Tessari (Italy/Spain 1965: Rizzoli Film, Balcázar Producciones Cinematográficas)
script: Duccio Tessari, Fernando Di Leo, Alfonso Balcázar
runtime: 96 minutes

The Revenge of Hercules (*La vendetta di Ercole*), dir. Vittorio Cottafavi (Italy 1960: Achille Piazzi Produzioni Cinematografica; CFFP; Produzione Gianni Fuchs)
script: Mario Baldi, Mario Ferrari, Duccio Tessari
runtime: 98 minutes (US: *Goliath and the Dragon*, 87 minutes)

Scipio Africanus (*Scipio l'africano*), dir. Carmine Gallone (Italy 1937: Consorzione 'Scipio l'Africano', ENIC)
script: Carmine Gallone, Camillo Mariani Dell'Aguillara, Sebastiano Luciani
runtime: 117 minutes

Sikandar, dir. Sohrab Modi (India 1941: Minerva Movietone)
script: Surdashan
runtime: 146 minutes

Spartaco (*Spartacus*), dir. Giovanni Vidali (Italy 1913)
runtime: 88 minutes

Spartaco (US: *Sins of Rome*), dir. Riccardo Freda (Italy 1953; Consorzio 'Spartaco', API Film, Rialto Film)
script: Maria Bory, Jean Ferry, Gino Visentini
runtime: 120 minutes (US: 71 minutes)

Filmography

Travelling Players (*O Thiasos*), dir. Theo Angelopoulos (Greece 1975: Papalios
  Productions)
  script: Theo Angelopoulos
  runtime: 230 minutes
Ulysses (*Ulisse*) dir. Mario Camerini (Italy 1954: Lux Film)
  script: Franco Brusati, Mario Camerini, Ennio De Concini, Hugh Gray, Ben
    Hecht, Ivo Perilli, Irwin Shaw
  runtime: 94 minutes
Ulysses' Gaze (*To Vlemma tou Odyssea*), dir. Theo Angelopoulos (Greece 1995:
  Greek Film Centre);
  script: Theo Angelopoulos, with Tonino Guerra, Petros Markaris
  runtime: 180 minutes
Voyage to Cythera (*Taxidi sta Kithira*), dir. Theo Angelopoulos (Greece 1983: Greek
  Film Centre)
  script: Theo Angelopoulos, with Thanasis Valtinos, Tonino Guerra
  runtime: 137 minutes
The Warriors, dir. Walter Hill (USA 1979: Paramount Pictures)
  script: Walter Shaber, Walter Hill
  runtime: 89 minutes (ultimate director's cut DVD 2005: 93 minutes)
The Weeping Meadow (*Trilogia I: To Livadi pou dakryzei*), dir. Theo Angelopoulos
  (Greece 2004: Hellenic Radio and Television)
  script: Theo Angelopoulos, with Tonino Guerra, Petros Markaris, Giorgio Silvani
  runtime: 185 minutes

Bibliography

All URLs were correct at the time this book went to press.

Aziza, C. (1998), 'Le mot et la chose', in C. Aziza, ed., *Le peplum: l'Antiquité au cinema = CinémAction* 89.4: 7-11.

Bergen, R. (2000), *The Coen Brothers*, London.

Bosworth, A.B. (1988), *Conquest and Empire: the Reign of Alexander the Great*, Cambridge.

Bowman, L. (2002), 'Buffy the Vampire Slayer: the Greek Hero Revisited', http://web.uvic.ca/~lbowman/buffy/buffythehero.html.

Bulwer-Lytton, E. (1834), *The Last Days of Pompeii*, London.

Burt, R. (1998), *Unspeakable Shaxxxspeares: Kiddie Culture, Queer Theory, and Loser Criticism*, New York.

Cammarota, M.D. (1987), *Il cinema peplum,* Rome.

Casty, A. (1966), 'The Films of Robert Rossen', *Film Quarterly* 20.2: 3-12.

Clark, M. (1989), 'Adorno, Derrida, and the *Odyssey*: A Critique of Center and Periphery', *boundary 2*, 16.2/3: 109-28.

Clauss, J.J. (1999), 'Descent into Hell – John Ford's "The Searchers" ', *Journal of Popular Film and Television*, 27.3: 2-17.

Coleman, K. (2005), 'The Pedant Goes to Hollywood: The Role of the Academic Consultant', in Winkler 2005a: 45-52.

Content, R., Tim Kreider and Boyd White (2001), review of *Oh Brother, Where Art Thou?* in *Film Quarterly* 55: 41-8.

Craigo-Snell, S. (2006), 'What Would Buffy Do? Feminist Ethics and Epistemic Violence', http://www.ejumpcut.org/archive/jc48.2006/BuffyEthics/index.html.

Cyrino, M. (2005), *Big Screen Rome*, Malden, MA.

Dalby, A. (1992), 'Greeks Abroad: Social Organization and Food among the Ten Thousand', *Journal of Hellenic Studies* 112: 16-30.

De Fornari, O. (1984), *Tutti i film di Sergio Leone*, Milan.

Dyer, R. (1997), *White*, London.

Elley, D. (1984), *The Epic Film,* London.

Fainaru, D., ed. (2001), *Theo Angelopoulos: Interviews.* Jackson, MI.

Farrell, J. (2001), *Latin Language and Latin Literature*, Cambridge.

Fitton, J.L. (2007), '*Troy* and the Role of the Historical Advisor', in Winkler 2007d: 99-106.

Frayling, C. (2005), *Once Upon a Time in Italy: the Westerns of Sergio Leone*, Los Angeles.

Fumento, R. and A. Williams, eds (1998), *Jack London's* The Sea Wolf: *a Screenplay by Robert Rossen*, Carbondale, IL.

Ghigi, G. (1977), 'Come si spiegano le fortune dei pepla su cui sembra si ritorni a puntare', *Cineforum* 17.12: 733-46.

Ghose, I. (2000), review of Burt (1998), *Early Modern Literary Studies* 6.2. 11.1-7.

Goodrich, P. (2003), 'Distrust Quotations in Latin', *Critical Inquiry* 29: 193-215.

Bibliography

Grobel, L. (1984), 'Playboy Interview (with Joan Collins)', *Playboy* 31.4: 55-70.

Gubar, S. (1996), 'Saphistries', in Ellen Greene, ed., *Re-Reading Sappho: Reception and Transmission*, Berkeley/Los Angeles: 199-217.

Günsberg, M. (2005), *Italian Cinema: Gender and Genre*, Basingstoke.

Hamilakis, Y. (2002), ' "The Other Parthenon": Antiquity and National Memory at Micronisos', *Journal of Modern Greek Studies* 20: 307-38.

Hedrick, D.K. (2000), review of Burt (1998), *Shakespeare Quarterly* 51.3: 390-3.

Hopkins, K. and M. Beard (2005), *The Colosseum*, Cambridge, MA.

Hornblower, S. (2004), 'This was Decided (*edoxe tauta*): The Army as *polis in* Xenophon's *Anabasis* and Elsewhere', in Robin Lane Fox, ed., *The Long March: Xenophon and the Ten Thousand*, New Haven, CT: 243-63.

Hornick, A. (2007), *Buffyology: an Academic Buffy Studies and Whedonverse Bibliography*, http://www.alysa316.com/Buffyology, updated 17 July 2007.

Horton, A. (1997a), *The Films of Theo Angelopoulos: a Cinema of Contemplation*, Princeton.

Horton, A. (1997b), *The Last Modernist: the Films of Theo Angelopoulos*, Trowbridge, Wilts.

Hughes, H. (2004), *Once Upon a Time in the Italian West*, London/New York.

Jenkyns, R. (2002), review of Kaveney 2001, *Prospect* 71, http://www.prospect-magazine.co.uk/article_details.php?id=4258.

Joshel, S.R. (2001), '*I Claudius*: Projection and Imperial Soap Opera', in Joshel, Malamud, McGuire 2001: 119-61.

Joshel, S.R., M. Malamud and D.T. McGuire, eds (2001), *Imperial Projections: Ancient Rome in Modern Popular Culture*, Baltimore, MD.

Kagan, N. (2000), *The Cinema of Oliver Stone*[2], New York.

Kaveney, R., ed. (2001), *Reading the Vampire Slayer*, London.

Koven, M.J. (2006), *La Dolce Morte: Vernacular Cinema and the Italian* Giallo *Film*, Lanham, MD.

Landry, M. (1996), ' "Which Way is America?": Americanism and the Italian Western', *boundary 2*, 23.1: 35-59.

Lane Fox, R. (1973), *Alexander the Great*, London.

Legrand, G. (1963), review of *Hercule à la conquête de l'Atlantide*, *Positif* 50-2.

Leone, S. (1983), 'To John Ford from One of his Pupils, with Love', in *Corriere della Sera*, 20 August 1983; translated in Frayling 2005: 167-9.

Lowe, N. (2004), 'Beware Geeks bearing Gifts', *Times Literary Supplement* 5279 (4 June): 18-19.

Lucas, T. (2007), *Mario Bava: All the Colors of the Dark*, Cincinnati, OH.

Malamud, M. and D.T. McGuire, Jr. (2001), 'Living like Romans in Las Vegas: The Roman World at Caesars Palace', in Joshel, Malamud and McGuire, 2001: 249-69.

McClelland, B.A. (2006), *Slayers and their Vampires: A Cultural History of Killing the Dead*, Ann Arbor.

Medak-Saltzman, D.F. (2006), 'Dances with Samurai', abstract of a paper presented at the annual meeting of the American Studies Association 2006 (http://www.allacademic.com/meta/p114137_index.html).

Mitchell, A. (1980), 'Animating Dead Space and Dead Time: *Megalexandros*', *Sight and Sound*, Winter 1980/81, reprinted in Fainaru (2001) 28-32.

Moravia, A. (1955), *Contempt*, trans. Angus Davidson (= *Il Disprezzo,* Milan 1954), London.

Moullet, L. (1961), *Cahiers de cinéma* review of *La Vengeance de Hercule*, reprinted in Pierpaolo Loffreda, ed., *L'éta dell' oro: cinema italiano 1960-1964* (Pesaro 2001) 124-5.

142

Bibliography

Murray, O. (2004), 'Introduction', E. Bulwer-Lytton, *Athens: its Rise and Fall,* London: 1-5.

Myrsiades, L.S. (1975), 'Legend in the Theatre: Alexander the Great and the Karaghiozis Text', *Educational Theatre Journal* 17.3: 387-94.

Nisbet, G. (2006), *Ancient Greece in Film and Popular Culture,* Bristol.

Nussbaum, G.B. (1997), *The Ten Thousand: A Study in Social Organization and Action in Xenophon's* Anabasis, Leiden.

Pomeroy, A.J. (2005), 'The Vision of a Fascist Rome in *Gladiator*', in Winkler 2005a: 111-23.

Raval, S. and Elisabeth Krimmer (2002), ' "Digging the Undead": Death and Desire in *Buffy*', in Wilcox and Lavery 2002: 153-64.

Reames, M.R. (2007), 'Beyond Renault: Alexander in Fiction 1920-Present', http://myweb.unomaha.edu/~mreames/Beyond_Renault/list.html

Reardon, B.P., ed. (1989), *Collected Ancient Greek Novels,* Berkeley/Los Angeles.

Riess, J. (2004), *What Would Buffy Do: The Vampire Slayer as Spiritual Guide,* San Francisco.

Rogers, B. and W. Scheidel (2004), 'Driving Stakes, Driving Cars: California Car Culture, Sex and Identity in *BtVS*', http://slayageonline.com/PDF/rogers_scheidel.pdf

Rutherford, R. (1986), 'The Philosophy of the *Odyssey*', *Journal of Hellenic Studies* 106: 145-62.

Schulz, G. (1999), 'I Shoot the Way I Breathe: *Eternity and a Day*', interview with Theo Angelopoulos in *Der Zeit*, February 1999, reprinted in Fainaru 2001: 117-22.

Siclier, J. (1962), 'L'âge du péplum', *Les Cahiers du cinéma* 131: 26-38.

Solomon, J. (2001), *Ancient World in the Cinema*[2], New Haven, CT.

Solomon, J. (2005), 'Gladiator from Screenplay to Screen', in Winkler 2005a: 1-15.

South, J.B., ed. (2003) Buffy the Vampire Slayer *and Philosophy: Fear and Trembling in Sunnydale*, Chicago, IL.

Sutherland, J. (2006), obituary of Mickey Spillane, *Guardian*, 18 July.

Tarn, W.W. (1948), *Alexander the Great*, 2 vols, Cambridge.

Toubiana S. and Frédéric Strauss (1988), '*Landscape in the Mist*', interview with Theo Angelopoulos, *Les Cahiers du cinéma* 413 (1988), reprinted in Fainaru 2001: 60-5.

Urbainczyk, T. (2004), *Spartacus*, London.

Van Steen, G. (2001), 'Playing by the Censors' Rules? Classical Drama Revived under the Greek Junta (1967-1974)', *Journal of the Hellenic Diaspora* 27: 133-94.

Van Steen, G. (2005), 'Forgotten Theater, Theater of the Forgotten: Classical Tragedy on Modern Greek Prison Islands', *Journal of Modern Greek Studies* 23: 335-95.

Vukanović, T.P. (1959), 'The Vampire', *Journal of the Gypsy Lore Society*, 3rd ser., 39: 44-55.

Walker, B. (2007), 'The Many Faces of Hercules at Tony's Drive-in Theater', http://www.briansdriveintheater.com/hercules.html.

Waquet, F. (2001), *Latin or the Empire of a Sign,* trans. J. Howe, London.

Wilcox, R.V. and D. Lavery, eds (2002), *Fighting the Forces: What's at Stake in Buffy the Vampire Slayer*, Lanham, MD.

Winkler, J.J. (1985), *Auctor & Actor: A Narratological Reading of Apuleius's* The Golden Ass, Berkeley/Los Angeles.

Winkler, M.M. (1995), 'Cinema and the Fall of Rome', *Transactions of the American Philological Association* 125: 135-54.

Bibliography

Winkler, M.M. (2000), '*Dulce et decorum est pro patria mori*? Classical Culture in the War Film', *International Journal of the Classical Tradition* 7: 177-214.

Winkler, M.M. (2001), 'The Roman Empire in American Cinema after 1945', in Joshel, Malamud and McGuire 2001: 50-76.

Winkler, M.M., ed. (2005a), *Gladiator: Film and History*, Malden, MA.

Winkler, M.M. (2005b), 'Neo-Mythologism: Apollo and the Muses on the Screen', *International Journal of the Classical Tradition* 11: 383-423.

Winkler, M.M., ed. (2007a), *Spartacus: Film and History*, Malden, MA.

Winkler, M.M. (2007b), 'Culturally Significant and Not Just Entertainment: History and the Marketing of *Spartacus*', in Winkler 2007a: 198-232.

Winkler, M.M. (2007c), 'The Holy Cause of Freedom: American Ideals in *Spartacus*', in Winkler 2007a: 154-88.

Winkler, M.M., ed. (2007d), *Troy: From Homer's* Iliad *to Hollywood Epic*, Malden, MA.

Winkler, M.M. (2007e), 'The *Iliad* and the Cinema', in Winkler 2007d: 43-67.

Wyke, M. (1997), *Projecting the Past*, London.

Wyke, M. (2002), *The Roman Mistress*, Oxford.

Yurick, S. (2003), *The Warriors*, New York (reprint of the 1965 novel with new introduction).

Index

79 A.D. (1962), 44
300 (2006), 2, 29, 99, 103, 113, 137
The 300 Spartans (1962), 43, 84, 113;
    epilogue, 131

Achilles, 50, 61-2, 74, 88, 100, 109
adaptation, for film, difficulties in, 63
Aeneid, see Vergil
Aeolus, 68, 77
AIDS, viii, 7-8
Airplane (1980), 29, 30, 32
Alessandro nell'Inde (opera), 104, 136
Alexander (the Great), 4, 11, 32, 44,
    50, 61, 84, 93, 95-113; as model for
    imperialism, 4, 95; Battle of
    Hydaspes, 96, 102, 104; career of,
    95-6; as focus of Balkan
    conflict,103; Hyphasis mutiny, 96,
    104, 134-5; novels about, 134-5;
    and Unity of Mankind, 97, 134;
    and Zoroastrians, 134
Alexander (2004), 4, 9, 100-3;
    construction of film, 100-1;
    homosexuality and American
    public, 101-2, 135; use of multiple
    perspectives, 102
Alexander the Great (1956), 4, 50, 84,
    96-9, 113; Macedon and America,
    97
All the King's Men (novel, 1946), 134
Alma-Tadema, Lawrence (painter),
    115
America, Middle, 2, 8
American International Pictures, 38
Americanism, 36
Amytis (love interest of Spartacus),
    31-2
Angel (tv, 1999-2004), 1, 19
Angelopoulos, Theo(doros) (director),
    4, 10, 63, 71, 79, 82-93, 103, 114;
    availability of films, 5; original
    Balkan gaze, 90-2; internalisation

of Greek myth, 85-6; trilogy of
    borders, 89-92; use of statuary, 84,
    87, 90-2, 132; use of name
    'Alexander', 135; use of trains, 86,
    132
animation, Japanese interest in
    Classical world, 4, 106-7; *Simpsons*
    and Classical world, 106; status in
    Japan, 106
anime, *see* animation (Japanese)
Antinea (Queen of Atlantis), 52, 80
apocalypse, 3, 7, 19, 108
Aramata, Hiroshi (novelist), 105, 107,
    111, 136
arête, 100
Argos (dog), 66, 88, 132
Aristotle, philosopher and tutor of
    Alexander, 95, 101, 104-5, 110;
    rules for drama, 62, 70, 81, 127
Ars Almadel, 119
art film/ art house, 18, 63, 79, 81, 92-3
L'Atlantide (novel, 1919), 125
Atlantis, 51-6
auteurs, 3, 17, 45, 58, 72
Aziza, Claude, 47, 125

bathos, 18
Bava, Mario (director), 45, 50, 54-9,
    62, 73, 78, 124-7
Ben Hur (1880 novel), 47; (1925 film),
    34; (1959 film), 37, 123-4, 136
Birth of a Nation (1915), 40
blockbuster, *see* spectacular
Bogans, 10, 115
Bond, James, 40, 54
Bonnard, Mario (director), 35, 122
Briullov, Karl (painter), *Last Day of
    Pompeii* (1834), 111
buff, 19
Buffy (Anne Summers), 13-28, 117
Buffy the Vampire Slayer (film, 1992),
    18

Buffy the Vampire Slayer (tv, 1997-2003), 1-2, 13-28; academic conferences, 1, 3, 17, 117; and Classicists, 17; philosophical implications, 21; ratings, 117
Buffyverse, 117
Bulwer-Lytton, Edward (novelist), 8, 30-43
Burt, Richard, 9

Cabiria (1914), 36-7, 40, 44, 48-9, 80
Caesar, (Gaius) Julius, *Commentarii*, 10; *veni, vidi, vici*,120
Calhoun, Rory (actor),43, 45
calligraphy, 14-15
Calypso, 64, 70, 80, 91
camp, as aesthetic term, 3, 29, 57
Campbell, Joseph (writer on mythology), 24, 119
Campion, Jane (director), 2, 115
Canale, Gianna Maria (actor), 32, 58, 121
capital, cultural, 28
capitalism, 36-7, 79-82, 97
Caserini, Mario (director), 8
Castellani, Bruto (actor), 36
censorship, in post-war Italy, 31, 121
Chaffey, Don (director), 45, 48
Charmed (tv, 1998-2006), 17, 117
Christian Democrats, 35, 41
Christianity, 7, 33-4, 37, 76, 78; and eschatology, 7; in film, 134; ideology, 9, 21, 130
Christians, as martyrs, 8, 10-11, 35, 38-9, 40, 44, 96, 99
Cinecittà (film studio), 31, 37-8, 44, 54, 61, 67, 81
cinema, international, 2, 93, 103, 113; *see also* Hollywood; Italian, 1950s-60s, 3; silent film, 3; use of Western dramas, 130
CinemaScope, 38, 81
Circe, 64-5, 68, 70-1, 74, 76, 80, 88, 92
'Classics', as term for Greek and Latin works, 22
Classics Comics/ Classics Illustrated, 10, 77, 115, 118-19
Cleopatra (1963), 48, 72
Coen, Ethan and Joel (directors), 4, 63, 73, 76-8, 130
Cold War, 63, 72, 99, 113

Coleman, Kathleen (academic), 9, 115, 121
Collins, Joan (actor), vii, 2-3, 7-9, 11, 28; on AIDS and end of Roman Empire, vii, 7
Colossus, as strongman, 124
Colossus of Rhodes (1961), 42-5
commensality, 3, 68-70
Constable, John (painter), *Hay Wain* (1821), 55
Contempt (1963), 4, 80-2, 130
Cooper, Merian C. (producer), 33, 35
Corbucci, Sergio (director, scriptwriter), 35, 48, 58, 73
Corman, Roger (director, producer), 131-2
corruption, political, 4, 33-4, 41, 99, 123
Cottafavi, Vittorio (director), 35, 45, 48, 50-4, 58-9, 72-3, 125-6; directors who admire, 124
Count of Monte Cristo, versions, 10-12, 116
Coyote, Wile E., 119, 137
Craven, Wes (director), 18
Crawford, Broderick (actor), 58
Crowe, Russell (actor), 40, 100-1
culture, gay, 12; guns and chequebooks, 81, 131; popular, 9-10, 13, 17, 21, 23, 29, 73; wars, 9; youth, 9, 13; *see also* high art, low art

Dallas (tv, 1978-91), 9
dance, ballet in *Spartaco*, 31; of Cleopatra, 59; dancing girls as feature of peplum, 53; of Ku Klux Klan, 77; of Odysseus and men, 77; Ponti dance, 88
D'Annunzio, Gabriele (poet), 122, 130
Darius (king of Persia), 96-8, 105, 109-10
Dawn (Summers), 24
De Concini, Ennio (scriptwriter), 35, 64, 122, 128
De Toth, André (director), 47
Deianeira, 52-7
Demetrius and the Gladiators (1954), 40
Demetrius Poliorcetes, 42
DeMille, Cecil B. (director), 34

Depression, 1930s, 4, 33-4, 76-8
dhampir, 20, 118
Dido, 10, 40
Dilessi murders, 83, 131
Diogenes (Cynic philosopher), 110, 136
Dionysius of Syracuse, 116
Douglas, Kirk (actor), 3, 32, 62, 64-7, 70-1, 76-8, 99
Dr Who, 62
Dreyer, Carl Theodor (director), 79, 93, 114
Drusilla, girlfriend of Spike, 26; sister of Caligula, 26
dubbing, of actors' voices, 36
Duck Dodgers ... (1953), 137
Dumas, Alexandre (playwright, novelist), 2, 10-12, 115-16
duumvir (Roman official), 40
Dynasty (tv, 1981-9), 7, 9
DVD, issues of films discussed, 5; PAL vs. NTSC, 5; zone settings, 5

education, elite formed by Classical languages, 2; in nineteenth-century France, 11; in twentieth-century USA, 11
Eisenstein, Sergei (director), 13
Eko Eko Azarak (films, 1995-), 119
Eliot, T.S. (poet), 133-4
Epstein, Edward Jay ('producer'), 85, 131-2
Esther and the King (1960), 8
Eumaios (swineherd), 64, 66, 74, 129
Euripides, 51, 62, 72, 80, 93, 126

Fabiola (1948), 35, 40
Fall of the Roman Empire, book (1776-89), 7; film (1965), 7
Fall of Troy (1910), 61
fans, as commentators, 17
fantasy, 3
Fascism, 35-6, 40, 50, 84, 98
Fast, Howard (novelist), 30
Fellini, Federico (director), 56, 72, 87
feminism, 12, 20
Festival of Peplum Film (Arles), 47
film, citation of titles, 5; different versions, 5
filone (stream, trend), 3, 48, 72
Finn, Riley, 21-2
First (Slayer), aka 'the Primitive', 18

Fistful of Dollars (1964), 38
Flaubert, Gustave (novelist), *Salammbo* (1862), 116
Ford, John (director), 62, 73
Fordism, 36
Forrest, Mark (actor), 51, 62
Francisci, Pietro (director), 35, 50, 57
Freda, Riccardo (director), 31-2, 45, 47, 57, 121, 124, 127
Fu Manchu, 40

Gaisford, Dean (Oxford Professor), 120
Gallone, Carmine (director), 32
Gaugamela, 9
Gellar, Sarah Michelle, 3
Gemma, Giuliano (actor), 5, 73, 126
genre, mauvais, 29, 32, 46
genres of film, 46, 76; boxing, 34; chain gang, 63, 73, 76; gangster, 34; High School drama, 1, 13; Hong Kong action, 13; horror, 13; kung fu, 13, 19; neo-realism/ social realism, 58, 64, 67, 76, 79-80; slasher 19; western 35, 38-9, 44-6, 48, 59, 62, 71-5
geography, bad, 53
giallo (crime thriller), 19, 48, 72, 74, 126-7
Giant of Marathon (1959), 46, 50, 58
Giants of Thessaly (1960), 45, 67, 125
Gibbon, Edward (historian), 7
Giles, Rupert, 13, 22, 24, 27; as academic role-model, 21
Giovagnoli, Raffaelo (novelist), 31, 120-1
Gladiator (2000), 2, 9, 35, 40, 43, 48, 50, 93, 99-101, 106; Latin in, 123; script versions, 128
Gli ultimi giorni di Pompeii (1908), 32; (1913), 8, 32, 121; (1926), 32; (1959), 35-46; box office receipts, 124
Godard, Jean-Luc (director), 4, 63, 79-82
Godzilla, 57, 106, 136
Goliath, 32, 45, 47, 51, 58
Goliath and the Vampires (1961), 58, 127
Golpho (*the Shepherdess*), 86, 132
Gómez, Ramiro (set designer), 42

The Good, the Bad, and the Ugly
(1966), 41
Goodbye Mr. Chips, film and
television versions, 118
Gray, Hugh (scriptwriter), 64, 128
Greece (modern), Civil War 84-6, 88;
English intervention in, 83-4; first
films, 89; foreign intervention, 4;
Goebbel's visit to Olympia, 132;
government involvement in film,
43, 84; independence struggle, 4,
10; marginalisation of left, 85;
migration, 4, 89, 133; nationalism,
84; Parthenon marbles question,
132; prison islands, 132; royalists
as film sponsors, 84
Greek, alphabet, 14; aphorisms in *300
Spartans*, 123; ancient vs. modern,
82-3; as esoteric knowledge, 24; in
film 43-4, 135; language 2, 25;
letters in names of fraternities, 25;
use for class differentiation, 82-3,
93; as visual wallpaper, 123
Greek romances, 31, 120-1
Greenaway, Peter (director), 16

Haidee (Epirot princess), 10
Hannibal, 40-9
Hannibal the Conqueror, 2
Harryhausen, Ray (animator), 24, 124
Häxan (1922), 117
Haydee (Byronic heroine), 10
Hecht, Ben (scriptwriter), 64, 128
Heemskerk, Marten (engraver), 43
Helen of Troy (film, 1956), 37, 50, 52,
61, 67, 72; Gig Young's
advertisements, 127-8; (tv, 2003),
62, 100
Helena (1924), 61
Hell, Christian, 45, 56
Hellmouth, 19, 20
Heracles, 24; *see also* Hercules
Herculaneum, 44
Hercules, 3, 24, 38
Hercules (1997), 32, 48
Hercules against the Moon Men
(1964), 58
Hercules and the Queen of Lydia
(1959), 35, 50, 53,
Hercules at the Centre of the Earth
(1961), 45, 54-8; alternate titles, 5;

lighting, 55; locations, 54, 126;
mise-en-scène, 55
Hercules Conquers Atlantis (1961), 45,
51-4; alternate titles, 5; lighting,
54; Woolner Bros. version, 125-6
Hercules, Samson, and Ulysses (1963),
57
Hercules, the Legendary Journeys (tv,
1995-9), 2-3, 48, 59, 113, 126
heroism, critiques of, 18, 23, 50-1, 63,
67, 70-2, 78, 84, 91-2, 97, 100-2,
108, 113
Hesperides (mythological figures), 56
high art, 2-3, 9, 23, 29, 32, 63, 76, 106,
114; *see also* snobbery
Hill, Walter (film director), 22-3, 82
Hollywood, 2-3, 9, 11, 30, 33-4, 37-8,
44, 48, 62, 67, 71-2, 74, 81, 93,
96-7, 99, 106; abandonment of
religious subtexts, 99; moral
nostalgia, 99; promotes family
values, 99-100
Homer, 10, 17, 22-3, 52, 61-83, 92,
100, 109, 127, 129, 131-3; in Greek
culture, 61, 127
homophobia, 29
humanism, 3, 71-2, 80
Hunchback of Notre Dame, film
versions, 23, 119
Hyllus, 51-3; as *eromenos*, 125

I Claudius (novel), 26; (tv, 1976), 26,
72
Iliad (Homeric epic), 22, 61-2, 73, 82,
85, 88, 93, 97
imperialism, American, 12, 107;
British, 104-5; European, 95,
102-4, 108; French, 12; Roman, 12,
31
intellectuals, and social
contradictions, 79, 81-2
Ione o Gli ultimi giorni di Pompeii
(1913), 32, 121
Ireland, as escape from Rome, 34
irony, 21
Iros (beggar in Odyssey), 70-1, 129

Jackson, Peter (director), 2, 124, 126
Jason and the Argonauts (1963), 3, 24
Jenkyns, Richard (academic), on
BtVS, 118

Jonathan (Levinson, character in *BtVS*), 25, 27

Kael, Pauline (critic), 22
Karaghiozis (puppet theatre), 84
Kazui, Fran Rubel (director), 18
kimota!, 26-7
kitsch, 29, 57
kleos, 100
kolossal, *see* spectacular
Kubrick, Stanley (director), 30, 40, 62

Labours of Hercules (1958), 35, 37, 39, 50-1, 57, 67; effect on Italian film industry, 122; introduces short dresses for heroines, 128
Landscape in the Mist (1988), 86-7
Lane Fox, Robin (academic), 9, 115
Lang, Fritz (director), 78, 80-1, 130
Last Days of Pompeii (1832 novel), 8, 30-1; (1935 film), 8, 33
The Last Legion (2007), 2
Latin, authenticity of in *BtVS*, 26; for bores, 26; Breton misinterpretation, 119; and Church, 25; emendation of, 26-7; errors in, 119; as esoteric knowledge, 22; in European education, 120; as language of power, 25; and legal community, 25; as sign of tradition, 25; for spells, 26; for taxonomy, 25-6; teaches humility, 28
Latin inscriptions, 42-4
Lawless, Lucy (actor), 113
Le Mépris (1964), 63, 79-82
Lee, Christopher (actor), 55, 57-8
Legions of Cleopatra (1960), 48, 51, 58-9, 129
Leone, Sergio (director), 30, 35-46, 123-4
LeRoy, Mervyn (director), 8, 128, 134
Les derniers jours de Pompeii (1948), 31, 35
lesbianism, 14, 16
Levine, Joe (Joseph) E., 37-8, 72, 80-1
Lion of Thebes (1962), 62
Livia, Augustus' wife 119; Tony Soprano's mother, 119
'loser criticism', 9
Lovecraft, H.P., cosmogony of, 19-20

low art, 2-3, 23, 80, 106; *see also* camp, kitsch, *genre, mauvais*
Lucretius Satrius Valens, Dec., 42
Luhrman, Baz (director), intended Alexander film, 135
Lumière brothers, 2, 131, 134

Maciste (strongman character), 32, 36, 45, 47, 50, 57-8; origin of name, 122
Maciste in Hell (1962), 45
Maggi, Luigi (director), 32
Malick, Terence (director), 82-3, 93
'Man of Constant Sorrow' (song), 76, 130
The Man Who Would be King (novel, 1888), 103; (film, 1975), 103-4
Manaki brothers (Yannaki and Milton) (film-makers), 63, 89-91, 132-3
Mangano, Sylvana, 128
Martin, Yves, creator of term 'peplum', 46
Marvelman/ Miracleman, 27
Marxism, 23, 35, 72, 84, 85, 97
Maté, Rudolf, 43
Medea, 24, 80, 93, 101, 114
Megalexandros, as folklore character, 84
Megalexandros (1980), 10, 83-4
Megali Idea, 84
Messalina (1960), 51, 58
Midnight Express (1978), 30
Minnelli, Vincente, 4, 81
Minoan art, 42, 64
Mitchell, Gordon (actor), 61
Miyu (Vampire Princess), 20, 118-19
modernism, 63, 67, 80
Moffa, Paul (director), 35
Moravia, Alberto (novelist), 79-82, 102
Morricone, Ennio (composer), 129-30
Morris, Kirk (actor), 57, 126
'Mosaic with Street Musicians', 42
Moullet, Luc (director), 51, 124, 126
Mussolini, Benito, 36; Abyssinian campaign of, 40, 49, 125
My Son, the Hero (1961), 73, 126
Mystery Science Theater 3000 (tv 1988-99), 32

Narona (daughter of Crassus), 30

Nausicaa, 65, 76, 80, 88, 92
Navarro, Nieves (actor), 74
nekyia, 64, 70
Nero, 7; *cupitor impossibilium*, 10; in
  Dead Man (1995), 116; in *The
  Producers* (1968), 116
New Zealand, location for filming tv
  series, 2
Niblo, Fred (director), 34
Nightmare on Elm Street, 18
Nisbet, Gideon, 9, 113, 120-1, 123-5,
  135
Noa, Manfred (director), 61
Noir (tv, 2001), 119
nomenclature, essential, 14;
  neo-Classical, 76

Odissea (1911), 64, 128
L'Odissea (1968), 3, 62, 64, 67-72, 78,
  80, 82; abbreviated version, 131;
  actors in, 129; availability, 5; blood
  feud settled, 70; costumes of
  Phaeacians, 128; costuming, 67;
  gods in, 130-1; hero's humiliation,
  70; joint venture, 128; processions
  in, 129; scriptwriters, 129;
  soundtrack, 129; theme of
  commensality, 68-70
Odyssey (Homeric epic), 3, 22, 52,
  61-93, 133; as aristocratic text,
  129; conclusion, 127
Odyssey (tv, 1997), 73, 127
Oechalia, 54-7
Oedipus myth, 80, 86, 101, 114
Oh Brother, Where Art Thou? (2000),
  4, 63, 76-9; nomenclature in, 130
Olympias (mother of Alexander), 95-6,
  109
Olympic Games, in *Days of 36* (1972),
  87; in *Labours of Hercules* (1958),
  57
Once Upon a Time in the West (1968),
  45-6
Once Were Warriors (1990 novel; 1994
  film), 118
Orestes, in Aeschylus, 89, 114; in
  Angelopoulos' films, 86-7, 103; as
  EAM rebel, 132
orgies, 8, 32, 34
Orientalism, 10, 33, 49, 102, 105, 109
OVA, defined, 118

Oveur, Captain, 29
Ovid, *Metamorphoses*, 11
Oz (Daniel Osborne, boyfriend of
  Willow), 27

Pagano, Bartolemeo (actor), 36
Palance, Jack (actor), 80
Palmeri, Amleto (director), 32
Paris Does Strange Things (1956), 62
Park, Reg (actor), 47, 49-59, 127
Parker, Alan (director), 30
Parmenion (general of Alexander), 96,
  98, 101
Parolini, Gianfranco (director), 44
Pasolini, Pier Paolo (director), 80, 114
Pastrone, Giovanni (director), 61
Penelope, 64-6, 71, 80-2, 87-8, 91
peplum, 3, 29-30, 32, 35, 38, 44-59,
  61, 63-4, 67, 71-3, 81, 113, 120,
  124-5; changed titles for, 121;
  decline of, 4; origin of term, 125;
  pronunciation of, 125;
  requirements for actors in, 58; use
  of recycled props, 58
Persephone (mythological figure), 56-7
Petronius (Nero's *arbiter elegantiae*),
  7, 115
Phaeacians, 63, 65, 67-8, 71, 92
Philip (father of Alexander), 95-6, 98,
  101
Pillow Book (Sei Shonagan's
  eleventh-century diary), blessing
  in, 16; (1996 film), 16
Pitt, Brad (actor), 62, 100
Plato (philosopher), 89, 110, 131
Platohedron, 107, 111
Playboy (magazine), vii, 7, 9
Podestà, Rosanna (actor), 61, 65, 67,
  127
Polyphemus, 3, 62, 64, 68, 77-8, 80, 92
Pompeii, 8, 30-47, 73, 106, 109, 111,
  114; film of Robert Harris' novel,
  114
Ponti, Carlo (producer), 80
Pontius Pilate, 33, 34, 121-2
Porus (Indian king), 96, 102, 104-5,
  110
Postmodernism, 13, 63, 79-81
praetorian guards, 39-40
Private Life of Helen of Troy (1927), 62
Procrustes (mythological figure), 56

Proteus (mythological figure), 52
Ptolemy (general and biographer), 101-2
Pyramus and Thisbe, 11
pyrodramas, 33

Quinn, Anthony (actor), 65, 67
Quo Vadis (1895 novel), 35; adapted as film, 8; adapted as opera, 8; adapted to stage, 7; (1912 film), 36; (1952 film), 8

racism, 4
railways, create demand for novels, 32
Rank Organization, 45
Rayne, Ethan (chum of Giles), 26-7
reception studies, 1
Reconstruction (1970), 86
Reeves, Steve (actor), 8, 35-40, 43, 47, 50, 53, 61, 81, 123
Reign, the Conqueror (tv 1999), 4, 105-11; dubbing, 106; faithfulness to tradition, 110; fantasy elements, 107-10; inauguration of Hellenistic philosophy and mathematics, 107; multiculturalism, 111; parallels with modern Japan, 107-8; Peter Chung's designs, 105, 108-9; recreation by destruction, 107-9; Samsung's investment in, 105, 136
Return of Martin Guerre (1982), 66
Return of Ringo (1965), 3, 38, 62, 73-5, 79, 129-30; racism in, 74
Revenge of Hercules (1960), 45, 51, 58, 125
Revolt of the Gladiators (1958), 35, 50
Revolutionary Girl Utena (tv 1997), dream of Scipio in, 106-7
Riefenstahl, Leni (director), *Triumph of the Will* (1935), 1, 87
The Robe (1953), 38, 96, 125
Rodolfi, Eleuterio (director), 32
Roman Empire, causes of downfall, 7, 28
Rome, comic treatments of, 114
Rome (tv series, 2005-7), 44, 72, 129; Latin in, 123
Romulus and Remus (1961), 58
Rossen, Robert (director), 4, 50, 84, 96-9, 101-2, 107, 110, 134-6; critique of individualism, 97, and

House UnAmerican Activities Committee, 4, 97, 134
Rossi, Franco (director), 62, 67-73, 78, 82
Roxane/ Roxanne, 97-8, 101-2, 104-5, 110
Ruapehu, Mt. (New Zealand volcano), 5

Samson, 32, 47, 57
sandaloni, 3, 29; *see also* sword-and-sandal, peplum
Sappho, inspiration for feminists, 119; *Ode* 1 (Hymn to Aphrodite), 14-16, 116-17
Sarajevo, 63, 89, 92
Schoedsack, Ernest B. (director), 8, 33
Schwarzenegger, Arnold (actor), 3, 48
Scipio l'Africano (1937), 40, 49-50, 125
Scoobie Gang, 13, 22, 26, 28
Scooby-Doo (tv, 1969-), 116
Scott, Ridley (director), 1, 35
Sea Wolf (novel, 1904), 134; (film, 1941), 134
Seferis, George (poet), 89-90, 133
Sernas, Jacques (actor), 61, 127
Shakespeare, William, 11, 17, 63, 73, 98, 105, 135-6
Siclier, Jacques (film critic), 45-8, 58
Sienkiewicz, Henryk (novelist), 7, 35
Sign of Cross (play, 1895), 8; (film, 1914), 8; (film, 1932), 8, 34
Sikandar (1941), 104-5, 110, 136; and Indian independence movement, 4, 105
Simpsons (tv, 1989-), 136
Sirens, 17, 24, 56, 65, 71, 76, 129
Slayer(s), 19-20
Sodom and Gomorrah (1961), 47
Solomos, Dionysius (poet), 89
Son of Spartacus (1963), 48
Sophocles, 80, 83-4, 86, 97, 114, 131
Sophonisba, 49
Sorbo, Kevin (actor), 48, 58
Sounis (mythological figure), 56
Spain, as filming location, 45, 59, 73
Spain, Fay (actor), 52, 58
Sparta, depiction, 113, 137
Spartaco (1874 novel), 31; (1913 film), 30-1; (1952 film), 31-2, 122

Spartacus (1951 novel), 30; (1960 film), 30, 48
spectaculars (*spectacolari, kolossals,* blockbusters), 38, 44, 48, 61-2, 64, 72, 80, 93
spells, languages in, 25
Spike (aka William the Bloody), 20, 24, 26, 120; on Caesar, 28
Spillane, Mickey (Frank Morrison) (novelist), 115
Ste. Marie, Buffy (singer), 117
Stewart, Rory (novelist), 100
Stone, Oliver (director), 4, 9, 100-2, 135; psychologising of Alexander, 101-2
Strabo (geographer), 61
Stravinsky, Igor (composer), *Oedipus Rex* (1927), 119
Sturges, Preston (director), 4, 76
Summers, Joyce (mother of Buffy), 13
Suspended Step of the Stork (1991), 87
sword-and-sandal, 3, 29-32, 35, 37-8, 44, 46-7, 61, 64; audience appeal in Italy, 37; audience appeal in USA, 37-8; *see also* peplum
Sybil, 56

Tacitus (Roman historian), 10
Tara (Maclay), 13, 21, 23, 116; as lesbian role model, 25
Tarantino, Quentin (director), 115
Tavernier, Bertrand (director), 46, 51, 124
Tcherina, Ludmilla (actor, ballerina), 31
Technicolor, 38, 64, 81
Telemachus (comic figure), 56-7
Telemachus (son of Odysseus), 64-5, 68-9, 74, 87-8
televangelism, 8
television, prestige productions, 72
Tessari, Duccio (director, scriptwriter), 3, 35, 54, 62, 73-5, 82, 114
Theodora, 64, 121
Theseus, 54-7
Thin Red Line (1962 novel), 131; (1998 film), 82-3; Homeric references in, 131; as Iliadic recreation, 83, 93
Thomson, Frederick A. (director), 8

The Travelling Players (1976), 86
Troy (2004), 53, 62, 67, 99-100, 106

Ulysses (1954), 3, 62, 64-7, 70, 72, 76-8, 80, 82, 93, 128
Ulysses' Gaze (1995), 4, 63, 79, 88-92; concluding soliloquy, 133-4; filming locations, 133
Ursus (strongman), 32, 36, 47, 58

Vampa, Luigi (brigand), 10-11
Vampire Hunter D., 20
Varinia (love interest of Spartacus), 31
Vergil, 28, 40, 56, 61, 120
Vesuvius (eruption AD 79), 8, 30-3, 35, 111
Vidali, Giovanni (director), 30, 32-3
Volonté, Gian Maria (actor), 52
Voyage to Cythera (poem by Baudelaire), 132; (1983 film), 88

Wallis, Lew (novelist), 47
Ward, Vincent (director), 2
The Warriors (1965 novel), 22; (1979 film), 22; and Homer, 22-3
Washington, Booker T. (educationalist), 120
Wasserstrasse, 62
The Weeping Meadow (2004), 85-6
West, Mae, and Sahara revue, 29, 120
Whedon, Joss (director, scriptwriter), 16-18, 20-1, 27, 117
Wicca (pl. Wiccan), 17, 25
Willow (Rosenberg), 13, 21-2, 25, 27, 116
Wise, Robert (director), 37
Wyke, Maria, 33, 35, 120-2
Wyler, William (director), 37

Xander (Alexander Harris), 13, 21-2, 24, 27
Xena, Warrior Princess (tv, 1995-2001), 2, 3, 48, 59; and Alexander, 135-6; as reversal of Classical Hercules, 113; subverts genre, 127
Xenophon (historian), *Anabasis,* 23, 118

Yojimbo (1961), 38
Yurick, Sol (author), 22-3